Emotions and Everyday Nationalism in Modern European History

This volume examines how ideas of the nation influenced ordinary people, by focusing on their affective lives. Using a variety of sources, methods and cases, ranging from Spain during the age of Revolutions to post-World War II Poland, it demonstrates that emotions are integral to understanding the everyday pull of nationalism on ordinary people.

Andreas Stynen (KU Leuven) is a Postdoctoral Assistant at the Research Group for Cultural History after 1750.

Maarten Van Ginderachter (Antwerp University) is a Professor of History at the PoHis Center for Political History.

Xosé M. Núñez Seixas (University of Santiago de Compostela) is a Professor of Modern European History.

Routledge Studies in Modern European History

For more information about this series, please visit: https://www.routledge.com/history/series/SE0246

Emotions and Everyday Nationalism in Modern European History

Edited by
Andreas Stynen, Maarten Van
Ginderachter and Xosé M. Núñez Seixas

Routledge
Taylor & Francis Group

LONDON AND NEW YORK

First published 2020
by Routledge
2 Park Square, Milton Park, Abingdon, Oxon OX14 4RN

and by Routledge
52 Vanderbilt Avenue, New York, NY 10017

Routledge is an imprint of the Taylor & Francis Group, an informa business

This book is part of the NISE proceedings

British Library Cataloguing-in-Publication Data
A catalogue record for this book is available from the British Library

Library of Congress Cataloging-in-Publication Data
Names: Stynen, Andreas, editor. | Ginderachter, Maarten Van, editor. | Núñez Seixas, Xosé M. (Xosé Manoel), 1966- editor.
Title: Emotions and everyday nationalism in modern European history / Andreas Stynen, Maarten Van Ginderachter, Xosé M. Núñez Seixas.
Description: Abingdon, Oxon ; New York : Routledge, 2020. |
Series: Routledge studies in modern European history |
Includes bibliographical references and index.
Identifiers: LCCN 2019058428 (print) | LCCN 2019058429 (ebook) |
ISBN 9781138354296 (hardback) | ISBN 9780429424939 (ebook)
Subjects: LCSH: Nationalism--Europe--History. | Emotions--Political aspects--Europe--History. | Nationalism--Europe--Psychological aspects. | Political psychology--Europe--Case studies.
Classification: LCC D359.7 .E56 2020 (print) |
LCC D359.7 (ebook) | DDC 320.54094--dc23
LC record available at https://lccn.loc.gov/2019058428
LC ebook record available at https://lccn.loc.gov/2019058429

ISBN: 978-1-138-35429-6 (hbk)
ISBN: 978-0-429-42493-9 (ebk)

Typeset in Times New Roman
by Taylor & Francis Books

Contents

Contributors

Thomas Blanck (University of Cologne) has a BA in Italian Studies (2011) and an MA in Public History (2014) from the Free University Berlin and Università degli Studi Roma Tre, funded by a scholarship from the Ev. Studienwerk Villigst. Since 2015 he has held a scholarship at the a.r.t.e.s. Graduate School for the Humanities, University of Cologne. His dissertation project is entitled: 'Mobilizing the Senses. Munich and Fiume in a State of Emergency, 1918–1922'. In the summer of 2016 he held a scholarship at the German Historical Institute, Rome.

Raul Cârstocea (University of Leicester) is Lecturer in Modern European History. He has previously worked as Lecturer in European Studies at the Europa Universität Flensburg, Germany (2017-2019), as Senior Research Associate at the European Centre for Minority Issues (2013–2017), as Teaching Fellow at University College London (2011–2012), and held research fellowships at the Imre Kértesz Kolleg Jena (2018) and the Vienna Wiesenthal Institute for Holocaust Studies (2012–2013). His research interests focus on anti-Semitism, Jewish history, nationalism, fascism, and the Holocaust, and more broadly on state formation and nation-building processes in 19th and 20th century Central and Eastern Europe and their consequences for minority groups. His most recent publication is *Modern Antisemitisms in the Peripheries: Europe and its Colonies, 1880–1945* (co-edited with Éva Kovács; Vienna, 2019).

José M. Faraldo (Universidad Complutense de Madrid) is Profesor Contratado Doctor (Assistant Professor, tenured). He received his PhD in History at the Universidad Complutense de Madrid with a work on Russian nationalism. After further studies in history and cultural studies in Moscow, Frankfurt/Oder and Poznań he worked from 1997 to 2002 at the European University Viadrina in Frankfurt/Oder (Germany). From 2004 to 2008 he was research fellow and project coordinator at the Center of Research on Contemporary History (ZZF) in Potsdam (Germany). Recent publications include: *Reconsidering a Lost Intellectual Project. Exiles' Reflections on Cultural Differences* (with Carolina Rodríguez-López; CSP, 2012]; *Europe, Nation, Communism. Essays on Poland* (Peter Lang, 2008);

Europe in the Eastern Bloc. Imaginations and Discourses (with Paulina Gulińska-Jurgiel and Christian Domnitz; Bohlau, 2008).

Josephine Hoegaerts (University of Helsinki) is Associate Professor at the Department of Cultures. She is the author of *Masculinity and Nationhood, 1830–1910* (Palgrave Macmillan, 2014). In her current research, she studies articulations of the self through vocal practices. Recent publications include 'Speaking Like Intelligent Men: Vocal Articulations of Authority and Identity in the House of Commons in the Nineteenth Century' (in *Radical History Review*, 2015) and (with dr. Goedele Declerck) 'Intercession, Emancipation and a Space In Between: Silence as a Mode of Deaf Citizenship in the Nineteenth Century and Today' (in *DiGeSt*, 2016).

Ville Kivimäki (University of Tampere) is a social and cultural historian of World War II and its aftermath. In his PhD thesis *Battled Nerves* (2013), he studied Finnish soldiers' war experiences, trauma and military psychiatry in 1941–44. Together with Prof. Tiina Kinnunen, he has co-edited a comprehensive anthology, *Finland in World War II: History, Memory, Interpretations* (Brill, 2012). Currently he is the 'Lived Nation' research team leader at the Finnish Centre of Excellence in the History of Experiences (HEX), where his own study is focused on the history of nation-state violence.

Wiktor Marzec (Central European University) holds a PhD in Sociology from the Department of Sociology and Anthropology of the Central European University, Budapest. His research interests include intellectual emancipation, political mobilization, ideological languages and conceptual innovation in early twentieth-century Russian Poland. His recent publications include articles in *Thesis Eleven, Journal of Historical Sociology* and *Eastern European Politics and Societies*. He is the author of *Rebellion and Reaction. The 1905 Revolution and Plebeian Political Experience in Russian Poland* (in Polish, with Lodz University Press and Universitas).

Raúl Moreno Almendral (University of Salamanca) is a lecturer in Modern and Contemporary History. He has held visiting positions at the London School of Economics and Political Science, L'École des Hautes en Sciences Sociales, the University of Lisbon and Harvard University, the last as a Fulbright Visiting Fellow. His doctoral thesis, defended at the University of Salamanca, was a comparative history of nationhood in British, French, Spanish and Portuguese personal narratives from the Age of Revolutions.

Martina Niedhammer (Collegium Carolinum, München) studied Slavonic languages and history in Munich, St. Petersburg and Prague. Her first book *'Nur eine Geld-Emancipation'? Loyalitäten und Lebenswelten des Prager jüdischen Großbürgertums 1800–1867* was awarded the Max Weber-Preis by the Bavarian Academy of Sciences in 2013. Since 2011, she has been a research associate at the Collegium Carolinum: Research Institute for the History of the Czech Lands and Slovakia in Munich. Currently, she is working on her postdoctoral research project 'The making of a mother tongue: Occitan, Yiddish and Belarusian in the context of regionalist enthusiasm, philological discourse, and national agitation' (advisor: Martin Schulze Wessel).

Xosé M. Núñez Seixas (University of Santiago de Compostela) is Professor of Modern European History. He has published widely on the comparative history of nationalist movements and national and regional identities. His recent publications include *Metaphors of Spain: Representations of Spanish National Identity in the Twentieth Century* (co-edited with Javier Moreno; Berghahn, 2017) and *Regionalism and Modern Europe. Identity Construction and Movements from 1890 to the Present Day* (co-edited with Eric Storm; Bloomsbury, 2019).

Joris Oddens (Leiden University) is a Postdoctoral Researcher at the Leiden University Institute for History. He has published widely on the political and emotional culture of the Netherlands around 1800. His dissertation (2012, which was awarded the D.J. Veegens Prize in 2016) dealt with the Dutch legislative assemblies during the age of revolution. In his current project he focuses on petitions as a means to study the negotiation of local and national identities in the Netherlands between 1750 and 1850.

Andreas Stynen (KU Leuven) is a Postdoctoral Assistant at the Research Group for Cultural History after 1750. In 2010 he received his PhD from the KU Leuven (Belgium) with an analysis of the manifold relationships between urbanity and naturalness in nineteenth-century Belgium. Afterwards he worked as a researcher at the ADVN, the archive of national movements in Antwerp, and as scientific coordinator of NISE, the international platform for the comparative study of national movements in Europe. His publications include several books and articles on popular music culture, memorials and trans-Atlantic migration. With Krisztina Lajosi he has co-edited *Choral Societies and Nationalism in Europe* (Brill, 2015) and *The Matica and Beyond: Cultural Associations and Nationalism in Europe* (Brill, 2020).

Maarten Van Ginderachter (Antwerp University) is Professor of History at the PoHis Center for Political History at Antwerp University. He is the author of *The Everyday Nationalism of Workers. A Social History of Modern Belgium* (Stanford University Press, 2019) and co-editor of *National Indifference and the History of Nationalism in Modern Europe* (with Jon Fox; Routledge, 2019) and *Nationhood from Below. Europe in the Long Nineteenth Century* (with Marnix Beyen; Palgrave-Macmillan, 2012).

Preface

This volume is the result of a workshop held at the Ludwig-Maximilian University in Munich (LMU) on May 31 and June 1, 2017, hosted by the Chair of Modern European History held at that time by Xosé M. Núñez Seixas, and organized by himself (today University of Santiago de Compostela), Maarten Van Ginderachter (Antwerp University) and Andreas Stynen (today KU Leuven, at the time affiliated to NISE) within the framework of the 'Nations and Nationalism from the Margins' project hosted by Van Ginderachter and the PoHis Center for Political History of Antwerp University.

We would like to express our appreciation to all participants in the workshop, most of whom have become contributors to this volume, as well as to Routledge for its interest in this project. The Hiwis of the chair of Modern European History at the LMU (Lisa Leuschel, Emanuel Steinbacher and Maximilian Heumann) provided great assistance in organizing the workshop. Finally we are grateful for the generous financing by the Flemish Research Foundation (International Scientific Research Program grant W0.017.14N) and for the additional support of NISE, the international platform for research and heritage on national movements in Europe. The current publication is the fifth volume in the 'NISE Proceedings' series and the fourth in the 'Nations and Nationalism from the Margins' project, after Jon Fox and Maarten Van Ginderachter (eds.), 'Everyday Nationalism's Evidence Problem', themed section of *Nations and Nationalism*, vol. 24, issue 3, 2018, pp. 546–623; Maarten Van Ginderachter and Jon Fox (eds.), *National Indifference and the History of Nationalism in Modern Europe*, London, Routledge, 2019; and Eric Storm and Maarten Van Ginderachter (eds.), 'Questioning the Wilsonian Moment. The Role of Ethnicity and Nationalism in the Dissolution of European Empires from the Belle Époque through the First World War', special dossier in the: *European Review of History / Revue européenne d'histoire*, vol. 26, issue 5, 2019, pp. 747–854.

Introduction

Emotions and everyday nationalism in modern European history

Andreas Stynen, Maarten Van Ginderachter and Xosé M. Núñez Seixas

This volume tackles one of the basic questions in nationalism studies as formulated by Katherine Verdery: How do people become national?[1] To examine how the nation entered ordinary people's 'insides', this book focuses on their affective lives. As such its objective is to bridge a double gap: the neglect of both emotions and the everyday realm in historical research on nationalism. On the one hand, Benedict Anderson's question, "Why [do nations] command such profound emotional legitimacy?",[2] has long befuddled historians, who have been late-comers to the so-called 'affective turn'.[3] On the other hand, historians have been taken to task for obsessing over the bells and whistles of nationalism and over-concentrating on the most articulate social groups. This collection of essays takes up the gauntlet. By analysing how nationalism harnesses, produces and feeds on emotions to pull ordinary people into its orbit, it refutes Anthony D. Smith's critique that everyday nationalism research is necessarily imbued with an "ahistorical blocking presentism".[4] Using a variety of sources, methods and cases, ranging from Spain and the Netherlands during the age of Revolutions, nineteenth-century France and Belgium over interwar Italy, Germany and Romania, to war-torn Finland and post-World War II Poland, this volume demonstrates that emotions are integral to understanding the everyday pull of nationalism on ordinary people.

In the seemingly endless succession of turns that the social sciences and humanities have witnessed in the last decades, there is one particular perspective that clearly stands out: the study of affects and emotions. Especially since the turn of the twenty-first century, a number of promising approaches has surfaced to help historians make sense of human experience without falling back on representation. The scholarly consensus about the theme's relevance, however, stands in sharp contrast to the lively debate on concepts and definitions, the nature of emotions (are they a biological or a cultural phenomenon?), their causality (what is the impact of environmental factors?) and the relationship with rationality and individual variance.[5]

Unsurprisingly the so-called affective turn has also manifested itself in nationalism studies. Indeed, national movements and state-led nationalisms alike abound with dramatic outcries, passionate pleas and heart-breaking mourning. Perhaps more striking is how long it took scholars to tackle the topic. In the introduction to his *Imagined Communities*, Benedict Anderson emphasized that in order to understand nationhood and related 'cultural artefacts' it was essential to consider why they exerted such a strong emotional pull on people. After raising the issue, Anderson further neglected it and implicitly subsumed it under vague terms.[6] Another revealing example is the 2001 *Encyclopedia of Nationalism*, edited by historian Alexander J. Motyl. Its two volumes do not only lack a chapter, but even an index entry on emotions, affects or other personal dimensions of nationhood.[7] The same applies to other readers on nationalism.[8]

Contributing to this lacuna is the effacement of the individual in many (historical) studies on nationalism.[9] In his *Ethnic Origins of Nations*, Anthony Smith stressed the defining role of the 'masses' in budding national movements:

> Just as in politics, elites must woo the 'masses' and compete for their votes, so the new imagination pictures the community as belonging to numerous, nameless, faceless but essentially identical men and women who embody the culture and meaning of the analogous but unique communities.[10]

Although emotions are a building block in explaining the wide appeal of national fervour, Smith's perspective overemphasizes matters of representation and ignores individual agency. How and why the anonymous crowds adopted the nationalist message remains unclear. Many scholars have implicitly or explicitly echoed the controversial 'contagion' model of mass psychologists like Gustave Le Bon: nationalism spreads as an infection among the unthinking and agency-less masses. This analytically problematic and normative view of nationalism dates back to the interwar period, when intellectuals blamed excessive patriotism for the slaughter of the Great War, with philosopher Everett Martin typically denouncing "the whole nation [as] a homicidal crowd".[11]

In the past two decades scholars have been challenging the view of the masses as automatically mimicking the nationalist fervour of elites. A more nuanced model was deemed necessary, especially as this perspective was symptomatic of a detrimental dualism in the entire field of nationalism studies: Western vs. Eastern, universal vs. particularistic and civic vs. ethnic nationalism. All too often these dichotomies were and are morally charged: whereas civic nationalism is seen as the desired type, characterized by inclusiveness and rationality, the ethnic pendant is to be eschewed, due to its exclusive nature and irrational emotionality. These are in fact a specific expression of the deeply rooted binary opposition between reason and emotion in Western culture. Inspired by a fundamental unease with everything considered non-rational some scholars have opted to ignore emotions altogether – at least on the surface, since emotions often return in disguise as 'interests', 'moral values' etc. To avoid such normative logic this volume consciously integrates the realm of emotions into accounts of nationalism. As Jonathan Heany recently stated, a thorough reappraisal of the relationship of emotions and nationalism can be very fruitful for our understanding of the latter.[12]

The possibilities of such an approach were convincingly demonstrated by, among others, Nicole Eustace in her study of revolutionary movements on both sides of the Atlantic in the decades around 1800. She analysed how combinations of reason and emotion provided the ground for political change in the United States, Haiti and France. Apart from showing the historiographical potential of emotional practices and discourses, Eustace's research reminds us that emotion itself is value-free, neither good nor bad. Her analysis was above all a political one: "It is in accepting and then analyzing the role of emotion in political change that scholars can gain strength from the power of feeling."[13] The ambition of historians of nationalism, however, must include other questions as well: not only how emotions left their mark on political matters, but also how the individual appropriated the nationalist fervour in his or her personal emotional life.

In the past two decades, top-down perspectives that take the impact of nationalism on the masses for granted have been challenged and complemented by bottom-up approaches that can be subsumed under the general heading of everyday nationalism research. These scholars study the concrete reproduction of nationhood in daily life. Unlike Michael Billig with his theory of banal nationalism, they see the masses not merely as passive recipients of nationalist propaganda, but also as active consumers and producers of their own sense of national belonging.[14] Yet, how emotions play into the way ordinary people appropriate nationalism has not been thoroughly tackled within this paradigm, and certainly not from a historian's perspective. More often than not, emotions are supposed to be inherently present when individuals – as implicitly passive recipients – consume national narratives, symbols and objects. Emotions also serve as a mechanism to explain how the different 'spheres' of nationalization (from above – the official public sphere, mainly represented by the state, institutions and the media; from below – the private sphere; and the intermediate sphere of organized social movements, associations and secondary groups that shape the 'non-official public sphere') interact and produce, in the end, 'nationalized' individuals who interiorize messages.[15]

Closing the gap

More than twenty years ago Katherine Verdery argued that scholars needed to 'direct attention away from the noisy and visible rhetorics of nationalists' to often invisible practices if they wanted to explain how the nation entered the individual's 'insides'.[16] Bridging the gap between the social and the individual is a difficult undertaking, and not only because of the methodological shift required. In the 1990s Anthony Cohen undertook a noteworthy attempt to disentangle the confusion between the nation, a grand generalization, and its individual members. Arguing against an all too easy (or even lazy) vision of individuals as merely defined by their membership of a collectivity, he emphasized the "mutual implication" of self and nation. Though Cohen's model of "personal nationalism" (cf. infra) had its benefits, he was aware of its short-comings, admitting that his musings about emotions were "essentially spec-ulative", a concession he succinctly summarized as: "I say 'I think' because I do not *know.*"[17] The German social historian Hans-Ulrich Wehler stated something similar some years later, as he questioned the objective nature of 'social classes' and considered them to be 'emotional classes' bound by myths, affects and emotions, which he tried to partly explain with sociobiological arguments.[18]

Cohen's doubt was motivated by a fundamental problem in the study of affects: can you ever be sure of someone's interpretation of the message (or representation) s/he received? Even words offer no direct access to a person's thoughts and feelings, being a translation and a context-specific expres-sion. This is a challenge all authors in the present volume deal with, especially those analysing the impact of elite nationalist messages on individuals.

Recently, several scholars of emotions have come to realize that dividing the representational (the discursive registers) from the non-representational (the affects involved) is not only a difficult but also a pointless endeavour: a rigid separation of discourse and affect renders written and spoken texts, narratives and other familiar objects of qualitative social research useless. The social psy-chologist Margaret Wetherell and her colleagues propose instead a synthesizing method, focusing on affective-discursive practices. Approaching emotions as a mysterious, intangible force makes it hard or even impossible to ascribe them any meaning, whereas assuming simultaneity of the embodied registration of an event and making sense of it justifies a reinvigorated reliance on discursive and other practices. It means the search for emotion does not require a new type of material; the sources are readily available to scholars willing to adopt a new perspective.[19] Nationalism research is no exception.

At first, the study of 'affective nationalism' in everyday practices may sound as an echo of Michael Billig's 'banal nationalism'.[20] But unlike the British sociopsychologist, who located the presence of the national *within* everyday markers such as coins, 'unwaved' flags or the weather forecast, a new generation of scholars looks at nationalism *between* bodies and objects, in their momentary encounters.[21] It is a much more dynamic perspective, adopted with great success, among others, by political geographers relying on auto-ethnographic methods: in close readings of first-hand experiences of affective encounters triggering nationalism, they reconstruct and even evoke the emotional responses during their field research.[22]

Obviously, this kind of participatory observation is barely possible for most historians. More than other social scientists, they are forced to rely on already extant sources in the analysis of emotions. The problem – or rather aware-ness – that words are the expressions of affects and hence no identical copy, is nowadays less considered an obstacle. Some accept that language is the prime medium of shaping and distributing individual emotions and as such the best entrance to past people's feelings.[23] The position of Barbara Rosenwein, one of the leading historians of the 'emotional turn', which has entered the discipline since 2010, is firmer: even if words are often inadequate, they are the material available to historians. Attempts to distinguish between 'expressed' and 'real' emotions are futile. Rosenwein's reaction to the question whether she is dealing with rhetoric rather than emotion is equally clear: "The answer is no. One cannot separate feeling from rhetoric, which is crucial for emotional expression."[24] It is a statement Wetherell would not disagree with.

Historians are becoming increasingly skilful – and confident – in addressing emotions, and they can build on a century of research. Among the first was Johan Huizinga's *The Waning of the Middle Ages* (1919), his influential analysis of late medieval courtly culture as a defence mechanism against the uncertainties and violence of the era. Lucien Febvre and his colleagues of the French *Annales* school assigned a key role to emotions in their history of mentalities ('mentalités'), as demonstrated by Lefebvre's classic study on the 'great fear' of 1789.[25] But the most impressive historiographical landmark is probably Norbert Elias's *Über den Prozeß der Zivilisation* [*The civilizing process*] (1939), his highly influential model of the internalization of self-restraint.[26] Unlike these precursors, today's historians are better aware of the distinctions between conventions and reality. No less important is the acceptance of emotions as being culturally construed instead of timeless and purely biological phenomena. In other words: in all eras and cultures emotions – there is hardly any consensus about a definition – have been learned (to a large extent at least), resulting in a multitude of meanings and an endless variety of practices.[27]

Making methodological choices

Accepting both the possibility and relevance of the history of emotions does not guarantee that sufficient tools are available to investigate this issue. As late-comers to the affective turn, historians have fewer concepts and methods at their disposal to study past feelings. Quite logically historians turn towards disciplines with a longer tradition in the study of emotions and affects. Social psychology in particular has been an inspiration, but some social psychologists (and historians) look sceptically at the choices made by some scholars, for example by neurohistorians, who assume basic emotions are hard-wired into mankind and who prefer (out)dated theories to more recent psychological research.[28]

There is no lack of historically interesting approaches and models in the (interdisciplinary) study of emotions. For the purposes of the current volume we will limit ourselves to an (inevitably cursory) overview of notions that have proven successful in studying the interplay between emotions and nationalism – something which has happened more often than Heany suggests.[29] Several of these models form the background against which the authors in this volume elaborate their cases.

As often in emotions research, feminist studies left their mark in assessing the relationship with nationalism. By integrating 'gender' and 'power' into the analysis of the nation, these scholars revealed how women were (and often are) prone to forms of repression in the national project. The insight that men and women have different roles meant a decisive step towards the dismantlement of the nation as a homogeneous whole – different roles equalled different identity constructions – turning attention towards its individual members.[30] Arguably the first stimulating notion was that of 'embodied nationalism', coined in the early 1990s by gender and colonial specialist Anne McClintock. Arguing against the abstract nature of much nationalism research, she started exploring how citizenship and other aspects of the political realm were present in bodily practices. In her South African case study, she focused on the division between the political and economic agency embodied by men and the moral and spiritual mission embodied by women.[31] Other scholars expanded upon this insight by investigating a plethora of embodied practices, including the use of rape as a weapon of war by Serbian militias in former Yugoslavia.[32] The notion of 'embodied nationalism' has proven itself a valuable step in nationalism research towards the revaluation of the personal, both in body and mind.

The inspiration for Cohen's notion of 'personal nationalism' was not feminist but anthropological. In trying to disentangle individual and collective identities, which tend to get easily conflated in nationalist discourse, he ascribed different roles to nationalist politicians and their audience. Whereas the first always had the intention of 'collectivizing' nationalism, the latter 'personalized' it, appropriating the message to their own experiences and expectations: "We listen to our leaders' vacuous rhetoric and render it meaningful by attributing our own sense to it, so that the sense we hear in the words being uttered is ours, not theirs. We hear their voices but listen to ourselves."[33] Cohen offered a suggestive explanation of how individuals, with all their individual differences, can identify themselves with a unifying message, but he offered fewer arguments *why* people choose to do so. What is their common interest in a collective identity? And what makes, among other options, the *national* narrative so convincing?

Though some scholars emphasize the parallels between Cohen and Billig, their focus was different, respectively on the individual and on the social. In 2007 the sociologist Jonathan Hearn proposed the concept of 'embedded nationalism' to bridge the gap between these two spheres. Hearn's model is indebted to Derek Layder's insight that individuals want to exert control over all unpredictability in their social environment. Emotions turn out to be the key medium in all attempts – not always successful – to achieve personal mastery and a stable sense of self. This power-seeking self is at work in several embedded layers of social interaction, from people's immediate surroundings, over social relations in institutions and organizations, to the encompassing environment of socially created materials and artifacts. Applied to nationalism such a scheme improves our understanding of how and why individuals incorporate all kinds of resources of national identities into their own sense of self: "National identity can suffuse certain social settings, becoming situationally relevant not just in the episodic interactions of individuals, but in the larger and more binding fates of organisations in which people become invested."[34] Hearn closed his article with a metaphor to clarify how nationalism is not sustained by just a few key carriers such as state discourse or the media; it should instead be seen "more like Velcro. Not one big hook and eye, but a multitude of small ones, tiny, daily points of attachment that together can bind very tightly".[35]

Though not always following the fine points of Hearn's 'embedded nationalism', many scholars agree that both personal and social dimensions of national identity are mediated in negotiated power relations. Integrating Sara Ahmed's "cultural politics of emotion", Wetherell for example fully endorses that such an identity is reproduced along a series of relations. In acknowledging that emotional experience is by definition directional – meaning that emotions always relate to an 'object' with its own meaning – she situates the essence of emotions in the relation between objects and subjects: "Affect is distributed. It is an in-between, relational phenomenon."[36] In a recent article on nationalism geographers Peter Merriman and Rhys Jones grounded their relational view of emotions in the theories of seventeenth-century philosopher Baruch Spinoza and his twentieth-century interpreter Gilles Deleuze. The resulting model of relations is a highly dynamic one, characterized by 'rhythmic refrains':

> These national and nationalist refrains are frequently characterized by consistent, relational and territorialized affective ties which take hold of, in and between bodies of different kinds. What the foregrounding and backgrounding of nationalist feelings, atmospheres, sensations and affects make apparent is the way in which new relations and attachments are continually formed, established relations gain consistency and meaning, and particular rhythmic refrains affect and connect in different ways, territorializing and deterritorializing bodies, assemblages and landscapes.[37]

Playing with Billig's notorious 'hot nationalism', Merriman and Jones also introduced the notion of 'flickering spatialities': only in certain relational configurations affective national sentiments appear.[38]

In his aforementioned plea for a reappraisal of the role of emotions in nationalism studies, Heany advocated a similar approach, one of 'process-relationism': in a transaction all units involved derive their meaning and significance from their current, momentary role. In the same vein he argued against the very notion of '(national) identity', preferring 'identification', due to its more processual nature, and – building on Pierre Bourdieu – 'national habitus'. Devoid of essentialist associations, these alternative terms leave more room for agency of local actors and organizations and are better suited to apprehend the emotional dimension of national solidarity – 'habitus' is very much an embodied system and "involves both the cognitive and emotional, conscious and non-conscious processes".[39] In fact, the late German social historian Hans-Ulrich Wehler also turned to 'habitus' as an explanatory tool to understand the binding power of national emotions, placing it in the buffer zone between the conscious and the unconscious sphere, as a cultural code assimilated by individuals in their early childhood. Yet, both Wehler and his pupils stuck to habitus as a social construction determined by institutional and human agency, seen as a consequence of the consolidation of national projects that were originally imposed from above.[40]

A focus on emotions and affects should never obfuscate people and their activities, organizations and relations. Emotions do not exist in isolation.[41] Closs Stephens's article on the so-called atmospheric operation of nationalism during the London 2012 Olympic Games is a case in point. Though correctly assessing the manifold origins of national feelings, the theory of 'affective atmosphere' – currently popular among cultural geographers – seems to be a step back in some ways: not only does the image of a "nebulous, diffuse atmosphere" lack precision, Closs Stephens's descriptions of nationalism as 'infectuous' and 'contagious' bear an uneasy resemblance to Le Bon's questionable ideas on crowd psychology.[42]

Other concepts are more useful tools in understanding affective nationalism. Several authors in the current volume (consciously) use the term 'belonging'. Though often put forward as a self-explanatory synonym of (national) identity or citizenship, human geographer Marco Antonsich has offered a framework for the study of belonging, which can be most revealing for the personal and emotional dimensions of nationhood. While in its first meaning (belonging as the personal, intimate notion of feeling at home) the term is under-researched but quite straightforward, its use as a discursive strategy is more complex. In claims of who is welcome and who should be excluded, the social dimensions of belonging are revealed. Politics of belonging always involve a process of negotiation, which are performed through individual and collective practices.[43] In case studies of affective nationalism the notion of 'belonging' deserves a central place.

Another fruitful concept which is explicitly applied in the current volume (see Faraldo's Chapter 9) is that of Rosenwein's 'emotional communities', which are defined as "groups [...] that have their own particular values, modes of feeling, and ways to express these feelings". Several emotional communities can (and do) exist in the same place at the same time. Often they overlap due to processes of imitation, borrowing and distancing.[44] In Chapter 4, Josephine Hoegaerts brings a historian's sensibility for historical change to the notion of emotional communities. Invoking the recent concept of 'emotional frontiers', Hoegaerts introduces the potential for both subtle and dramatic changes. Individuals try to meet the emotional imperatives of a given social environment, including its hierarchies and structures. Yet, in case these same individuals fail to understand the cultural and emotional codes that are proper to that situation, breaking the social and cultural frontiers also becomes a painful, deeply emotional experience.[45]

It is hard, but probably unnecessary, to prioritize between the available models and concepts. With its wide-ranging theoretical background this volume aims at stimulating and feeding the debate on the relationship between emotions and nationalism from a historical perspective, exploring the possibilities of the available theoretical and methodological tools. In the spring of 2017, during the workshop held at the Ludwig-Maximilians University of Munich where earlier versions of the chapters were presented and discussed, the participants – today's authors – shared the intention to attribute a key role to emotions in nationalism studies. We are confident that the chapters in the current volume reflect both the ambitions of and debates among the authors.

Guide to this volume

The contributions to this volume explore and analyse a wide variety of cases, offering a panorama of nations and emotions in Europe since the end of the eighteenth century. First is Raúl Moreno Almendral's chapter 'Feeling nationhood while telling lives: ego-documents, emotions and national character during the Age of Revolutions'. Drawing on a corpus of 170 diaries, journals, memoirs and travel-books written between the 1780s and the 1830s from Great Britain, Spain and France, Moreno Almendral explores the links between emotions and self-narration as a site of potential nation-building in a key moment in the history of nationalism. His contribution highlights how the political intensification of the Age of Revolutions merged with the strong emotionalized tools that individuals use to express their national allegiances. He argues that emotions could only become so intense and politicized on a personal level precisely because of the shaping role of the new languages of nation.

In Chapter 2, 'So close and yet so far: degrees of proximity in pauper letters to Dutch national power holders around 1800', Joris Oddens studies petitions of poor people within the broader context of the Netherlands' shift from a confederate, oligarchic republic to a centralized monarchy. The connection Dutch paupers exhibited in their letters to king-like power holders ranged between the paradoxes of an emotion-less closeness and an affectionate distance. When they envisaged their power holders as 'ordinary' mortals belonging to the same community, a personal, emotional bond was generally missing in the letters. At the other end of the spectrum, some paupers looked up to their 'betters' as monarchical rulers by divine right. Despite their sense of social separation, they felt a close emotional connection that was reminiscent of their relationship to God. In all letters a strong sense of nationhood was lacking. Paupers expressed their 'subjecthood' as local, partisan or religious rather than national. In this sense the emotional appeal of kingship still had a pre-modern character. Only during the second half of the nineteenth century would the Dutch monarchy become nationalized among the populace at large.

In Chapter 3, '"Lou tresor dóu Felibrige": an Occitan dictionary and its emotional potential for readers', Martina Niedhammer investigates dozens of personal letters addressed to Frédéric Mistral (1830–1914), the most prominent leader of the Occitan movement, from the late 1860s through 1886. She sheds light on the construction of a distinct Occitan 'groupness' and on the emotional and personal dimensions of region- and nation-building. Praised by its proponents for its noble, antique past which can be traced back to the medieval troubadours, but taunted by its opponents as a 'patois', Occitan was never able to shed its status as a 'minor' language. Nevertheless it developed a highly emotional appeal for its supporters and established strong ties of individual belonging. In this respect Niedhammer problematizes the emotional interstices between nationhood, ethnicity and regionalism.

Chapter 4, Josephine Hoegaerts' 'Learning to love: embodied practices of patriotism in the Belgian nineteenth-century classroom (and beyond)', takes up Monique Scheer's suggestion that "the body is not a static, timeless, universal foundation that produces ahistorical emotional arousal, but is itself socially situated, adaptive, trained, plastic, and thus historical". Hoegaerts applies this notion to primary school children, and to the arousal of love for the fatherland. How, this chapter asks, were children expected to acquire the vocabularies and practices connected to patriotism, and how did they appropriate what they were taught? Hoegaerts draws on a variety of sources relating to geography teaching in the nineteenth-century primary city schools of Antwerp (Belgium). Her dataset consists of manuals for geography, teacher education, correspondence and, most importantly perhaps, documents pertaining to the organization of school excursions, including reports of these trips written by pupils. Even though the latter bear the hallmarks of educational normativity, they show some level of agency, especially in the way pupils connected individual corporeal experiences and practices (such as seeing, walking, eating and singing) with the more collective and abstract notions of the nation and patriotism.

In Chapter 5, 'Performing and remembering personal nationalism among workers in late Russian Poland', Wiktor Marzec examines the emotional commitment to nationalism of industrial workers at the turn of the nineteenth and twentieth centuries. The Revolution of 1905 brought about massive political participation of urban workers. Using a corpus of ca. 110 autobiographical testimonies written by proletarian militants from various political backgrounds, this chapter exposes the tension between, on the one hand, 'emotives', as William Reddy would call the expression of feelings in a language which circulated in nationalist propaganda, and, on the other hand, the emotions articulated by the workers writing about their pasts. Marzec demonstrates how emotives were successfully appropriated in ego-writing to justify a nationalist commitment that went against the mainstream of working-class memory and to validate 'fratricidal' practices like strike breaking and anti-Semitism.

Chapter 6, Thomas Blanck's 'In search of the true Italy: emotional practices and the nation in Fiume 1919/1920' focuses on Gabriele D'Annunzio's annexation of Fiume, the multicultural port city in the northern Adriatic that was mostly inhabited by Italian- and Croat-speakers. Fiume became an allegory for a vital, young, emotionally charged 'new Italy', which attracted numerous men and women to the port city. Based on autobiographical and archival sources of the legionaries involved, Blanck investigates the strong connection between national and emotional loyalty and the close association between bodily affects and nationalism. While the old Italy was no longer able to evoke feelings, the new one naturally inspired love and desire. Through public speeches, rallies and festivities Italian legionaries successfully aroused shared bodily affects and thereby conveyed the idea of an inclusive emotional community. From late 1919 onwards, however, this sense of belonging together with the emotional community of the new Italy proved to be short-lived and highly dysfunctional. The emotional practices which had initially been so successful were now turned against their very creators.

In Chapter 7, Raul Cârstocea spotlights how Romania's interwar fascists instrumentalized public funerals, mourning and the assorted emotions that these induced to attract mass support in the face of harsh state repression. On February 13, 1937 Bucharest was the scene of the massively attended funeral of Ion I. Moța and Vasile Marin, two of the Iron Guard's most prominent members, who were killed in combat in the Spanish Civil War. Their burial exemplifies the 'thanatic nationalism' of Romanian fascism. Using archival sources and the coverage of the funeral in the contemporary press, Cârstocea argues that this "unique death cult, unusually morbid even for a fascist movement" (Payne) represented a fine-tuned and skilfully employed tool of emotional mobilization. It struck a sensitive chord with many ordinary people who had recently experienced personal loss of close ones in World War I. This emotional sense of nationhood had more popular appeal than the state's modernizing project, which hinged on notions of accelerated development modelled on Western patterns that remained alien to a predominantly 'peasant' population.

In his contribution, Chapter 8, 'Feeling the Fatherland: Finnish soldiers' lyrical attachments to the nation during the Second World War', Ville Kivimäki investigates a collection of ca. 850 unpublished frontline poems gathered by the Information Department of the Finnish Army High Command. Despite the evident propaganda purposes these poems were supposed to serve, they also offer rare insight into the reciprocal interaction between the 'official' wartime rhetoric and the idealized sentiments of war among the frontline soldiers themselves. It is obvious that they often reacted allergically to any patronizing attempt to promote patriotism from above, and it is equally clear that they grew disillusioned with the lofty nationalistic rhetoric as the war dragged on. But to become disillusioned, there must first be something that is consequently exposed as an illusion. Thus, the topic of this chapter is: Finnish soldiers' emotional attachment to the nation before the apparent disillusionment; and what this tells us about the power and emotional attraction of nationalism.

Using a dynamic interpretation of Barbara Rosenwein's concept of 'emotional communities' José-María Faraldo, in Chapter 9, examines how Polish-speaking settlers came to grips with their new lives on the so-called Western territories as an instance of 'emotional reconstruction'. These Western regions were an area of around 103,000 km² of former German territories that came 'under Polish administration' after the Second World War. After the expulsion of about eight million German-speakers, millions of Polish-speakers came to live in these urbanized and partially industrialized regions. The new inhabitants found a 'foreign', 'alien' land- and cityscape which they associated with the 'Germans', the people who had occupied their country and caused so much pain in their recent history. The settlers' experience was not only a private, subjective matter. It was part of a larger social process, governed by a nationalizing state that harnessed ideology, politics and cultural pressure to foment emotional acceptance of a new political (and national) situation. The source material used includes as much as 800 diaries and memoirs, as well as documents of the Polish national and regional archives.

This volume has the ambition to improve our understanding of the dynamics between emotions and nationalism. Through a set of diverse case studies that hail from several geographical contexts and use a wide array of methodologies and sources, it offers a multifaceted approach that goes beyond the neat dichotomies which have plagued nationalism studies for too long.

Antwerp, Leuven and Santiago de Compostela, October 2019

Notes

1 Verdery, 'Whither "nation" and "nationalism"?', p. 41.
2 Anderson, *Imagined Communities*, p. 4.
3 Boddice, 'The affective turn'.
4 Smith, 'The limits', pp. 565–566.
5 Eustace et al., 'AHR Conversation', p. 1487; Seyfert, 'Beyond personal feelings', pp. 27–31; Plamper, *The History of Emotions*.
6 Anderson, *Imagined Communities*, p. 4. See Heany, 'Emotions and nationalism', p. 248.
7 Greenfeld, 'Etymology, definitions, types', pp. 259–260.
8 Thus, the only contribution that approaches the issue of "nationalism from below" in John Breuilly's edited *The Oxford Handbook of the History of Nationalism* barely deals with emotions (Déloye, 'National identity and everyday life'). Other readers on nationalism and ethnicity do not include emotions at all (see Guibernau and Rex, *The Ethnicity Reader*).
9 See on this issue: Beneš, *Workers and Nationalism*; Van Ginderachter and Beyen, *Nationhood from Below*. See also Van Ginderachter, *The Everyday Nationalism*.
10 Smith, *The Ethnic Origins of Nations*, p. 171.
11 Martin, *The Behavior of Crowds*, p. 79. See Garcia-Garcia, 'After the Great War', p. 114.
12 Heany, 'Emotions and nationalism', pp. 246–248.
13 Eustace, 'Motion and political change', p. 181.
14 On everyday nationalism see: Fox and Miller-Idriss, 'Everyday nationhood'; Knott, 'Everyday nationalism'; Skey and Antonsich, *Everyday Nationhood*; McCrone and Bechhoffer, *Understanding National Identity*; Goode and Stroup, 'Everyday nationalism'. For a critique, see Smith, 'The limits'.
15 Quiroga, 'The three spheres'.
16 Verdery, 'Whither "nation" and "nationalism"?', p. 41.

17 Cohen, 'Personal nationalism', pp. 804, 809, 812.
18 Wehler, 'Emotionen in der Geschichte'.
19 Wetherell et al., 'Settling space', pp. 57, 59–60.
20 Billig, *Banal Nationalism*.
21 Merriman and Jones, 'Nations, materialities and affects', p. 602.
22 Militz and Schurr, 'Affective nationalism'.
23 Matt, 'Recovering the invisible', pp. 42–43.
24 Rosenwein, *Generations of Feeling*, pp. 4–9. See also Stalfort, *Die Erfindung*, pp. 19–167.
25 See Lefebvre, *La Grande Peur*.
26 Matt and Stearns, 'Introduction', p. 3.
27 Reddy, *The Navigation of Feeling*, p. xi.
28 Leys, 'The turn to affect', pp. 437–440; Wetherell, 'Trends', pp. 141–142.
29 Heany, 'Emotions and nationalism', p. 248.
30 See Frevert, *Emotions in History*, pp. 87–148.
31 McClintock, 'No longer in a future heaven', p. 109; Idem, 'Family feuds', pp. 61–62, 66. McClintock gained more attention for this breakthrough in her *Imperial Leather*, pp. 352–389.
32 Mayer, 'Embodied nationalisms', pp. 155–157.
33 Cohen, 'Personal nationalism', p. 807.
34 Hearn, 'National identity', pp. 666–670 (quot. p. 671).
35 Hearn, 'National identity', p. 672.
36 Wetherell, 'Trends', pp. 154–158. See also Ahmed, *The Cultural Politics*.
37 Merriman and Jones, 'Nations, materialities and affects', pp. 603–605.
38 Ibid.
39 Heany, 'Emotions and nationalism', pp. 251–257, 261. See also Goltermann, *Körper*.
40 Wehler, *Nationalismus*.
41 See Wetherell, 'Trends', p. 159; Antonsich and Skey, 'Affective nationalism', p. 845.
42 Closs Stephens, 'The affective atmospheres', pp. 182, 184.
43 Antonsich, 'Searching for belonging'.
44 Rosenwein, *Generations of Feeling*, pp. 3–4.
45 Vallgårda, 'Divorce, bureaucracy, and emotional frontiers', pp. 86–87.

References

Ahmed, Sara, *The cultural politics of emotion*, New York, Routledge, 2004.

Anderson, Benedict, *Imagined communities. Reflections on the origin and spread of nationalism*, London, Verso, 1994 [1983].

Antonsich, Marco and Skey, Michael, 'Affective nationalism: Issues of power, agency and method', in: *Progress in Human Geography*, vol. 41, no. 6, 2017, pp. 843–845.

Antonsich, Marco, 'Searching for belonging – An analytical framework', in: *Geography Compass*, vol. 4, no. 6, 2010, pp. 644–659.

Beneš, Jakub S., *Workers and nationalism: Czech and German Social Democracy in Habsburg Austria, 1890–1918*, Oxford, Oxford University Press, 2016.

Billig, Michael, *Banal nationalism*, London, Sage, 1995.

Boddice, Rob, 'The affective turn: Historicizing the emoticions', in: Tileagâ, Cristian and Byford, Jovan (eds), *Psychology and history. Interdisciplinary explorations*, Cambridge, Cambridge University Press, 2014, pp. 147–165.

Breuilly, John (ed.), *The Oxford handbook of the history of nationalism*, Oxford, Oxford University Press, 2013.

Closs Stephens, Angharad, 'The affective atmospheres of nationalism', in: *Cultural Geographies*, vol. 23, no. 2, 2016, pp. 181–198.

Cohen, Anthony P., 'Personal nationalism: A Scottish view of some rites, rights, and wrongs', in: *American Ethnologist*, vol. 23, no. 4, 1996, pp. 802–815.

Déloye, Yves, 'National identity and everyday life', in: Breuilly, John (ed.), *The Oxford handbook of the history of nationalism*, Oxford, Oxford University Press, 2013, pp. 615–634.

Eustace, Nicole *et al.*, 'AHR Conversation: The historical study of emotions', in: *The American Historical Review*, vol. 117, no. 5, 2012, pp. 1487–1531.

Eustace, Nicole, 'Motion and political change', in: Matt, Susan J. and Stearns, Peter N. (eds), *Doing emotions history*, Urbana Ill., University of Springfield Press, 2014, pp. 163–183.

Fox, Jon E. and Miller-Idriss, Cynthia, 'Everyday nationhood', in: *Ethnicities*, vol. 8, no. 4, 2008, pp. 536–563.

Frevert, Ute, *Emotions in history – Lost and found*, Budapest – New York, Central European University Press, 2011.

Garcia-Garcia, Juan, 'After the Great War: Nationalism, degenerationism and mass psychology', in: *Journal of Social and Political Psychology*, vol. 3, no. 1, 2015, pp. 103–123.

Goltermann, Svenja, *Körper der Nation. Habitusformierung und die Politik des Turnens 1860–1890*, Göttingen, Vandenhoeck & Ruprecht, 1998.

Goode, James Paul and Stroup, David R., 'Everyday nationalism: Constructivism for the masses', in: *Social Science Quarterly*, vol. 96, no. 3, 2015, pp. 717–739.

Greenfeld, Liah, 'Etymology, definitions, types', in: Motyl, Alexander J., *Encyclopedia of nationalism, vol. 1: Fundamental themes*, San Diego: Academic Press, 2001, pp. 251–265.

Guibernau, Montserrat and Rex, Jon (eds.), *The ethnicity reader. Nationalism, multiculturalism and migration*, Cambridge, Polity, 2nd edition, 2010.

Heany, Jonathan, 'Emotions and nationalism: A reappraisal', in: Demertzis, Nicolas (ed.), *Emotions in politics. The affect dimension in political tension*, London, Palgrave-Macmillan, 2013, pp. 243–263.

Hearn, Jonathan, 'National identity: Banal, personal and embedded', in: *Nations and Nationalism*, vol. 13, no. 4, 2007, pp. 657–674.

Knott, Eleanor, 'Everyday nationalism: A review of the literature', in: *Studies on National Movements*, vol. 3, 2015, available at: http://snm.nise.eu/index.php/studies/article/view/0308s (accessed 21 October 2019).

Lefebvre, Georges, *La Grande Peur de 1789*, Paris, Armand Colin, 1932.

Leys, Ruth, 'The turn to affect: A critique', in: *Critical Inquiry*, vol. 37, no. 3, 2011, pp. 434–472.

Martin, Everett Dean, *The behavior of crowds. A psychological study*, New York, Harper & Brothers, 1920.

Matt, Susan J. and Stearns, Peter N., 'Introduction', in: Matt, Susan J. and Stearns, Peter N. (eds.), *Doing emotions history*, Urbana Ill., University of Springfield Press, 2014, pp. 1–13.

Matt, Susan J., 'Recovering the invisible: Methods for the historical study of emotions', in: Matt, Susan J. and Stearns, Peter N. (eds.), *Doing emotions history*, Urbana Ill., University of Springfield Press, 2014, pp. 41–53.

Mayer, Tamar, 'Embodied nationalisms', in: Staeheli, Lynn, Kofman, Eleonore and Peake Linda (eds.), *Mapping women, making politics: Feminist perspectives on political geography*, New York, Routledge, 2004, pp. 153–167.

McClintock, Anne, '"No longer in a future heaven": Women and nationalism in South Africa', in: *Transition*, vol. 51, 1991, pp. 104–123.

McClintock, Anne, 'Family feuds: Gender, nationalism and the family', in: *Feminist Review*, vol. 44, 1993, pp. 61–80.

McClintock, Anne, *Imperial leather: Race, gender and sexuality in the colonial context*, New York, Routledge, 1995.

McCrone, David and Bechhoffer, Frank, *Understanding national identity*, Cambridge, Cambridge University Press, 2015.

Merriman, Peter and Jones, Rhys, 'Nations, materialities and affects', in: *Progress in Human Geography*, vol. 41, no. 5, 2017, pp. 600–617.

Militz, Elisabeth and Schurr, Carolin, 'Affective nationalism: Banalities of belonging in Azerbaijan', in: *Political Geography*, vol. 54, 2016, pp. 54–63.

Motyl, Alexander J., *Encyclopedia of nationalism*, San Diego: Academic Press, 2001.

Plamper, Jan, *The history of emotions. An introduction*, Oxford – New York, Oxford University Press, 2015.

Quiroga, Alejandro, 'The three spheres. A theoretical model of mass nationalisation. The case of Spain', in: *Nations and Nationalism*, vol. 20, no. 4, 2014, pp. 683–700.

Reddy, William M., *The navigation of feeling: A framework for the history of emotions*, Cambridge – New York, Cambridge University Press, 2001.

Rosenwein, Barbara H., *Generations of feeling. A history of emotions, 600–1700*, Cambridge, Cambridge University Press, 2015.

Seyfert, Robert, 'Beyond personal feelings and collective emotions: Toward a theory of social affect', in: *Theory, Culture & Society*, vol. 29, no. 6, 2012, pp. 27–47.

Skey, Michael and Antonsich, Marco (eds.), *Everyday nationhood. Theorizing culture, identity and belonging after banal nationalism*, Basingstoke, Palgrave Macmillan, 2017.

Smith, Anthony D., 'The limits of everyday nationhood', in: *Ethnicities*, vol. 8, no. 4, 2008, pp. 563–573.

Smith, Anthony D., *The ethnic origins of nations*, Oxford, Blackwell, 1986.

Stalfort, Jutta, *Die Erfindung der Gefühle. Eine Studie über den historischen Wandel menschlicher Emotionalität (1750.1850)*, Bielefeld, Transcript, 2013.

Vallgårda, Karen, 'Divorce, bureaucracy, and emotional frontiers: Marital dissolution in late nineteenth-century Copenhagen', in: *Journal of Family History*, vol. 42, no. 1, 2017, pp. 81–95.

Van Ginderachter, Maarten and Beyen, Marnix (eds.), *Nationhood from below. Europe in the Long Nineteenth Century*, Basingstoke, Palgrave-Macmillan, 2012.

Van Ginderachter, Maarten, *The everyday nationalism of workers. A social history of modern Belgium*, Stanford CA, Stanford University Press, 2019.

Verdery, Katherine, 'Whither "nation" and "nationalism"?', in: *Daedalus*, vol. 122, no. 3, 1993, pp. 37–46.

Wehler, Hans-Ulrich, 'Emotionen in der Geschichte. Sind soziale Klassen auch emotionale Klassen?', in: Dipper, Christof (ed.), *Europäische Sozialgeschichte. Festschrift für Wolfgang Schieder*, Berlin, Duncker und Humblot, 2000, pp. 461–473.

Wehler, Hans-Ulrich, *Nationalismus: Geschichte – Formen – Folgen*, Munich, Beck, 2001.

Wetherell, Margaret *et al.*, 'Settling space and covering the nation: Some conceptual considerations in analysing affect and discourse', in: *Emotion, Space and Society*, vol. 16, 2015, pp. 56–64.

Wetherell, Margaret, 'Trends in the turn to affect: A social psychological critique', in: *Body & Society*, vol. 21, no. 2, 2015, pp. 139–166.

1 Feeling nationhood while telling lives

Ego-documents, emotions and national character during the Age of Revolutions

Raúl Moreno Almendral

Introduction: emotions and personal approaches to nationhood

In late 1812, the Napoleonic army that had invaded the Russian Empire some months before was in a disastrous retreat. Being chased down by the enemy, a band of French soldiers was lucky enough to come across a Polish baron who gave them shelter in his estate near Białystok.[1] According to the memoirs of one of them, former sailor Henri Ducor, the nobleman could speak French fluidly and, while feeding the group, enthusiastically informed them of Napoleon's victories at Lutzen, Bautzen and Wurschen (May 1813). The baron spoke of the Russians as though they were animals and barbarians. Apparently, they had offered him a position in the imperial administration of Poland, but he had refused.

> I would like them [the Russians] to be properly penetrated by the cordial hatred that my fellow-countrymen and I have for their nation. That would be a sort of revenge and compensation. This hatred, we know how to instil it into our children, because it must survive us, it must be everlasting, and, thank God, our children will understand us. Sooner or later, they will be their parents' avengers, and the liberators of their country.[2]

Ducor seemed to be unbothered by the oxymoron "cordial hatred" and went on to write: "We could only applaud the baron's generous feelings." It is not clear whether the adjective 'generous' is intended to be applied to the hatred itself, or rather to its employment towards the emancipation of an oppressed nation, which was a morally elevated cause for allegedly rational enlightened and first-generation liberals.

This way of talking and thinking belongs to a fundamental period in the history of nationalism and raises basic questions about the relation between nations and emotions. Almost intuitively many claims of national belonging are expressed in emotional terms: love for the country, pride of one's nation and its achievements, shame when one's nation or one of its members does not live up to the imagined standards, contempt for other supposedly inferior peoples, etc. Conversely, if emotions are shaped by cultural frameworks and mindsets, nationalism would definitely have had an impact on the way human beings have felt for at least the last few centuries. Ducor's words also uncover other issues, such as the coexistence of apparently contradictory emotions and the individual/collective tension that is familiar to any nationalism scholar.

The history of emotions and the history of nationalism have recently gone through major transformations that reinforce the possibility of an analytical interaction between both fields of enquiry. As Jan Plamper outlines in his introductory survey, the recent academic interest in emotions constitutes a serious attempt to overcome the old debate between universalism (emotions are essentially the same over time and space) and culturalism (emotions are profoundly shaped by societal ideas and practices about feelings, so variations in time and space can be critical).[3] Concepts such as Barbara Rosenwein's 'emotional communities' and William Reddy's 'emotional regime' have gained traction and have been widely debated. These scholars do not deny the biological basis of emotions, but they assert the existence of different systems of feeling. Clearly, this has implications for every scholar working with phenomena that are based in perceptions of community: how do these emotional communities relate to more classic, 'identitarian' communities, based on nationhood, race, gender, social class, etc.? When analysing how these perceptions of commonality are created and reproduced, do emotions explain how identities work and/or do identities explain how emotions are felt? Are they imbricated, identical or separate?

Within nationalism studies, there has been an even more fundamental transformation. Object and agent are no longer conflated, at least in theory. Thus, nations are not the actors of their own formation, but the result of a process in which individuals and their asymmetric interactions should be studied as its actual agents. Reified abstractions such as 'nation', 'people' or 'State' are no longer unquestioned analytical tools. Historians and social scientists have started to develop specific concepts in what we can call the 'cognitive' and 'agency turns' within nationalism studies.[4] Thus, concepts such as 'personal nationalism', 'experiences of nation', 'nationhood from below', 'everyday nationalism' and 'national indifference' are being extensively explored and discussed.[5] Equally, more scholars are trying to gauge the thoughts and feelings of non-elite groups.[6]

This chapter hinges on personal or self-narratives as a way of addressing these issues. Self-narratives and ego-documents are separate but at the same time overlapping source types.[7] A letter or a recorded conversation can be classified as an ego-document, but not as a personal narrative. Conversely, every self-narrative is an ego-document. In this chapter, I will only draw on self-narratives, which usually have a more elaborate narrative structure, a more emphatic presence of memory processes, and an explicit but problematic claim of correspondence between author and narrator and/or main characters.[8]

In concreto, this chapter draws on a corpus of 170 British, French, Spanish and Portuguese diaries, journals, memoirs and travel books written from the

1780s to the 1830s, compiled in the course of my PhD research on personal nationhood during the Age of Revolutions. In this period the concept of nation received its modern content. Although the term 'nation' is very old, it was usually employed as an exonimic of 'tribe' until early modern times. During the seventeenth and eighteenth centuries, some intellectuals started to talk of nations as the basic organizational units of human diversity. They drew more and more systematized charts of peoples to which specific 'national characters' were associated. By the late Enlightenment, these features included a link between psychology, morality and political institutions. Individuals from the Age of Revolutions, especially the most educated ones, had this in mind when faced with what has been called 'modern nationalism'.[9]

In this chapter I will only use the British, French and Spanish narratives from my broader corpus.[10] These materials are very heterogeneous: archival or published, amounting to dozens or thousands of pages, written by people from different walks of life in terms of profession, education, gender, literacy and provenance. Out of the forty-seven British accounts, 49 per cent can be considered elites, 38 per cent had a professional link to the military, 38 per cent were from peripheral, i.e. non-English, regions and 13 per cent were women.[11] The figures in the forty-five French narratives are 62 per cent elites, 44 per cent non-central origin (not raised in the Île-de-France and nearby departments), 69 per cent military and 13 per cent women. In the Spanish case, 60 per cent elites, 22 per cent military, 62 per cent non-Castilian and 9 per cent women.[12]

As the three major European transoceanic monarchies in the Early Modern Period, Britain, France and Spain shared the systemic political crisis that shook the *status quo* during the Age of Revolutions and all of them played significant roles in the so-called Revolutionary and Napoleonic Wars. Nonetheless, there were three important differences: first, Britons did not experience the large-scale total war and revolutionary breakdown of the state which continental French and Spanish subjects/citizens did. Second, Britain in the late eighteenth and early nineteenth century presents a specific political culture where the notions of 'people' and 'nation' were shaped by the seventeenth-century parliamentary revolution's legacy. Thus, while the French and Spanish liberals proclaimed the nation as sovereign during their revolutions, 'nation' was a much more cultural and flexible concept in Britain as sovereignty was attached to "the people in Parliament" together with the King. Obviously, the power of the King and the force of absolutism were much stronger in Spain than in France. In fact, while Louis XVI was killed, the Monarchy in Spain as an institution was never seriously questioned.

Drawing on these sources I will explore how the political intensification brought about by the Age of Revolutions produced parallel evolutions in nationhood semantics and emotional displays. Then I will look at how those situations created by the revolutionary and Napoleonic wars provided some of my corpus individuals with situations of boundary-making where emotions played a shaping role. Finally, I will turn from the 'external other' to the 'internal' one, discussing tensions within the nation that were also framed in emotive terms. I conclude my chapter with a reflection on whether nations and emotional communities are the same thing.

A changing world of nations: from moral sentiments to (anti) revolutionary passions

The idea of the world as a mosaic of nations that are collective subjects endowed with specific and distinctive traits, agency and, in the case of Britain, France and Spain, a political entity, was already in place by 1780. This was no longer the original ancient-medieval *natio*'s meaning or, arguably, the early modern 'ethnotypes'. However, its role and even inclusion in the history of nationalism is and will always be disputable. I argue that the Enlightened, Liberal and Romantic ways of imagining the nation (as a public spirit, as a sovereign community, as a cultural reflection of genuineness and mystic distinctiveness) are decisive turning points in the rise of modern and contemporary nationalism.

The evidence of the first and second usages is clear and consistent for highly educated subjects and for memoirs and self-narratives that were meant to be published. The situation is more debatable and ambiguous for other social groups and for diaries and more private memoirs, but the case is still strong. It is also clear that the experience of revolution introduces decisive qualitative and quantitative changes (especially regarding French and Spanish experiences). It is, for instance, common to find the image of the British as a superior people because they had attained the best institutional system that granted them true liberties without bloodshed and the destruction of valuable traditions, while the French imagined themselves as superior because they were the supposedly most civilized nation and, with the Revolution, they truly conquered freedom. Both of these tropes lean on the kind of liberal universalism that would shape the political history of the first half of the nineteenth century. By contrast, this was very unlikely in Spanish sources, which relied more on the defence of Catholic and Monarchist authenticity and national independence.

The presence of the emotive element in picturing that world of nations and explaining the nature of its bonds is undeniable. For instance, the English painter Joseph Farington wrote in his diary entry of the 12th of April 1799 about that day's dinner table conversation. His interlocutor spoke of "the wretched state of France", but he deemed its destruction unlikely because, contrary to the situation in other countries, "the French are a very national people". According to Farington, he told him that the English were "the most national people in Europe", and after them, the French and the Swiss. "The Germans, the Italians have no national feeling, – Prussians, Austrians etc only feel for those they are associated with, viz. for their neighbours, – they do not feel for the Country, – like Englishmen & Frenchmen."[13]

In the self-narratives, being national was often associated with "feeling for the country", but in this case there was no further elaboration on what 'feeling' and 'country' meant. In other cases, the feeling itself was at least specified beyond a mere attachment. It is striking how Anglican vicar Joseph Townsend and Scottish official Alexander James agreed on the way they expressed their pride for their Britishness while being abroad with more than forty years' difference. Townsend travelled around the Iberian Peninsula in 1786–87. He sailed past Gibraltar when it was under siege by the Catholic King. "[I] had the satisfaction to view the proud rock, at the sight of which every British heart should triumph in the recollection."[14] For his part, James was sent to 1830s Portugal, where, as in Spain, liberals and absolutists were clashing and fighting a civil war. He described his feelings as his ship approached Porto:

> If there is a spark of patriotism in the breast of a Briton, it must be elicited on seeing a British frigate on a foreign sea; there is nothing in the world so calculated to warm one's heart and cause it to exult in our country's greatness as this.[15]

This tone contrasts with that of individuals who had first-person lived experiences of intense and intimate violence. Renée Bordereau wrote (or dictated) her memoirs while she was in prison in 1814. Two decades before, she had been one of the leaders of the *Armée catholique et royale* (dressed as a man). She described very vividly why she started fighting a war that she would eventually in 1814 consider to be a civil war between Frenchmen:

> The royalist insurrection in La Vendée in 1793 attracted to our country [*notre pays*] the armies of the republicans, which ravaged and massacred without mercy. I saw forty-two relatives of mine die successively, but the death of my father, perpetrated right in front of me, sent me into transports of rage and distress [*rage et désespoir*]. From that moment on, I decided to sacrifice my body to the King, offer my soul to God, and swear that I would fight until death or victory.[16]

More indirect, symbolic and/or distant acts could also be framed in equally intense displays of emotion. A case in point is Laure Permon, general Junot's wife. She composed her eighteen-volume memoir, published in the early 1830s, without any restraint on including her reactions to hearsay events. Very supportive of Napoleon, she mentioned that 'a foreigner' had dared to appear before the King of France with a *giberne* (a cartridge pouch) with the inscription 'Waterloo' on it:

> Shame! Infamy! Then what?, have we become so contemptible that a friend more insolent and dishonourably outrageous than an enemy can come to the palace that the nation has given to its kings and insult our supposed weakness? [...] [What he has done is the same as saying:] 'You are the king of a petty nation; I mock you.' I am only a woman, but I clenched my fists, my breast set on fire, my eyes got teary, and my heartbeat

speeded up until almost hurting; and I am just a woman! But this woman has seen all the glories of the Republic and the Empire, this woman is French ... she is a patriotic Frenchwoman ... she has cried out of joy when seeing the tricolour flag. [...] The king of the French must have really suffered watching such an insult to the nation that has chosen him.[17]

Apart from its interest from a gender perspective (the stereotype of women being more emotional than men clashes here with the men as supposedly more active, decided and politically involved subjects), the excerpt reveals a basic model of emotionality that was hegemonic in the Western world throughout modern times: emotions are intimate and internal reactions to certain stimuli or situations, often unleashed after a process of accumulation or 'boiling'. Applied to the issue of nationalism, concrete emotions shape a more general national belonging.

However, we can also find accounts that depict emotions as 'a flow' or 'an atmosphere' that is originally external to individuals and engulfs or seizes them. Laure Junot herself described a sort of collective ecstasy that supposedly took place in the town of Vizille, near Grenoble, when Napoleon made an appearance on his way to Paris in 1815. According to her, "almost every youngster had tricolour ribbons on their hats and preceded the emperor singing *La Marseillaise* and *Le Chant du Départ!*" She also pointed out that "there was something old and beautiful, as in the memories of ancient Roman times, in those popular celebrations and in this driving force (*élan*) of an entire free nation in the expression of its love".[18] In this picture, the behaviour of the inhabitants of Vizille was not an individual response to personal inputs, but rather it sprouted as healthy and worthy branches from something bigger, a collective spirit that went beyond those particular circumstances. Thus, it seems that, like in Ducor's case, Junot assumed the existence of a sort of national *Geist* that 'penetrates them' and made them feel accordingly.

The parallel and reciprocal political/emotional intensification as a major factor in the nationalizing experience of the Age of Revolutions is also visible in Spain. One of the key moments is the spring/summer of 1808, when the 2nd of May uprising in Madrid ended in the breakdown of the Old Regime Monarchical State, in a process of resistance and collaboration, and in the inception of a liberal revolution. Anti-liberal Juan Gabriel del Moral, a lower *hidalgo* from the Alpujarra, composed a private memoir, probably in the late 1820s, in which the *Dos de Mayo*, usually presented as a liberal myth, is remembered as a purely national deed. For him, the French invasion was a divine punishment because the Spaniards had betrayed their traditions and, importing 'French ideas', had become "lovers of living in complete liberty, independent of God, its holy Church and its ministers". This was especially true for the rich and the intellectuals, who had handed the country over to the "tyrant of Europe" by supporting the king appointed by Napoleon, his brother Joseph. But the ordinary Spanish people stayed true to the nation's essence and defended its independence against pro-foreigner elites and the invaders, an event that Del Moral praised as a positive surprise:

The fury (*el fuego*) of the 2nd of May in Madrid travelled through air (*penetró por el aire*) so quickly to every city, town and village in Spain that (rare thing) it [the uprising] was known almost by the same courier in Toledo, Figueres, Cádiz, Pamplona, Badajoz, Seville, Guadalajara, etc.

The entire nation rose up in mass almost at once. The men, women and children that had the joy of true patriotism went out of their houses breathing the most intense hatred (*respirando el más acalorado odio*) towards the French and their friends. All of them, as a single voice, without fear or hesitation, cried: Hail the Catholic religion! Long live Ferdinand VII! Death to the French and the Spanish traitors that are their friends![19]

Feeling at home and discerning foreigners in times of total war

Del Moral's perception is quite far removed from how historians now interpret the social involvement in anti-French resistance during the Peninsular War.[20] In fact, it is much more in line with the (even contemporary) Spanish nationalist narrative of the event. Del Moral is an example of an anti-liberal nationalist. He also shows how the inclusion/exclusion dynamic can be very lively and powerful when it is deployed and developed on familiar ground. Identifying external others, such as the French in the previous case, is a long-known basic part of the cognitive process involved in nation-building. Nonetheless, life narratives allow a better grasp on what individuals call 'home' and 'abroad' and the Age of Revolutions provides situations of total war that put them into very pressing circumstances. Coping with a trying experience is very likely to produce emotional outcomes in terms of friend/enemy, but we must not lose sight of the same dynamic working in less distressful environments and/or less political frameworks, as well as the necessary role of previous ideas of collective belonging.

In his account of his years in the British West Indies accompanying his father, writer Frederick Bayley made a revealing comment when describing the post office. Living a relatively calm life, he recalled how "the sight of the packet from England occasions a great sensation among the colonists". Every European colonist (lawyers, clerks, soldiers, planters …) rushed to the office: "the parcels are opened in a moment, the news spreads like a pestilence in a plague-struck city; and before ten minutes have passed away every one is acquainted with what is going on at home". He elaborated on this idea, which he defined as 'a feeling':

This word *at home* is the common expression of the West India settlers. England, Scotland, or Ireland is still their home. Unlike the inhabitants of the French colonies, they look upon the island in which they reside as a place to which they are, as it were, exiled for a certain period; as a place containing their properties, and, therefore, of the greatest consequence to them; but very few of them expect to die on those properties. Those who can afford it are in the habit of making trips every three or four years to the United Kingdom; and nearly all look forward to spending their last days in the land of their birth.[21]

Thus, according to this first generation European settlers were still attached to "their original lands" through a sort of nostalgic emotional link. For individuals with more ordinary trajectories the most common experience that crystallizes the cognitive map underlying national identity comes from the variegated consequences of war. Jean-Baptiste Godin was a soldier born in Condé-sur-l'Escaut, today's department of Nord. He returned to France in the Napoleonic final retreat from the Iberian Peninsula. In 1815 he wrote: "we were lucky throughout the rest of the route and, after five days walking, we could see from the mountains' heights the beloved plains of our homeland (*les plaines chéries de notre patrie*)".[22] Royal painter Vigée Le Brun showed more mixed emotions when coming back, according to her own life narrative (in 1789 she had fled, spending twelve years in exile): "the pain, the fear, the joy that convulsed me by turns (since there was a bit of everything in the thousand sensations that shook my soul)". She claimed that she cried for "the friends that I had lost to the gallows, but I was going to see those that had survived". The France to which she returned had been "the theatre of the most atrocious crimes", but that France was her 'homeland' ("*mais cette France était ma patrie!*").[23]

Picardian soldier Charles François took part in Napoleon's expedition to Egypt. In his journal, he mentioned that he spotted an Englishman among a group of prisoners of war. The prisoner talked to him in Arabic and, receiving no answer, François asked: "Are you English?" He replied in "German mixed with English". Once convinced that he was English, the French soldier "blew his brains out" (*je lui brûlais la cervelle*). "That way I proved my hatred for this nation, who is the cause of all our misfortunes."[24]

There is no doubt that François crafted that story because it was useful, even needed, for his particular situation (which, we should not forget, included a British naval blockade and direct support to the Ottoman armies). Our identities are the stories we tell about ourselves to make sense of our social world, and this kind of evidence provides excellent opportunities to see that idea at work. When personal experiences and these narratives about how our nation is or should be do not coincide, an internal conflict occurs. The individual must readjust the narrative or use it against those that do not comply with it. 'Home' was quite far away when English sailor James Choyce was captured by the Spaniards in the Pacific. He was later transferred to a depot in Orleans, where he was visited by "an English gentleman living at Orleans, who was commissary for English prisoners". He did not attend to them as he should have and the sailor thought this was shameful:

> Blush Britons! Sorry I am to say that an Englishman should have so little feeling for a dozen or so of his poor, miserable, half-starved countrymen. [...] this act of the noble lord made such an impression on my heart that time will only blot it out by death.[25]

Of course, this interplay is not just about coming home from abroad, but also receiving the *aliens* in what you consider your territory. Antoine Vincent Arnault was a secretary born into a middle-class family in Paris and later a writer, as Bayley. In his memoirs, he clearly stated that he was not a revolutionary. In fact, having lived through the excesses of the revolution he had generated 'an aversion' towards it. At some point, he attended a spectacle in Lille, a city that had been under siege and partially destroyed by the (Austrian) Imperial army in 1792. He declared that he had forgotten the name of the play, but what he firmly remembered was the moment *La Marseillaise* was performed. "I realised that I was French because of the feeling with which I heard that call to national revenge in the middle of the ruins created by Austrian jealousness in one of our most beautiful cities."

Later on, being in Italy during the *Directoire*, he wondered why he reacted negatively towards Italian criticism of the French government even if he did not sympathize with "the revolutionary doctrine". His answer, published during the same Orleanist regime that reinstalled the tricolour revolutionary flag, was rooted in the pride he felt "of our military glory". He could not bear that "those who have been incapable of defending our flags in the battlefield" were the same that insulted them "when their heroic colours are paraded" (in clear reference to the French expansion). He had never had that feeling in France, "where so far they [the tricolour flags] had only been for me the banners of a party", but it 'dominated' him since he was abroad (*me domina dès que je fus chez l'étranger*) "because I could only see the colours of my nation".[26] This quote elucidates both the force and limitations of "flagging the flag".[27] The same tricolour Arnault rejected as a partisan symbol within France became a token of nationhood when his *habitus* was broken abroad.

One of the territories where the French certainly paraded those 'heroic colours' was Spain. The city of Barcelona had harboured French troops since before the 2nd of May 1808 and was only 'liberated' by the very end of the war. During that period, its citizens had to learn to deal with the situation. Catalan priest Raymundo Ferrer wrote a detailed journal about life during what he felt was an occupation. In his account, it is clear that his displays of Spanish nationalism were intimately related to experiences of otherness vis-à-vis the French. For example, he relished in telling how young boys from the city used to play mock Spanish–French combat. One day in April 1810, at the height of the French power, over a hundred boys clashed near the *Palacio de la Capitanía General*, a key headquarters of the military government. Those that played 'the Spaniards' ran around yelling "*Viva España, viva Fernando!*" and played the *Marcha española* (supposedly the *Marcha Real*) on drums. Ferrer affirmed that the French grenadier guards, believing that it was a real attack, became frightened and hid in a nearby inn. For Ferrer, such embarrassment satisfactorily showed 'the fear' of the French garrison and roused pride among local adults for "the bravery of their youngsters in shouting in the streets such odious words for the French", adding: "If these are the feelings of the kids of Barcelona, you can infer those of the parents."[28]

The emotional construction of inner otherness and the foundations of state-nationhood

The French occupation experience of Spain did not only engender strong anti-French feelings of otherness (which, by the way, Ferrer did not translate into committed actions of opposition); it also created a solid rejection of the supporters of the French government, the *afrancesados*, the *agavatxados*, the bad Catalans, or simply the traitors to the nation. This sort of 'internal other', who can become an 'enemy within', is inevitable in all collective phenomena. Although there is a unifying and homogenizing impetus in every nation-building project, it can never merge all the differences among the members of the nation. Obviously, this also happens with those who, according to the nationalists, do not know that they belong to the nation, those who are confused about it and make wrong decisions, or those who stubbornly deny complying with their nature (for example, being French and not speaking French or being Spanish but not adhering to Catholicism).[29] Internal others can be labelled as defective or unworthy members of the community, in opposition to the good ones, or can be expelled from the nation since they are not true Spaniards, French, British, etc. These kinds of conflicts are very common and delicate at the same time, since individuals under pressure can develop alternative national projects and the nation can be torn apart.

There are two major realms in which these conflicts over the definition of the nation take place. The first is primarily political and it affects the discussions on sovereignty, citizenship, individual rights, political management of material inequalities, religious cleavages and the practical access to power. Here we find the political cleavage that is often pointed out in progressive and conservative versions of the same nationalism. In the Age of Revolutions this was clearly shaped by the divides between revolution and reform, absolutism and liberalism, royalism and republicanism.

The second is primarily cultural and deals with the diversity of linguistic modalities, local customs and traditions, hierarchical organization of cultural expressions (including standardization) and differing perceptions of community. This part has not been well studied, since cultural diversity has too often been taken for granted, as something objective that 'simply exists'. It can be shaped, accommodated, even destroyed by acculturation, but as such it always presents something that is given, a 'pre-political' nucleus (like 'a distinctive language' or 'a history of one's own'). In fact, many explanations of sub-state nationalisms, such as the Catalan or the Scottish, contain that assumption (that peoples are 'of course' as they are). In my view, this is a form of essentialism. The management of cultural diversity and the creation of an idea of commonality cannot be separated from the former's definition and reproduction. As nations are not naturally unitary entities but lean on perceptions of unity, cultural diversity is also a matter of territorialized perception of difference. The way these perceptions are worded and framed into identity narratives is not incidental but vital for their own existence and political performance.[30]

Identity politics and state nationalism emerge from the overlapping of both realms. The British, French and Spanish cases, particularly at this time, are clear examples of Old Regime monarchical States turning into nation-states by dealing with political struggle and high levels of cultural diversity throughout the entire long nineteenth century. Thus, we can say that one of the social foundations of state-nationhood is precisely keeping in check the tensions and conflicting stereotypes that spawn from heterogeneity within the same polity. In analytical terms, the ultimate goal should be to find out the tipping points between a more or less troublesome integration and a symbolic 'mental' and 'emotional' breakup. This sort of 'symbolic secession' would eventually happen in areas such as Ireland and Catalonia through stateless nationalist movements in the late nineteenth century, but it had previously operated when many Anglo-Americans, *hispanoamericanos* and *luso-brasileiros* ceased imagining themselves as members of European nations in other continents.

These processes are deeply embedded in the histories of imperial crisis that Western European monarchies went through during the Age of Revolutions, but the perception of intense cultural cleavages predates this and affected its supposedly 'nuclear' parts. Réunion Creole slave-holder Henry Panon-Desbassayns travelled to 'metropolitan' France twice, both before and during the revolution. In July 1785 he was in Nîmes, in an Occitan linguistic area, and wrote in his diary:

> I became upset in the Languedoc due to the patois. The people I deal with, who are ordinary people, speak only that. At the inns, the household staff usually speaks only the patois; a foreigner cannot understand anything he is said.[31]

Panon's experience was overtly negative: he claimed to have been badly treated and that everything was dirty and malodorous. Later on, his anger turned to satisfaction in Lyon. "I realise that I am in France and that French is spoken here. What a difference with all the Languedoc, Dauphiné and the Provence!" His overall assessment of the place was now positive.[32]

Of course, personal experiences and previously built stereotypes are reciprocal and profoundly shaped by the histories and political culture in which they were built. The aforementioned particular trajectory of Britain in this regard ensured that perceptions of internal diversity were placed into English, Scottish, Welsh and Irish categories. The concepts of 'British' and 'English' were usually conflated, even in the non-English self-narratives of our corpus. The attachment to the idea of Britishness varied, but there was never an outright rejection. The interplay of stereotypes did not always follow centre-periphery dialectics. For example, the Anglo-Irish soldier Robert Blakeney, born in Galway, narrated how he enlisted in 1804 and his regiment moved to Kinsale in order to drive back a French invasion.

As soon as the fight was over, the men sat down to dine with all those proud feelings which soldiers are wont to entertain after a victory. Never shall I forget the thrilling emotion which agitated my whole frame at seeing the blood fall from the hand of one of the soldiers, wounded through the clumsy manner in which he fixed his flint. I eyed each precious drop that fell with glowing sensations such as would blaze in the breast of a Napoleon on beholding an old dynasty diadem, or inflame the heart of a Scot in contemplating a new place in the Treasury.[33]

It comes as no surprise that the Irish case is somewhat different from the British one, given, among other things, the violent attempt of secession in 1798 and the subsequent repression. Representations of the Irish in English accounts tended to show contempt, and some displayed a certain civilizational superiority reminiscent of certain stereotypes about Southern Europe, Africa or Asia. However, the Irish were still conceived as part of the British world. Blakeney, for instance, reproduced a long argument between an English and an Irish sergeant in which the former stated that England was the mother-country of Ireland, to which the latter replied: "I don't understand how you make out England to be our mother-country. Step-mother is the proper term to give her; and, faith! a true step-mother she has proved herself to be."[34]

Indeed, once the collective *self* stops being considered as completely unitary, family metaphors become handy because they can effectively suggest mixed feelings, long-lasting ties and long-suffering relationships. Besides, they can be elaborated on derivative ideas such as 'divorce', 'emancipation', 'brotherhood' or the previously mentioned 'motherhood'. The term 'mother-country', '*la madre patria*', was also applied to Spain by Spanish Americans during and after the Ibero-American secessions, another product of the Age of Revolutions. When the Spanish Monarchy crisis broke out in 1808, the American creole families had already developed a composite concept of the Spanish nation, encompassing European and American Spaniards.[35] The 1812 Cádiz Constitution did not proclaim that "The Spanish Nation is the meeting of all the Spaniards of both hemispheres" gratuitously. Arguably, this was the very first expression of the idea of 'internal otherness' in the modern history of Spanish nation-building. In some of the analysed self-narratives, the 'imagined separation' existed before the first *Juntas*; in others, it did not fully develop until the 1820s. Of course, some of these individuals would see themselves as Spaniards until the end of their lives, as happened with many British-American royalists after 1783.

The most interesting subjects are those who wrote their ego-documents while their identifications were in transition. Fray Servando Teresa de Mier is a case in point. He was a secularized Dominican born in Monterrey and would later become a hero of Mexican independence, proclaimed in 1821. He was banished to the Iberian Peninsula for having suggested that the cult of the Virgin of Guadalupe had Pre-Hispanic origins. He fought in the Spanish War of Independence and then went back to New Spain. His published memoirs are actually the result of several versions, the 1818–19 one being the most complete. Although very caustic when criticizing the Monarchy and 'the Spaniards' when construed in contrast with the (Spanish-)Americans (*americanos*), there are passages in which he included himself in the Spanish nation and spoke of the Spaniards in the first person plural.[36] "When the felony of Napoleon against our kings electrified the entire nation, breathing myself the same indignation, I came to the aid of Catalonia with the Spanish troops that were France's prisoners in Portugal, as a military priest."[37] Later, he commented on the American demands in the Cádiz Cortes:

> Does the Cortes want to treat the *americanos* fairly? Start by giving the *americanos* all the commands and appointments. [...] Promises come too late. The same ones that were made to them by the King from Valencia were horribly broken [when returning from his prison in France in 1814, Ferdinand VII had promised the liberals that he would maintain the constitutional regime, but he abolished it instead]. Those who once lied cannot expect to be believed now.
>
> I am a son of Spaniards; I don't hate them but as oppressors, and my life, exposed so many times fighting for them, is irrefutable evidence. But I speak politically: without these guarantees, the *americanos* will not admit any proposition, because without them the Constitution will be at best what the Laws of the Indies were, words and names.[38]

We should not fall into the trap, nonetheless, of accepting that every demand of secession (or autonomy) came after a previous process of cognitive differentiation and emotional disentanglement during a political crisis. Juan Antonio Posse was another clergyman, born in Soesto, a Galician hamlet. He was a rural priest in León, writing his memoirs probably in the 1830s. Throughout the document he identified himself as Spanish and spoke of 'the nation' to which he belonged, referring to Spain. However, when a group of liberal officials led by Rafael del Riego overthrew the absolutist government in 1820 and forced Ferdinand VII to restore the Cádiz Constitution, he described his pessimism and his conversations about it with relatives and a fellow priest. He stated that the same political elites of 1814 would do even more harm in 1820. They were greedy and too compliant (*pasteleros*). They only saw to their appointments and their friends, pushing aside "the best men of the nation". They did not have sufficient intelligence (*luces*) and good faith. In this respect, the nation was in danger because it was attached to a disastrous state. Thus, he conceived of a rational political secession while staying Spanish in emotional terms:

> Because of this distrust and having a presentiment about our ruin, I wrote to La Coruña and my country [perhaps referring to Galicia, perhaps to the region around his original town, comparable to the French *pays*] so that it could become independent as a Republic, free and

separate from the others, since they had everything necessary to rule themselves. And in this case, they could confederate with the other Spaniards, become preferential allies to the English, and other things that I came up with at that time.

This proposal was not well received at all, and it was even a cause for people considering me insane henceforth. Thus, I needed to back down and I never spoke about it again.[39]

Concluding remarks: are nations communities of feeling?

Interpreting Posse's words is certainly difficult, especially as historians tend to expect from their sources the necessary coherence for inferential treatment. However, his environment's reaction and the effect that it had on him seem revealing about the inter-subjective character of nation-building processes. It also leads us back to the issues raised in the introduction. In my view, the evidence presented in this work from the British, French and Spanish cases supports that the Age of Revolutions was a nationalizing experience because, among other factors, the political intensification of total war and the breakup of traditional frames of power produced, and were at the same time amplified by, intense emotions of hatred, love, pride, shame and contempt. The tendency towards linking sentiments and morality to the different national characters in Europe was a feature of Enlightenment thought. However, symbolic and physical violence arising from revolutionary political conflicts engenders noticeable passions, both when constructing external and internal 'others'.

Personal experiences, usually full of sensorial stimuli affecting both the elites and ordinary people, were the best way to generate or underpin ideas of collective suffering or glory, going beyond mere rational considerations and opening further discussions: did these individuals suffer actual psychological transformations during their lives due to these processes or did genre conventions regarding self-narratives amplify their statements? Besides, in these narratives one could also identify the transition between different regimes of agency, leading to the rise of modern individualism, and regimes of sentimentality, shifting from external to internal models of emotion-making. In the end, the evidence presented here suggests that individuals *did* feel strongly for their nation because it was an operative way to understand the political intensification that their world was going through. They *could* do so because the new semantics of the nation provided them with the suitable tools.

Having said that, caution is advised. Emotions, both positive and negative, can be a means to nation-building, being socially transversal and spreading easily; nation-building cognitive processes (identity, narrativity, otherness, projection, normativity, etc.) can be a key for modern historians of emotions, but the fact that nationhood is based on feelings of community does not automatically create a community of feeling. Actually, we would be very wrong if we defined the nature of national belonging in exclusively emotional terms. First, because there are many situations in which individuals, including those from my corpus, express their national allegiance without loving, hating or despising anyone or anything. Second, because the line between the emotional and rational is actually blurry, so we might be focusing too much on just one part of the picture. Finally, explaining individual nationalization through emotions might seem feasible, but when we turn to a macro-scale, we still have the same problem: people using the same word for more or less different things, and people meaning the same thing with different words, people living in the ambiguous, sometimes ineffable edge between the familiar and the unknown.

Notes

1 Research grant HAR2017–87557-P. All translations to English are the author's.
2 Ducor, *Aventures d'un marin*, vol. 2, p. 264.
3 Plamper, *The History of Emotions*.
4 Brubaker, *Ethnicity Without Groups*, 7–27; Calhoun, *Nationalism*.
5 Cohen, 'Personal nationalism'; Archilés, 'Lenguajes de nación'; Van Ginderachter and Beyen, *Nationhood from Below*; Molina Aparicio, 'La nación desde abajo'; Goode and Stroup, 'Everyday nationalism'; Fox and Miller-Idriss, 'Everyday nationhood'; Van Ginderachter, *The Everyday Nationalism of Workers*; Zahra, 'Imagined noncommunities'; Van Ginderachter and Fox, *National Indifference*.
6 The binary conceptualization of elite vs non-elite is problematic, but it is an understandable point of departure as top-down approaches have long been dominant in nationalism studies. Identifying who belong to the 'elite' and who are 'ordinary people' is much more contextual and subjective than what should be desirable for such a widely used analytical category. A parish priest could be considered a member of the local elite, but compared with a bishop he would be part of the non-elite realm. A writer could be classified as a member of an intellectual elite, but he could also live in precarious material conditions that might be very similar to those that we classify as 'ordinary people'.
7 Fulbrook and Rublak, 'In relation'.
8 Among others: Maftei, *The Fiction of Autobiography*; Marcus, *Auto/biographical Discourses*; King, *Memory, Narrative, Identity*. The following publications have used autobiographies for the study of national identity, with different procedures and outcomes: Hunsaker, *Autobiography and National Identity*; Lynch, *Irish Autobiography*; Kumar, *Dalit Personal Narratives*.
9 For this argument, see Leerssen, *National Thought in Europe*. The modern/premodern polemic can be surveyed in Gorski, 'The mosaic moment'; Breuilly, 'Changes in the political uses of the nation'; Reynolds, 'The idea of nation'; Grosby, Leerssen and Hirschi, 'Continuities and shifting paradigms'.
10 There is a considerable literature on nation-building in the British, French and Spanish states during this period, e.g. Colley, *Britons*; Bell, *The Cult of the Nation in France*; Baycroft, *Inventing the Nation: France*; Álvarez Junco, *Spanish Identity in the Age of Nations*.
11 See previous note about the problems of the idea of 'elite'. In my corpus the elites consist of the university-educated, high state officials or large property owners.
12 The complete study can be found in Moreno Almendral, *Nación vivida, nación narrada*.
13 Farington, *The Diary of Joseph Farington*, pp. 1197–1198 and 1251.
14 Towsend, *A Journey through Spain*, vol. 3, p. 2.
15 Alexander, *Sketches in Portugal*, pp. 8–9.

16 Bordereau, *Mémoires*, p. 9.
17 Abrantes, *Mémoires*, vol. 10, pp. 158–160.
18 Abrantes, *Mémoires*, vol. 18, p. 355.
19 Moral, *Las memorias de un alpujarreño*, p. 69.
20 Esdaile, *Fighting Napoleon*.
21 Bayley, *Four Years' Residence*, pp. 291–292.
22 Godin, 'Abrégé de mes voyages', p. 98.
23 Vigée-Lebrun, *Souvenirs*, vol. 3, p. 138.
24 Jourquin, *Journal du Capitaine François*, p. 375.
25 Choyce, *The Log of a Jack Tar*, p. 161.
26 Arnault, *Souvenirs d'un sexagénaire*, vol. 1, p. 444; vol. 3, pp. 312–313.
27 See Billig, *Banal Nationalism*.
28 Ferrer, *Barcelona cautiva*.
29 This relates to the issue of national indifference. Van Ginderachter and Fox, 'Introduction'.
30 On nation, conflict and war, see Hutchinson, *Nations as Zones of Conflict*; Hutchinson, *Nationalism and War*.
31 Panon-Desbassayns, *Petit journal*, pp. 146–147. For the linguistic issue in the French Revolution, a classic is Certeau, Julia and Revel, *Une politique de la langue*.
32 Panon-Desbassayns, *Petit journal*, p. 169.
33 Blakeney, *A Boy in the Peninsular War*, pp. 1–2.
34 Blakeney, *A Boy in the Peninsular War*, p. 174.
35 See Herzog, *Defining Nations*.
36 See e.g. Mier, *Memorias*, pp. 52, 64. In his later writings, the cognitive separation is obvious.
37 Mier, *Memorias*, p. 192
38 Mier, *Memorias*, p. 282. On the cuestión americana, see, among others, Chust, *La cuestión nacional americana*.
39 Posse, *Memorias*, p. 249.

References

Abrantes, Duchesse d', *Mémoires*, Paris, Ladvocat, vol. 10/18, 1834.

Alexander, James E., *Sketches in Portugal, during the Civil War of 1834*, London, James Cochrane and Co., 1835.

Álvarez Junco, José, *Spanish identity in the age of nations*, Manchester, Manchester University Press, 2011 (1st ed. in Spanish, *Mater Dolorosa*, 2001).

Archilés, Ferran, 'Lenguajes de nación. "Las experiencias de nación" y los procesos de nacionalización: propuestas para un debate', in: *Ayer*, no. 90, 2013, pp. 91–114.

Arnault, Antoine Vincent, *Souvenirs d'un sexagénaire*, Paris, Librairie Duféy, 1833.

Baycroft, Timothy, *Inventing the nation: France*, London: Hodder Education, 2008.

Bayley, Frederick W.N., *Four years' residence in the West Indies, during the Years 1826, 7, 8 and 9*, London, William Kidd, 1830.

Bell, David, *The cult of the nation in France. Inventing nationalism, 1680–1800*, Cambridge MA, Harvard University Press, 2001.

Billig, Michael, *Banal nationalism*, London, Sage, 1995.

Blakeney, Robert, *A boy in the Peninsular War*, ed. Sturgis, Julian, London, John Murray, 1899.

Bordereau, Renée, *Mémoires de Renée Bordereau, dite Langevin, touchant sa vie militaire dans la Vendée*, Paris, L.G. Michaud, 1814.

Breuilly, John, 'Changes in the political uses of the nation: continuity or discontinuity?', in: Scales, Len and Zimmer, Oliver (eds.), *Power and the nation in European history*, Cambridge, Cambridge University Press, 2005, pp. 67–101.

Brubaker, Rogers, *Ethnicity without groups*, Cambridge MA – London, Harvard University Press, 2004.

Calhoun, Craig, *Nationalism*, Minneapolis, The University of Minnesota Press, 1997.

Certeau, Michel de, Julia, Dominique and Revel, Jacques, *Une politique de la langue. La Révolution française et les patois: l'enquête de Grégoire*, Paris, Gallimard, 1975.

Choyce, James, *The log of a jack tar*, Maidstone, George Mann, 1973.

Chust, Manuel, *La cuestión nacional americana en las Cortes de Cádiz (1810–1814)*, Alzira, Fundación Instituto de Historia Social, 1999.

Cohen, Anthony, 'Personal nationalism. A Scottish view of some rites, rights and wrongs', in: *American Ethnologist*, vol. 23, no. 4, 1996, pp. 802–815.

Colley, Linda, *Britons: Forging the nation, 1707–1837*, New Haven, Yale University Press, 1992.

Ducor, Henri, *Aventures d'un marin de la garde impériale, prisonnier de guerre sur les pontons espagnols, dans l'île de Cabréra, et en Russie*, Paris, Ambroise Dupont, 1833.

Esdaile, Charles J., *Fighting Napoleon: Guerrillas, bandits and adventurers in Spain, 1808–1814*, New Haven, Yale University Press, 2004.

Farington, Joseph, *The diary of Joseph Farington, vol. III. September 1796 – December 1798; vol. IV. January 1799 – July 1801*, eds. Garlick, Kenneth and Macintyre, Angus, New Haven – London, Yale University Press, 1979.

Ferrer, Raymundo, *Barcelona cautiva, ó sea, Diario exacto de lo ocurrido en la misma ciudad mientras la oprimieron los franceses, esto es desde el 13 de febrero de 1808 hasta el 28 de mayo de 1814; acompaña a los principios de cada mes una idea del estado religioso-político-militar de Barcelona y Cataluña*, appendix to Moliner Prada, Antonio, *La Guerra del Francès a Catalunya segons el diari de Raimon Ferrer*, Bellaterra, Servei de Publicacions de la Universitat Autònoma de Barcelona, 2010.

Fox, John E. and Miller-Idriss, Cynthia, 'Everyday nationhood', in: *Ethnicities*, vol. 8, no. 4, 2008, pp. 536–576.

Fulbrook, Mary and Rublak, Ulinka, 'In relation: The 'social self' and ego-documents', in: *German History*, vol. 28, no. 3, 2010, pp. 263–272.

Godin, Jean-Baptiste, 'Abrégé de mes voyages faits pendant les années 1808–1809–1810–1811–1812 et 1813', in: *La Giberne*, vol. 10, no. 9, 1909.

Goode, John P. and Stroup, David R., 'Everyday nationalism: Constructivism for the masses', in: *Social Science Quarterly*, vol. 96, no. 3, 2015, pp. 717–739.

Gorski, Philip S., 'The mosaic moment: an early modernist critique of modernist theories of nationalism', in: *American Journal of Sociology*, vol. 105, no. 5, 2000, pp. 1428–1468.

Grosby, Steven, Leerssen, Joep and Hirschi, Caspar, 'Continuities and shifting paradigms. A debate on Caspar Hirschi's "The origins of nationalism"', in: *Studies on National Movements*, vol. 2, 2014, pp. 1–48.

Herzog, Tamar, *Defining nations: Immigrants and citizens in early modern Spain and Spanish America*, New Haven – London, Yale University Press, 2003.

Hunsaker, Steven, *Autobiography and national identity in the Americas*, Charlottesville, University Press of Virginia, 1999.

Hutchinson, John, *Nationalism and war*, Oxford, Oxford University Press, 2017.

Hutchinson, John, *Nations as zones of conflict*, London, Sage, 2005.

Jourquin, Jacques (ed.), *Journal du Capitaine François, dit le Dromadaire d'Egypte 1792–1830*, Paris, Tallandier, 2003.

King, Nicola, *Memory, narrative, identity: Remembering the self*, Edinburgh, Edinburgh University Press, 2000.

Kumar, Raj, *Dalit personal narratives. Reading caste, nation and identity*, New Delhi, Orient Blackswan, 2012.

Leerssen, Joep, *National thought in Europe. A cultural history*, Amsterdam, Amsterdam University Press, 2006.

Lynch, Claire, *Irish autobiography. Stories of the self in the narrative of a nation*, Oxford, Peter Lang, 2009.

Maftei, Micaela, *The fiction of autobiography. Reading and writing identity*, New York – London, Bloomsbury, 2013.

Marcus, Laura, *Auto/biographical discourses*, Manchester, Manchester University Press, 1994.

Mier, Servando Teresa de, *Memorias. Un fraile mexicano desterrado en Europa*, ed. Ortuño Martínez, Manuel, Madrid, Trama Editorial, 2006

Molina Aparicio, Fernando, 'La nación desde abajo. Nacionalización, individuo e identidad nacional', in: *Ayer*, no. 90, 2013, pp. 39–63.

Moral, Juan G. del, *Las memorias de un alpujarreño: D. Juan Gabriel del Moral Villalobos. Entre Fondón y Berja (1796–1826)*, ed. Sánchez Ramos, Valeriano, Almería, Arráez Editores, 1999.

Moreno Almendral, Raúl, *Nación vivida, nación narrada: una historia de lo nacional en el Reino Unido, Francia, España y Portugal, c. 1780–1840*, PhD dissertation, Universidad de Salamanca, 2018.

Panon-Desbassayns, Henri P., *Petit journal des époques pour servir à ma mémoire (1784–1786)*, Saint-Gilles-Les-Hauts, Musée historique, 1990.

Plamper, Jan, *The history of emotions: An introduction*, Oxford, Oxford University Press, 2015.

Posse, Juan Antonio, *Memorias del cura liberal Juan Antonio Posse*, ed. Herr, Richard, Madrid, Centro de Investigaciones Sociológicas, 1984.

Reynolds, Susan, 'The idea of nation as a political community', in: Scales, Len and Zimmer, Oliver (eds.), *Power and the nation in European history*, Cambridge, Cambridge University Press, 2005, pp. 54–66.

Towsend, Joseph, *A journey through Spain in the years 1786 and 1787*, vol. 3, London, C. Dilly, 1792.

Van Ginderachter, M. and Fox, Jon E. (eds.), *National indifference and the history of nationalism in modern Europe*, Abingdon – New York, Routledge, 2019.

Van Ginderachter, Maarten and Beyen, Marnix (eds.), *Nationhood from below. Europe in the long nineteenth century*, Basingstoke, Palgrave-Macmillan, 2012.

Van Ginderachter, Maarten and Fox, Jon, 'Introduction', in: Van Ginderachter, M. and Fox, Jon E. (eds.), *National indifference and the history of nationalism in modern Europe*, Abingdon – New York, Routledge, 2019, pp. 1–14.

Van Ginderachter, Maarten, *The everyday nationalism of workers. A social history of modern Belgium*, Stanford, Stanford University Press, 2019.

Vigée-Lebrun, Louise-Élisabeth, *Souvenirs*, vol. 3, Paris, H. Fournier, 1837.

Zahra, Tara, 'Imagined noncommunities: National indifference as a category of analysis', in: *Slavic Review*, vol. 69, 2010, pp. 93–119.

2 So close and yet so far

Degrees of emotional proximity in pauper letters to Dutch national power holders around 1800

Joris Oddens

There is an impressive body of historical scholarship on what Martyn Lyons has recently described as 'writing upwards': the epistolary genre used by the weak who wrote to the powerful in pursuit of their personal interests.[1] Historians have various names for such writings – letters, petitions and supplications, to mention only the most common English terms. This genre is often investigated in case studies that focus on a specific time and place, and on letters addressed to a specific type of recipient. Such case studies can have different objectives, ranging from contributing to the history of poverty and poor relief to the study of ordinary people's literacy and writing practices.

Quite a few of these studies deal, in some way or other, with the question of why writers wrote what they wrote in the way they wrote it. A crucial point of reference for historians asking this question is the work of James C. Scott. For Scott, letters produced by subordinate groups in society are 'public transcripts', a term he uses to describe the public discourse the powerful deploy to legitimize their power, which is subsequently adopted by subordinates, in whose interest it is to tell those in power what they want to hear. Scott juxtaposes public transcripts with 'hidden transcripts', a discourse that is used 'off-stage', where the powerful cannot see or hear them.[2] It is possible to ask, as Maarten van Ginderachter has done for the writers of letters to the Belgian royal family around 1900, to what extent the weak are successful in reproducing the official public transcripts of the powerful.[3]

Such a question presupposes that practitioners of the genre of writing upwards saw their letters primarily as public interventions, and not as private communication between writer and addressee. That this is not always the case was recently suggested by Tanya Filer, who found that the possibility of writing letters directly to the Argentinian president Carlos Menem in the 1990s created in the eyes of some citizens a safe space, in which they felt they could freely speak their mind to Menem and even criticize him without doing public damage to his reputation. Filer proposes to understand the language used by these letter writers as a third category of transcript, the 'intimate transcript', with which subordinate groups may speak to those in power in 'off-stage' contexts.[4]

While I don't think that we would benefit from an inflation of transcripts, Filer does touch on an important issue with regard to the genre of writing upwards. Even if we look at letters from the same time and place, by writers who are more or less in the same situation, the differences between such letters can sometimes be so substantial that it does not seem that all writers were even trying to relate to the same official transcript: some of them, for instance, exhibited an attitude of familiarity vis-à-vis power holders, while others displayed an attitude of deference and awe.[5]

It is possible to understand these different approaches as emotional styles. Monique Scheer has proposed the notion of 'emotional style' as an alternative to 'emotional regime' (William Reddy) and 'emotional community' (Barbara Rosenwein). To Scheer the latter concepts, both of which are well known in the history of emotions, run the risk of being seen as "rather static systems of shared values". Scheer prefers the notion of emotional style because it acknowledges that different emotional styles can co-exist in a society and that one and the same individual, while remaining part of the same socio-cultural group, can switch between multiple emotional styles.[6] Which emotional style is adopted in a certain situation is dependent on individual agency and contextual factors. Benno Gammerl has drawn attention to the importance of the spatial context in particular: "How specific emotions like grief, happiness or affection are generated, handled and expressed depends to a large degree on *where* they occur."[7]

The spatial dimension also seems relevant when studying emotional styles in ordinary writings within the context of emerging nationalism, specifically in the more relative sense of proximity versus distance. The rise of the nation-state involved the centralization of power and the creation of new types of power holders. This opened new avenues for those seeking support from the powerful. The figures of power they might now resort to were in many cases geographically, socially or symbolically more distant from them than the predominantly local power holders they had dealt with in the past. Is this also reflected by the emotional styles they exhibited in their letters? Did subordinates, in their interactions with rulers, establish (the suggestion of) affectionate bonds of a new type, which can be connected to a (growing) sense of nationhood?

In this contribution I will investigate these questions in a case study of the Netherlands in the age of revolutions. Around 1800 the Netherlands changed from a confederate, oligarchic republic into a centralized monarchy. In the context of this volume this is a particularly interesting moment, because in Dutch historiography this process of state-building has been seen as a catalyst for the production of nationhood, in the sense that the nation and its symbols started to take on new meanings for individual Dutch citizens. The aim of this contribution is to assess the different ways in which a group of practitioners of the genre of writing upwards addressed national power holders in this period.

In this chapter I will focus on pauper letters, a subtype of the genre of writing upwards involving paupers who ask for support in money or in kind. Most of the evidence that I will present comes from letters written by poor women, because they constitute a relatively homogeneous subordinate group in the sense that they often found themselves in similar circumstances, fully

deprived of formal or informal power. Moreover, female paupers in the Netherlands around 1800 surprisingly often wrote their letters themselves, without the
assistance (or so it seems) of family members or scribes. This helps me to avoid –
in this chapter at least – the discussion about authenticity and authorship that is
so often central to studies of the genre of writing upwards.[8]

The Netherlands, in the early modern period a confederacy of autonomous
provinces, underwent drastic transformations between 1780 and 1815. In the
early 1780s, Stadtholder William V of Orange, officially the first servant of the
state but in practice a quasi-monarchical figure since the office of stadtholder
had been made hereditary in the mid-eighteenth century, was challenged by a
citizen movement known in Dutch historiography as the Patriot movement.
William V suppressed the revolt of the Patriots in 1787, with the military
support of a Prussian army.[9] The Patriots in turn chased the stadtholder away
in 1795, this time with the support of a French army, and founded the Batavian Republic, one of the revolutionary sister republics in the French sphere
of influence. The Patriots set in motion a process of democratization and
centralization, which in 1798 resulted in the ratification of a constitution that
abolished the sovereignty of the provinces and created a unitary state.[10]

From the turn of the century French influence grew and many democratic
reforms were cancelled, but the foundations of the unitary state remained
intact. In 1806 Napoleon Bonaparte, unhappy with what he considered a
Dutch reluctance to support France in its military endeavours, pressured the
Dutch into transforming their republic into a monarchy, the Kingdom of
Holland, and accepting his brother Louis Bonaparte as their king. To the
emperor's dismay, his brother identified with his new people and did not
always behave like the puppet he was supposed to be. In 1810 Napoleon
ended his brother's reign and incorporated the Netherlands into the French
Empire. The emperor sent Charles-François Lebrun, a veteran of the revolutionary and Napoleonic administration, to the new departments of Holland
as governor-general. Lebrun remained in office until November 1813.[11] After
the defeat of Napoleon a new government was established in the name of
William Frederick, prince of Orange and son of the deposed stadtholder
William V, who had returned from exile and was first given the title of
Sovereign Prince of the Netherlands. Later, in 1815, William Frederick
became King William I of the United Netherlands, which also included the
former Austrian Netherlands, present day Belgium.[12]

The decades around 1800 are usually considered to have been a period of
growing national awareness among the people of the Netherlands.[13] Historians have different views on the exact significance of the Kingdom of Holland
in this process. It is a fact, however, that the reign of the French-born Bonaparte represents the first moment in Dutch history when the entire Dutch
nation was united under a single monarchical ruler in a (at least nominally)
sovereign Dutch state. It is usually agreed that Louis Bonaparte succeeded to
some extent in personifying the Dutch nation in the eyes of his subjects,
against the will of his brother, the emperor.[14] By contrast, there was no longer

a Dutch state between 1810 and 1813. Historians have recently emphasized how in the Netherlands, as elsewhere in Napoleonic Europe, the years of incorporation have been crucial in the development of a Dutch national identity in a shared resistance against the French occupation.[15]

In this chapter I will consider pauper letters to Louis Bonaparte and Charles-François Lebrun, as well as letters to William V. For the reign of the King of Holland, pauper letters are available in abundance, mostly archived together in the collection of a relief committee that Bonaparte instituted in response to the many requests for support he received.[16] The archives of Bonaparte's secretarial office also hold a collection of miscellaneous petitions, including pauper letters, to Charles-François Lebrun from the year 1811.[17] The stadtholderate of William V has left fewer archival traces than subsequent regimes, and it is unclear how common the practice of presenting pauper letters to the stadtholder was, as he seems to have preferred personal audiences.[18] Nevertheless, I have identified a small number of letters written to the stadtholder by needy supporters, all from the restoration years between 1787 and 1795.[19]

To get a better sense of how we should value the emotional styles adopted in letters to these national power holders, I will compare them with pauper letters as we best know them from the literature, sent to local poor relief services. In the Netherlands requests for local poor relief were made in person rather than in writing around 1800. Paupers were forced to periodically appear before the boards of regents of religious or municipal poor relief institutions.[20] Written requests do sometimes seem to have been made as well, but they were never systematically studied by historians and no archival collection is readily available. The situation in Dutch historiography stands in sharp contrast to that in Great Britain, where thousands of extant pauper letters from the eighteenth and nineteenth centuries have been identified and extensively studied.[21] In the English poor relief system anyone not living in their parish of settlement had to apply in writing to that parish for relief. Some 750 extant letters from the county of Essex, mainly written during the first half of the nineteenth century, have been studied by Thomas Sokoll, who has also published the letters.[22] This enables me to compare the letters from the Netherlands with a contemporaneous corpus of letters to local institutions in England. Although the Essex pauper letters come from a different national context, they are helpful in identifying elements in the Dutch letters that are not exclusive to interactions between subjects and national power holders.

The template of the familiar letter

In his study of the Essex pauper letters, Thomas Sokoll identified three distinct literary types: formal petitions, ordinary letters and oral writing. Formal petitions followed strict petitionary conventions, such as formulaic opening and closing sentences and the use of the third person singular.[23] Ordinary letters – or familiar letters as they are often called – used a plain style, but like the petitions still followed a classical rhetorical model.[24] Oral writing is the term Sokoll reserved for letters that were written in the first person, did not respect epistolary conventions, lacked punctuation, had little sense of layout, contained idiosyncratic or phonetic writing and grammatical errors, and on the whole bore the characteristics of an oral performance, a speech act as it might have been performed before the overseers of the poor in person.[25]

While the Essex pauper letters contain relatively few formal petitions, it is in practice difficult to draw a sharp line between familiar letters and oral writing, and the style and tone sometimes even change within the same letter. Many of the English pauper letters seem to have been written with the assistance of more experienced writers (for example local notables and parish officials), which may explain differences in the degree to which epistolary standards are respected.[26] What most letters in this corpus have in common is that they adopt a relatively familiar tone, with few deferential markers. To make this more concrete, I shall give the example of one letter, written in 1817 by Sarah Hall in Chelmsford to the overseer of St Botolph:

> Sir
>
> My Present Necessity Obliges me to Send you Another Letter Concerning My Money for I Am in great Disttress For it My Parents Cannot Aford to Maintain me & the Child Without my Alowance for I Cant get Anything To Do I Am in Vew of A Place in Chelmsford But I Cant go to it Without the money to get me A thing or tow to go in for i am in Wants Of things & I Shall Be Oblige to you to get the money for me or I Shall Not know What Cource to take Sir I Shall be Oblige to you to Send me An Answer by the Return of Post
>
> Sarah Hall
> Chelmsford
> March the 31 1817[27]

Now let us compare this letter with one written by a female writer from Amsterdam, identifying herself as "the widow Bakker", addressed to Charles-François Lebrun in 1811:

> Your August Majesty
>
> I humbly beg you for forgiveness that I have to bother your majesty again the unbearable poverty that increases daily obliges me I recently wrote to your majesty that from the lord intendant of the crown I received nothing but 5 guilders and 50 *stuivers* [pence] and as your majesty can imagine I cannot go to the hague with that nor do anything else so a poor widow with two unhappy children begs for god's sake to be helped by you to a piece of bread to feed my household that has perished for want and misery I have at present nothing from which I can make something in my house all has been consumed I had humbly begged your highness for an answer but as I have received none I fall with my two poor and unhappy

children before your majesty's feet so that we don't perish and that it will please your majesty to help us to a piece of bread and if that cannot be oh that it will please your highness to give me travel money so that I can go with my children to the hague to my other children for this will humbly pray and wait in despair

Your majesty's humble servant
the widow Bakker
Amsterdam 20 April 1811[28]

There are important similarities between both letters, as well as some differences. One clear difference is in the address: whereas Hall plainly uses 'Sir', Bakker addresses Lebrun as 'your majesty' and 'your highness'. There is considerable variety in the forms of address used in pauper letters to Bonaparte, Lebrun and William V: we find the equivalents of 'prince', 'king', 'monarch', 'sire', often used in combination with adjectives such as 'high', 'mighty', 'august' or 'beloved'. All these various forms indicate that the writers formally recognized their addressees as monarchs. Technically they were not wrong in bestowing this honor on them – after all Lebrun was a duke and William V a prince – but it seems to have mattered preciously little to them that only the King of Holland could claim sovereign power over the territories they lived in.

In the opening sentence of her letter, the widow Bakker humbly begs for forgiveness for having to bother Lebrun (again). Begging for forgiveness is also a standard element of the Essex pauper letters. It expresses a minimal degree of deference. Bakker returns to the phrase of humbly begging a few times in the letter. She also mentions falling down before Lebrun's feet with her two children, albeit with little enthusiasm: she gives the impression of kneeling with some reluctance, and only because a previous letter had received no response. We do not find references to kneeling or prostrating in the Essex pauper letters, but they had been standard elements in letters and petitions to monarchs throughout Europe for centuries. They are common in the pauper letters to Napoleon and Lebrun, which is intriguing because we tend to think of the Netherlands before the Napoleonic era as lacking a real monarchical tradition. That said, in the small number of extant pauper letters to Stadtholder William V, Dutch subjects also metaphorically threw themselves before the feet of (the person they perceived as) their monarch.[29]

Overall, Bakker's letter is not particularly humble. She writes in the same informal first person singular that is adopted by Hall. She refers to an earlier request she made to Lebrun about a sum of money she received from one of the king's civil servants and clearly implies that this sum was far from sufficient: "as your majesty can imagine I cannot go to [T]he [H]ague with that nor do anything else". We find such complaints also in other Napoleonic pauper letters, such as that written by Nannet Bulcourt, a single parent with an infant and a sick mother, to Louis Bonaparte in 1808: "I have addressed myself to mister lombardie for [support] because I know that he is a member of the council he sent me a guilder wonder majesty if that helps a sick mother who is dying in misery."[30] The use of direct, even blunt, language has also been observed by Sokoll in the Essex pauper letters, while there are indications that Dutch paupers, too, could be rather straightforward when they appeared before the administrators of poor relief institutions.[31]

In her letter to Lebrun, Bakker tries to persuade her addressee by confessing that in her house she has "nothing from which she can make something", she is entirely out of resources. Many other letters in the Napoleonic collections of pauper letters also provide details about the terrible situation the writers and their families were in. The widow Geertruy Harmse had no bread for her six starving children and no clothes to cover their nakedness. Geesje Kooymans, also a widow with young children, had no chair to sit on and no bed to sleep in. The widow Elsman, an older woman, did not have a bed either, while the widow Uriot, who had given birth to twenty-two children, nine of whom were still alive, had slept on a chair for ten years, without a blanket. The widow Ruel had neither bread to eat nor clothes to wear. One of Hinderik van den Berg's five children had "cancer in the mouth". Rachel Jacob Proops, a single woman, had temporarily been deprived of her eyesight, while Kaatje Kalkman, whose husband and four children had died, had lost her sanity for eighteen months.[32]

Such references to dire material circumstances or bad health are also among the dominant motives in the Essex pauper letters: Sarah Hall, like the widow Bakker, just writes that she is "in Wants Of things", but many others provide much more detail. It has been argued that the narratives provided by the writers of pauper letters should not necessarily be seen as realistic descriptions, but belong to the rhetorical repertoire of pauper agency along with the formulaic expressions of deference. Peter Jones, for example, has demonstrated that the many references to nakedness in English pauper letters did not always literally mean that the letter writers were naked, even if want of clothing could be a real concern.[33] The writers of pauper letters appealed to the moral responsibility of their addressees – whether these represented parishes or the nation – to improve their situation.

The similarities between the English and Dutch letters are interesting in light of what Peter Jones and Steven King have recently written in an attempt to explain why the writers of the English letters opted for the informal model of the familiar letter rather than for that of the formal petition, while the petition had for centuries been the standard epistolary form to solicit favour or patronage. According to Jones and King, the use of the petition implied a type of relationship whereby "a low-status petitioner is granted an audience with someone of much higher status (so high in fact, that they would normally be far outside the petitioner's sphere of influence) and who is in a position to intercede on their behalf", while the use of the familiar letter implied "a conversation between, if not equals, then at least parties who are entitled to approach each other directly, and to expect a considered response to that approach".[34] Indeed, the collection of Essex letters contains many letters by paupers who wrote more than once and were involved in an ongoing dialogue with their overseers: of Sarah Hall, quoted above, seven letters survive.[35]

The explanation offered by Jones and King sounds convincing for the institutional dynamics governed by the English Old Poor Law, but it does not seem to explain why the collections of pauper letters to Bonaparte and Lebrun contain, besides formal petitions drawn up by scribes, many letters that at best tried to follow the model of the familiar letter. From a present-day perspective the Napoleonic power holders definitely qualified as addressees "of much higher status", and although several women wrote multiple letters, there was little chance for a direct conversation with their addressees. Before I try to make sense of this I will first proceed to discuss another emotional style that was employed in Dutch pauper letters around 1800, for which in my view neither the petition nor the familiar letter served as a model.

The template of petitionary prayer

In the summer of 1808 Louis Bonaparte received a letter written by a Mrs Vighart from Arnhem, in the east of the country. Vighart wrote that her first husband, with whom she had had two children, had passed away thirteen years earlier, while her second husband had recently left her. She now found herself in a state of dire poverty, and the municipality had declined her request for support, supposedly because she was a Catholic. What follows is a substantial part of her long letter:

> most merciful majesty I fall down on my knees here before your royal feet to be granted a request or beg for me poor mother who can get counsel nor solace from nobody o most merciful king I take refuge in you majesty to make my bitter poverty known for 18 months I have earned the bread of my 2 children alone and now I am exhausted it is as if my strengths diminish because of grief and poverty [...] now my god has reminded me of his most holy mother to whom I have prayed for 9 consecutive days while lighting a candle and I called on her to find salvation now by the grace of god and his holy mother I hope to have found your lord's help [...] o merciful king please have mercy with me and with my 2 children your merciful king has had compassion with my brother bernardus busser his majesty's fisherman and has released him from his poverty o bountiful king please help me too and stand by me I will give rest to all who are weary and burdened that is also why I come to you o merciful king and confess before god and before you my miserable state I hope to be heard by god by you o king because for me no counsel nor solace is to be found in my wretched poverty but from you o merciful king please don't despise me I pray you merciful king for god's sake don't let my child depart from your majesty without solace but I pray you to give me a little support for me and my two children even if it is only 80 guilders per year or similar if it were to please god and your majesty I would be more than content oh if the good god and his most holy mother were so merciful to me my heart would be full of joy o I would thank god and his holy mother maria and you my king for the mercy that I received o holy mother

anna whom I daily honor with my two children please help me stand by me in my poverty now and at the hour of my death

I remain your royal highness
your most humble and most submissive
servant Mrs. Vighart[36]
with haste and sadness

Vighart's letter, like Bakker's letter in the previous section, is written in an unconventional, idiosyncratic Dutch without punctuation. It also contains, in the part of the text that I did not provide here, a number of motifs that we find in other letters to Napoleonic power holders as well: Vighart writes, for instance, that she has not rested on a bed or a mattress for seventeen months; that she is unable to support her children; and that she has long tried to hide her poverty. Yet, despite such common motifs, it will be clear that Vighart's letter is really quite different from that written by the widow Bakker. Vighart's does not resemble a letter to a family member or to a local notable, nor does it evoke a person appearing before the boards of regents of a poor relief institution. This letter is governed by a different kind of logic, that of a petitionary prayer. Whereas Bakker shows emotional restraint and is relatively concise, limiting herself to providing essential information, Vighart seems little concerned that her addressee may have many demands on his time. She writes as if she is in the business of praying to God, for whom time obviously is no issue.

The language of Vighart's long letter is repetitive and reads more like a stream of consciousness than an oral performance. What stands out is the repeated use of the vocative case ('o merciful king'), common in Christian worship, and the paraphrasing of fragments of religious texts, such as the lines "I will give rest to all who are weary and burdened that is also why I come to you" (Matthew 11:28) and "stand by me in my poverty now and at the hour of my death" (Hail Mary). Vighart addresses Bonaparte as her saviour, a last resort suggested to her in her prayers (although she also hints that she writes to the king because her brother had received support from him before). She repeatedly establishes an analogical relationship between her addressee and God, confessing "before God and before you my miserable state", and hoping "to be heard by God by you". She gives the impression that she is at the same time writing to Bonaparte and God and that were she to receive support, she would consider this an act of grace from God and Maria as well as from the king.

In a study of early modern England, the political theologian David Nicholls has observed that there were "significant analogies between civil petition and petitionary prayer", which drew on an underlying analogy between divine and civil government. For Nicholls this meant first of all that people prayed to God as if they were petitioning the king, and interestingly enough he seems to have thought mostly of public petitions with political objectives rather than of the genre of writing upwards.[37] The prayer does not seem to have functioned as a model in English pauper letters: Thomas Sokoll does not include it in his typology of literary styles, and neither do Peter Jones and Steven King refer to it in their study of the genre.

Although the pauper letters in the Napoleonic collections typically make use of the straightforward register of the familiar letter, they do abound, unlike the Essex pauper letters, in the use of the vocative case and allusions to prayers and the addressee's proximity to God. While the religious conviction of the female writers is not always so explicitly stated as in the case of Vighart (a Catholic woman writing to a Catholic king, in a state where Calvinism had been the dominant religion since the Reformation) sometimes educated guesses can be made. Rachel Jacob Proops, who had a Jewish name and lived in the house of a Samuel Eliazer Levij, in the Jewish quarter of Amsterdam, wrote that until the end of her days she would ask God in her prayers to protect her king. Kaatje Kalkman wrote to Bonaparte that she had "nobody left but God and his majesty to whom I pray with tears in my eyes and folded hands", while Johanna Christina Boom, a widow with three young children, promised Lebrun that she would "recognize you my supreme majesty as my benefactor next to God".[38]

The model of petitionary prayer seems not only to have been available to Dutch female paupers from different denominations, but its use also preceded the founding of the Kingdom of Holland. This becomes clear when we turn to the example of a letter to Stadtholder William V, who had a staunchly Calvinist reputation. Clara Cornelia van Kervel was a widow living in The Hague in the 1780s, when the rebellious Patriots forced the Stadtholder William V of Orange to leave his residence and temporarily move into a palace in Nijmegen, at the eastern border of the Dutch Republic. Upon the stadtholder's return to The Hague in 1787, after the Patriot movement had been suppressed, Van Kervel, a fierce supporter of the stadtholder in his conflict with the Patriots, wrote him a letter in which she welcomed him back as a saviour. Her letter is written in a profoundly associative religious register, full of references to the Psalms:

Most merciful monarch and lord

I find myself wishing you beloved monarch with the utmost humbleness and frankness all the imaginable hail and blessing for your joyous entry in the hague may the lord bless you and your august house with all the blessings that can be prayed from heaven the jehovah god shows us more and more the effects of your beloved monarch's joyous entry so that we unfortunates can behold the hand of the almighty and cry out lord not for our but for your name's sake that you have saved us when we were afraid o beloved monarch, may this simple but sincere pure blessing of mine please you beloved monarch, I don't have more to offer to you dear and highly beloved monarch than a gratefulness that is full of tears of joy [and] praise my creator all days of my life for still being so good and merciful to our dear nation and returning to us our beloved monarch what else can we do to repay the lord for his benevolence but to bend our knees before our heart for the benevolence shown to us now beloved monarch beloved hereditary stadtholder of the netherlands may jehovah god protect you like the white of the eye and place a heavenly guard of angels around your beloved high person who guard you in your rising and reclining as he does to all of the august house of orange until its last offspring [...] oh dearest beloved monarch be good to me I very humbly pray you just like jehovah god has graced us with his bene-volence when he saved us, save me too now that you have come beloved monarch.[39]

Van Kervel's letter problematizes what might have been offered as one possi-ble explanation for the occurrence of very different degrees of emotional proximity in pauper letters around 1800. Like most of the women writing to Bonaparte and Lebrun, the widow Bakker lived in Amsterdam, and both the King of Holland (at least during the year of 1808, from which the letters referred to in this study date) and the *Prince de l'Empire* also resided in the city. Louis Bonaparte and Charles-François Lebrun both had the reputation of being relatively accessible (they were after all products of the revolution). It is possible that letters could sometimes even have been handed to them in person, as implied by Kaatje Kalkman, who began her letter to Bonaparte by stating that she had given him two letters before.[40]

Natives of Amsterdam such as Bakker and Kalkman, it might be argued, could perceive Bonaparte and Lebrun as primarily *local* authority figures, especially since they had no previous experience with power holders repre-senting anything other than the local government in their city. Mrs Vighart lived in Arnhem, far from the locus of monarchical power. This cannot be said of Van Kervel, who was an inhabitant of The Hague, the seat of Stad-tholder William V, and who turned his 'joyous entry' into that city into a messianic narrative. While Van Kervel does mention William V's official title of hereditary stadtholder of the Netherlands, her use of the word 'nation' (*vaderland*) seems first of all to refer to the local context of The Hague. Finally, to complicate matters further, there are also letters to Wil-liam V from distant places like Sint Oedenrode, in the countryside of States-Brabant, which are very direct in tone. A certain De Cocq, a man for once, informed his monarch in 1791 that he had already written him so many letters that the cost of that alone had left his wife and him poor, and boldly urged the stadtholder to finally compensate him for the fact that during the time of the conflict with the Patriots he had always stood up for him in every conversation.[41]

Taken together, the examples of Bakker, Vighart, Van Kervel, De Cocq and others mentioned in this chapter show the full range of self-written, informal pauper letters to national power holders in the Netherlands around 1800, from concise, business-like and very straightforward to lengthy, spiritual and full of awe. All writers addressed the recipients of their letters as monarchs, and most writers payed their addressees at least a minimum of formulaic respect, but otherwise their letters are worlds apart: while some would have seemed hardly out of place in the everyday correspondence between English paupers and their overseers (and most probably neither in the Dutch local poor relief system), others evoked an emotion-charged triangular relationship between writer, addressee and God.

Conclusion

When the weak wrote to the powerful they obviously did not write things that might harm their interests. In that sense all their writings were 'public transcripts', but they did not always act alike. There have been many times and places in history where it was clear to members of a given community that in order to successfully solicit a favour, authorities had to be addressed in a certain way and no other. Writings in such times often took the shape of formal petitions, the drawing up of which was left to a scribal elite. There have also been times and places where the desired form and contents of written requests were less standardized, and it was left to the interpretation of those who had something to request as to which strategy was best to follow.

The English pauper letters to local overseers of the poor are an example of the latter situation from the period around 1800. English paupers could choose the template of the formal petition, but rarely did so because it was more in their interest to create the suggestion of an ongoing, informal dialogue by using the template of the familiar letter (costs probably also played a role because such letters could be written by semi-experienced writers instead of professional scribes). By the nineteenth century, the informal language used in the English pauper letters had more or less crystallized, as the overseers accepted this more straightforward style of communication.

The Dutch letters to national power holders introduced in this chapter present a different stage of this process. There had been little opportunity for crystallization to take place. Poor women (and also men) who wanted to solicit William V, Louis Bonaparte or Charles-François Lebrun for support could choose to do so in multiple ways. And although these women found themselves in similar circumstances, they made very different choices. Some of them hired a scribe to write a formal petition. Most women decided to write a request themselves. When they did, they had the choice of at least two ideal-typical templates; one resembling the familiar letter or the oral performance, and one resembling petitionary prayer, each with its own emotional charge. In practice, women sometimes used elements of both of these ideal-types in their letters.

I started the research for this chapter with the hypothesis that I would find different emotional styles in pauper letters to power holders representing different loci of identification. The outcome of this study turns out to be ambiguous, but is perhaps no less relevant for it. It is hard to predict the degree of proximity or distance female paupers suggested between power holders of whatever kind and themselves. The official political status of a power holder seems not necessarily to have been decisive in determining this. William V, Louis Bonaparte and Lebrun were equally addressed as monarchs. I found no significant differences between the language used in letters to Bonaparte and Lebrun. While Vighart's letter to Bonaparte seems to have been something of an extreme case, Lebrun, though he was 'only' the emperor's governor-general, could all the same be represented as a ruler with a divine right. Conversely, the King of Holland, like Lebrun, could be addressed more or less in the same way as a local poor relief administrator would have been. Finally, the small number of letters to the stadtholder of the United Provinces does not allow for any definitive statements, but one thing seems clear. While paupers writing to William V may have considered him the leader of an Orangist faction rather than the symbol of a nation, they nonetheless drew from the same emotional repertoire as those writing to the Napoleonic power holders.

When I try to generalize from these results, I come first of all to the observation that there can be not only different degrees but also different kinds of emotional proximity to national power holders. At one end of the spectrum, we find a tendency to see these powerholders as 'ordinary' mortals, in which case the perceived social distance is relatively small, and the power holders are considered to belong to the same, even local, community, without there necessarily being the sense of an affectionate bond. At the other end of the spectrum, we see a propensity to look up to national power holders as rulers with a divine right. Practitioners of the genre of writing upwards who tend towards this view can feel emotionally close to their rulers, just as they feel close to God, but the other side of the coin is that they have the sense of much greater social distance. It is interesting that the option of viewing national power holders as endowed with a divine right seems to have been readily available to poor women in a state that between the sixteenth century and 1806 had been a republic, without an indigenous tradition of sacred kingdom, but also that these women differentiated little, perhaps exactly because such a tradition was lacking, between the various types of national power holders they saw themselves confronted with around 1800.

For women on both sides of the spectrum no strong sense of nationhood seems to have been in place, at least not if we conceive nationhood as identification and solidarity with a national community. Their subjecthood was local, partisan or spiritual rather than national, and thus essentially pre-modern. It remains to be seen precisely when in Dutch history popular monarchism came to coincide with popular nationalism, as was the case at the end of the nineteenth century.[42] Recent preliminary investigations point in the direction of a gradual process, in which the accession of a monarch from the House of Orange in 1813 did not mark the end, but only the beginning.[43]

Notes

1 Lyons, 'Writing upwards'.
2 Scott, *Domination and the Arts of Resistance.*
3 Van Ginderachter, 'Public transcripts of royalism'.
4 Filer, 'Letters to the President'.
5 See also Würgler, 'Asymmetrie und reziprozität'.
6 Scheer, 'Are emotions a kind of practice', pp. 216–217.
7 Gammerl, 'Emotional styles', p. 164.
8 See, about this problem for pauper letters in particular: Jones and King, 'From petition to pauper letter'. For more about the importance of scribes in the genre of writing upwards more generally, see Lyons, 'The power of the scribe'; Dabhoiwala, 'Writing petitions'.
9 See, on the Patriot Era: Klein, *Patriots republikanisme*; Velema, *Republicans*, 2007.
10 See, on the Batavian Republic: Oddens, *Pioniers in schaduwbeeld*; Rutjes, *Door gelijkheid gegrepen*, 2012; Grijzenhout, Van Sas and Velema, *Het Bataafse experiment*; Oddens, Rutjes and Jacobs, *The Political Culture.*
11 See, on the Napoleonic era in the Netherlands: Joor, *De adelaar en het lam*; Jensen, *Verzet tegen Napoleon*; Verheijen, *Nederland onder Napoleon.*
12 See, on the (United) Kingdom of the Netherlands: De Haan, De Hoed and Te Velde, *Een nieuwe staat*; Aerts and Deneckere, *Het (on)verenigd koninkrijk*; Van de Perre and Judo, *Belg en Bataaf.*
13 About this process, see: Van Sas, *De metamorfose van Nederland.*
14 See Grijzenhout, 'Lodewijk Napoleon', p. 13; Jensen, '"See our succumbing Fatherland"'. For a different perspective: Jourdan, 'Staats- en natievorming'.
15 Jensen, *Verzet tegen Napoleon*; Verheijen, *Nederland onder Napoleon.*
16 I looked at letters dating from 1808: National Archives The Hague (NA), 2.01.01.07, Staatssecretarie tijdens Koning Lodewijk Napoleon, Commissie van Onderstand, inv. no. 662.
17 NA, 2.01.01.07, Secretariaat van het gouvernement-generaal der Hollandse departementen van het Franse keizerrijk, inv. no. 480.
18 Woelderink, *Inventaris*, p. 22; Van Meerkerk, *Willem V en Wilhelmina.*
19 The letters I used can be found in Royal Collections The Hague (RC), A31, Collection William V, inv. no. 1003; and NA, 3.02.32, Collection Bentinck van Rhoon, inv. no. 16.
20 See for example: Pot, *Arm Leiden*, p. 172; Spaans, *Armenzorg in Friesland*, pp. 258–259; Buursma, *'Dese bekommerlijke tijden'*, p. 96.
21 See King, 'Pauper letters as a source'.
22 Sokoll, *Essex Pauper Letters.*
23 For the formal conventions of the petition, see: Houston, *Peasant Petitions*, pp. 73–107.
24 See Fitzmaurice, *The Familiar Letter.* For the Netherlands, see Ruberg, *Conventional Correspondence.*
25 Sokoll, 'Writing for relief', pp. 91–111.
26 Jones and King, 'From petition to pauper letter', pp. 54–55, 64–69.
27 Sokoll, *Essex Pauper Letters*, pp. 302–303.
28 NA, 2.01.01.07, 480, the widow Bakker to Charles-François Lebrun, 20.4.1811.
29 See for example RC, A31, 1003, Egber Willem Cramer to William V, 16.3.1777; NA, 3.02.32, 16, Clara Cornelia van Kervel to William V, 1787.
30 NA, 2.01.01.07, 662, Nannet Bulcourt to Louis Bonaparte, 27.6.1808.
31 Sokoll, 'Writing for relief', p. 102; Buursma, *'Dese bekommerlijke tijden'*, p. 355.
32 NA, 2.01.01.07, 480, Geesje Kooymans to Lebrun, Leeuwarden 1811; the widow Uriot to Lebrun, Amsterdam, 4 April 1811; the widow Ruel to Lebrun, Amsterdam, 23 March 1811; NA, 2.01.01.07, 662, Geertruy Harmse to Louis Bonaparte, 1808; the widow Elsman to Louis Bonaparte, 1808; Hinderik van den Berg to

Louis Bonaparte, 1808; Rachel Jacob Proops to Louis Bonaparte, 1808; Kaatje Kalkman to Louis Bonaparte, 27.6.1808.

33 Jones, "'I cannot keep my place'".
34 Jones and King, 'From petition to pauper letter', p. 72.
35 Sokoll, *Essex Pauper Letters*, letters nos. 291, 293, 294, 295, 313, 315 and 321.
36 NA, 2.01.01.07, 662, Mrs Vighart to Louis Bonaparte, 1808.
37 Nicholls, 'Addressing God as ruler', p. 138.
38 NA, 2.01.01.07, 662, Kalkman to Bonaparte; Proops to Bonaparte; Johanna Cristina Boom to Louis Bonaparte, 1808.
39 NA, 3.02.32, 16, Van Kervel to William V.
40 NA, 2.01.01.07, 662, Kalkman to Bonaparte.
41 RC, A31, inv. no. 1004, J.C.A. de Cocq to William V, 20 November 1791.
42 Petterson, *Eigenwijs vaderland*.
43 Judge and Oddens, 'Father figures and faction leaders'.

References

Aerts, Remieg and Deneckere, Gita (eds.), *Het (on)verenigd koninkrijk, 1815-1830-2015*, Rekkem, Ons Erfdeel, 2015.

Buursma, Albert, *'Dese bekommerlijke tijden'. Armenzorg, armen en armoede in de stad Groningen 1594–1795*, Assen, Van Gorcum, 2009.

Dabhoiwala, Faramerz, 'Writing petitions in early modern England', in: Braddick, Michael J. and Innes, Joanna (eds.), *Suffering and happiness in England 1550–1850: Narratives and representations*, Oxford, Oxford University Press, 2017, pp. 127–148.

De Haan, Ido, Den Hoed, Paul and Te Velde, Henk (eds.), *Een nieuwe staat. Het begin van het Koninkrijk der Nederlanden*, Amsterdam, Prometheus Bert Bakker, 2013.

Filer, Tanya, 'Letters to the President: Participation beyond the public sphere in Argentina, 1989–1999', in: *Journal of Iberian and Latin American Studies*, vol. 23, no. 3, 2017, pp. 317–339.

Fitzmaurice, Susan M., *The familiar letter in early modern English: A pragmatic approach*, Amsterdam, Benjamins, 2002.

Gammerl, Benno, 'Emotional styles: Concepts and challenges', in: *Rethinking History* vol. 15, no. 2, 2012, pp. 161–175.

Grijzenhout, Frans, 'Lodewijk Napoleon. Beeld en zelfbeeld', in: Rem, Paul and Sanders, George (eds.), *Lodewijk Napoleon. Aan het hof van onze eerste koning*, Zutphen, Verloren, 2006, pp. 9–17.

Grijzenhout, Frans, Van Sas, Niek and Velema, Wyger (eds.), *Het Bataafse experiment. Politiek en cultuur rond 1800*, Nijmegen, Vantilt, 2013.

Houston, R.A., *Peasant petitions: Social relations and economic life on landed estates, 1600–1850*, Basingstoke, Palgrave, 2014.

Jensen, Lotte, '"See our succumbing fatherland, overwhelmed by disaster, woe and strife": Coping with crisis during the reign of Louis Bonaparte', in: *Dutch Crossing*, vol. 40, no. 2, 2016, pp. 151–164.

Jensen, Lotte, *Verzet tegen Napoleon*, Nijmegen, Vantilt, 2013.

Jones, Peter and King, Steven, 'From petition to pauper letter: The development of an epistolary form', in: Jones, Peter and King, Steven, *Obligation, entitlement and dispute under the English poor laws*, Cambridge, Cambridge Scholars, 2016, pp. 53–77.

Jones, Peter D., '"I cannot keep my place without being deascent": Pauper letters, parish clothing and pragmatism in the south of England, 1750–1830', in: *Rural History*, vol. 20, no. 1, 2009, pp. 31–49.

Joor, Johan, *De adelaar en het lam. Onrust, opruiing en onwilligheid in Nederland ten tijde van het Koninkrijk Holland en de inlijving bij het Franse keizerrijk (1806–1813)*, Amsterdam, De Bataafsche Leeuw, 2000.

Jourdan, Annie, 'Staats- en natievorming in de tijd van Lodewijk Napoleon. Nederland als "objet de désir"', in: *De Negentiende Eeuw*, vol. 30, no. 3–4, 2006, pp. 132–146.

Judge, Jane and Oddens, Joris, 'Father figures and faction leaders: Identification strategies and monarchical imagery among ordinary citizens of the northern and southern low countries (c. 1780–1820)', in: *BMGN – Low Countries Historical Review*, vol. 133, no. 3, 2018, pp. 72–97.

King, Steven, 'Pauper letters as a source', in: *Family & Community History*, vol. 10, no. 2, 2007, pp. 167–170.

Klein, S.R.E., *Patriots republikanisme. Politieke cultuur in Nederland (1766–1787)*, Amsterdam, Amsterdam University Press, 1995.

Lyons, Martyn, 'The power of the scribe: Delegated writing in modern Europe', in: *European History Quarterly*, vol. 44, no. 2, 2014, pp. 244–262.

Lyons, Martyn, 'Writing upwards: How the weak wrote to the powerful', in: *Journal of Social History*, vol. 49, no. 2, 2015, pp. 317–330.

Nicholls, David, 'Addressing God as ruler: Prayer and petition', in: *The British Journal of Sociology*, vol. 44, no. 1, 1993, pp. 125–142.

Oddens, Joris, *Pioniers in schaduwbeeld. Het eerste parlement van Nederland 1796-1798*, Nijmegen, Vantilt, 2012.

Oddens, Joris, Rutjes, Mart and Jacobs, Erik (eds.), *The political culture of the sister republics, 1794–1806: France, the Netherlands, Switzerland, and Italy*, Amsterdam, Amsterdam University Press, 2015.

Petterson, Anne, *Eigenwijs vaderland. Populair nationalisme in negentiende-eeuws Amsterdam*, Amsterdam, Prometheus, 2017.

Pot, G.P.M., *Arm Leiden: Levensstandaard, bedeling en bedeelden 1750–1854*, Hilversum, Verloren, 1994.

Ruberg, Willemijn, *Conventional correspondence: Epistolary culture of the Dutch elite, 1770–1850*, Leiden, Brill, 2011.

Rutjes, Mart, *Door gelijkheid gegrepen. Democratie, burgerschap en staat in Nederland*, Nijmegen, Vantilt, 2012.

Scheer, Monique, 'Are emotions a kind of practice (and is this what makes them have a history)? A Bourdieuian approach to understanding emotion', in: *History and Theory*, vol. 51, no. 2, 2012, pp. 193–220.

Scott, James C., *Domination and the arts of resistance: Hidden transcripts*, New Haven, Yale University Press, 1990.

Sokoll, Thomas, 'Writing for relief: Rhetoric in English pauper letters, 1800–1834', in: Gestrich, Andreas, King, Steven and Raphael, Lutz (eds.), *Being poor in modern Europe: Historical perspectives 1800–1940*, Oxford, Lang, 2006, pp. 91–111.

Sokoll, Thomas, *Essex pauper letters, 1731–1837*, Oxford, Oxford University Press, 2001.

Spaans, Joke, *Armenzorg in Friesland 1500–1800. Publieke zorg en particuliere liefdadigheid in zes Friese steden*, Hilversum, Verloren, 1997.

Van de Perre, Stijn and Judo, Frank (eds.), *Belg en Bataaf. De wording van het Verenigd Koninkrijk der Nederlanden*, Kalmthout, Polis, 2015.

Van Ginderachter, Maarten, 'Public transcripts of royalism: Pauper letters to the Belgian royal family (1880–1940)', in: Deploige, Jeroen and Deneckere, Gita (eds.), *Mystifying the monarch: Studies of discourse, power, and history*, Amsterdam, Amsterdam University Press, 2006.

Van Meerkerk, Edwin, *Willem V en Wilhelmina van Pruisen. De laatste stadhouders*, Amsterdam, Atlas, 2009.

Van Sas, N.C.F., *De metamorfose van Nederland. Van oude orde naar moderniteit, 1750–1900*, Amsterdam, Amsterdam University Press, 2004.

Velema, Wyger R.E., *Republicans: Essays on Eighteenth-Century Dutch Political Thought*, Leiden, Brill, 2007.

Verheijen, Bart, *Nederland onder Napoleon. Partijstrijd en natievorming 1801–1813*, Nijmegen, Vantilt, 2017.

Woelderink, B., *Inventaris van de archieven van stadhouder V, 1745–1808 en de Hofcommissie van Willem IV en Willem V, 1732–1794*, Hilversum, Verloren, 2005.

Würgler, Andreas, 'Asymmetrie und reziprozität. Herrschaft und protektion in suppliken der frühen neuzeit', in: Haug, Tilman, Weber, Nadir and Windler, Christian (eds.), *Protegierte und Protektoren. Asymmetrische politische Beziehungen zwischen Partnerschaft und Dominanz (16. bis frühes 20. Jahrhundert)*, Cologne, Böhlau, 2016, pp. 281–294.

3 'Lou tresor dóu Felibrige'

An Occitan dictionary and its emotional potential for readers

Martina Niedhammer

Occitan as a 'minor' language

> The Provençal language is definitely disappearing. It is not part of our agenda
> to examine the legitimacy of the regrets we have heard about the loss of this
> language; however, we could reply to them that it is the fault of Provençal
> itself after all if it disappears. Why has it not produced some masterpieces or
> at least remarkable works?[1]

The way Charles de Gabrielli, the author of a grammatical manual, described Provençal (Occitan) in 1836 is quite typical for the attitude of French
intellectuals and officials of that time towards the old Romance language,
which is mainly spoken in Southern France.[2] According to Gabrielli and his
contemporaries, Occitan could not be regarded as a 'fully-fledged' language
in its own right because it was not a prestigious literary language like
French nor was it academically institutionalized. Nevertheless, Occitan was
perceived as a constant internal threat to the French language, whose high
linguistic status ran the risk of being undermined by Occitan native speakers. The only possibility to escape their harmful influence was education:
those who spoke Occitan on a daily basis should be trained in the equivalent
French vocabulary, morphology and syntax. They should also lose their
characteristic Provençal accent. Therefore, Gabrielli and others sought to
convince their Occitan readers to study French grammar and to learn by
heart correct versions of frequent 'mistakes'.[3]

What seems unusual about Gabrielli's approach is the fact that he quite
openly discusses the exclusiveness and intolerance of French language politics,
which lack the generosity of "Roman Jupiter who welcomed all deities he had
successfully defeated on the Capitol".[4] While Gabrielli admitted that Occitan
had certain lexical qualities missing in French, which had to be given up for
the sake of France's linguistic unity,[5] Occitan was often simply dismissed as a
deformed French dialect ('patois', "langage vulgaire"). In fact, there was little
willingness to accept the linguistic independence of Occitan.

This perception is, of course, crucial, when it comes to the question of
Occitan nationhood, which is highly controversial to this day. Occitan is not

an official language in France[6] where the majority of its speakers live and it is mainly restricted to the private sphere. According to the UNESCO, the linguistic status of Occitan is severely endangered because it is mostly spoken by members of the older generation among themselves, people whose children and grandchildren do not use or even understand the language.[7] Poor external recognition, however, is only one side of the coin. Occitan lacks a stable basis also from an internal, linguistic and political perspective. There is no consensus about the dialect base for a standard written language – something that becomes obvious by the absence of an orthographic standard – nor is there a social or political programme that successfully targets a broader Occitan speaking audience.[8]

Hence, the Occitan movement is described both in terms of regionalism and nationalism. What seems to be contradictory at first glance reflects not only the parlance of the nineteenth century and the early twentieth century, which sometimes did not clearly distinguish between both related movements, for instance, for strategic reasons,[9] but also the fact that regionalists repeatedly tried to tap into the success of major national movements by claiming the uniqueness of their region.[10] In the case of France, the latter can be linked to the concept of *petite patrie* that arose during the Third Republic. In contrast to the *grande patrie* France, which one learns to love by civic education, the *petite patrie* is a place to which one is personally attached in a way that resembles the love of a child for his mother. As Anne-Marie Thiesse has shown, the *petite patrie* served as a role model for the *grande patrie* in schools, where pupils were taught how to embrace France on the basis of their affection for their region.[11] Regional and national identities were then considered as complementary, which in the beginning facilitated the activities of proponents of the Occitan language, especially until the early 1890s, when local languages were completely banned from the classroom.[12]

In this chapter I will argue that even though Occitan was never able to shed its status as a 'minor' language it developed a highly emotional potential for its supporters and thus established strong ties of individual belonging. The analysis of how speakers and followers of Occitan built their own self-understanding upon the idea of a distinctive Occitan groupness during the late nineteenth century allows us to gain insight into the personal aspects of nation- and region-building on a small scale. According to Rogers Brubaker, the concept of groupness makes visible the variability of groups which are not 'given', but characterized by "moments of intensively felt collective solidarity" and phases of discontinuity.[13] The proponents of Occitan who tried to strengthen its role in public French culture had one desire in common which served as a basis for their group cohesion: they wanted to increase the prestige of their native language by the development of a modern Occitan literature – in order to promote those chefs-d'œuvre whose absence had been criticized by Gabrielli. The 'category' of literary achievement is thus a valuable tool to analyse the emotional process of group-formation by considering the degree this category is propagated by Occitan language proponents, and embedded and internalized by their audience.[14]

The 'Felibrige' and the Occitan 'renaissance'

During the second half of the nineteenth century and the early twentieth century, Occitan experienced a revival which is very well documented by archival sources including a huge number of personal notes and letters. They are mainly connected with a small group of activists who tried to spread the idea of Occitan cultural, regional, and to some extent also national, 'renaissance' throughout Southern France. In 1854, seven young men met at castle Font Séguigne near Avignon and founded a circle called 'Felibrige'[15] (derived from Occitan 'felibre', meaning 'pupil') in order to promote their mother tongue by strengthening its 'purity' and thus establishing a common literary standard.[16] However, the initiative of the Felibrige did not come out of thin air. It reflected a general European cultural trend of the nineteenth century that led to the foundation of many language movements based on regional identity, which later, often but not necessarily, turned into national identification.[17] A glorious linguistic (and sometimes also political past) would become an important reference point in order to legitimate public and ideological support. The Felibrige regularly referred to the troubadours of the middle ages who had been the first to write important texts in Provençal; this is why medieval Provençal, which preceded the other Romance languages, had been "the only light [of civilization, MN] in the darkness of barbarism" according to the Felibrige.[18] Over the decades, the felibres (members of the Felibrige) developed a whole programme of cultural heritage and folklorism.[19] In 1891, they began publishing a popular journal called *L'Aiòli* which defended the Occitan identity of the Midi and propagated a federal organization of France.[20] Five years later, the first plans for the 'Museon Arlaten' in Arles were made. It was designed as a kind of *Biblia pauperum* for those indifferent or ignorant about Occitan language and culture[21] and displayed objects from the local area within a carefully chosen historical setting.[22]

What distinguishes the Felibrige from similar movements was its internal hierarchical structure on the one hand and the 'personal union' between its members and the idea of a new 'Occitanism' on the other hand. In fact, both aspects are two sides of the same coin. The Felibrige was deeply influenced by Frédéric Mistral (1830–1914), an Occitan writer who won the Noble prize for Literature in 1904 and was by far the most prominent felibre of his time. Because of the popularity of his poems and books and the fact that he outlived most of his early fellow felibres, he was able to shape the Felibrige according to his personal beliefs. The Felibrige was organized in four sections (*mantenènços*) that represented the main regional varieties of Occitan. These were divided into several subgroups (*escolos*) and managed by a central office headed by the *capoulié*,[23] a position held by Mistral for several years. Over time, Mistral gained the status of the 'king' of Occitan which made it impossible for anyone to promote Occitan language, culture or politics without his support or at least his consent. His position among his fellow felibres can be understood best when looking at postcards and leaflets that were published on behalf of the costume festival 'Fêtes d'Arles' or the fiftieth anniversary of the publication of *Mirèio* ('Mireille'),[24] his major work, in 1909.[25]

Therefore, it is no wonder that many projects of the Felibrige were initiated by Frédéric Mistral himself. One example is the above mentioned 'Museon Arlaten', another good one is the monumental dictionary *Lou tresor dóu Felibrige* (literally 'The treasure of Felibrige') which was compiled by Mistral from the late 1860s through 1886.[26] While Mistral was working on the *Tresor* and especially after its publication, he received hundreds of letters from admirers and opponents. They provide a glimpse into the readers' emotional perception of the Occitan language and its national connotation in their private value system. These letters are the main source for this chapter, although they very often lack emotive terms in the strict sense of the word. Tracing and describing the feelings Mistral's subscribers developed and articulated when reading the *Tresor* shows the difficulties of an emotional approach to historiography: should we analyse emotions as single feelings, as norms, styles or even as a set of practices?[27] In the absence of many concise emotional expressions in the letters to Mistral, this chapter draws on the very process of writing them by focusing on the 'doing' of emotions: it is the habit or manner Mistral's correspondents chose when mentioning the *Tresor* and the Occitan language that can reveal something about their affective belonging.

'Lou tresor dóu Felibrige' and Mistral's appeal to emotion

The *Tresor* was by no means the first modern Occitan dictionary to appear for a broader audience. As we have already seen, manuals and grammars that targeted Occitan native speakers in order to improve their knowledge of French sometimes also provided vocabularies. An early dictionary that was not intended to 'convert' Occitan natives into French speakers was published by a certain Avril in 1839.[28] Instead, his *Dictionnaire Provençal-Français* was meant to help those who had a professional need to know Occitan because of their clients who did not speak proper French: in the preface Avril mentioned doctors, lawyers, civil servants, merchants and clergymen as his intended audience.[29] The fact that he added a second, albeit smaller, French–Occitan word list to make it easier for French natives to learn some Occitan,[30] points in the same direction. In Southern France Occitan was regarded as a necessary part of daily life that had to be mastered instead of eliminated. But the scope of Avril's dictionary was quite narrow; it referred only to those Occitan dialects that were spoken in the Provence.[31]

In the late 1840s, the physician Simon-Jude Honnorat (1783–1852) published a bilingual dictionary in two volumes in which he combined Occitan expressions from all over the Midi with French explanations.[32] Like Frédéric Mistral, he was a linguistic amateur and an ardent language activist who wanted to help improve Occitan speakers' knowledge of their mother tongue and to enable foreigners to learn some Occitan before travelling through

Southern France. For this purpose, Honnorat added separate French–Occitan word lists which were even longer than the ones published by Avril in 1839.[33] Moreover, he asked his readership for feedback in order to augment the vocabulary of his dictionary.[34]

Despite this 'didactic' impetus, Honnorat's *Dictionnaire provençal-français* was far less popular than its successor. This is even more remarkable because Mistral did not change very much in the structure of his dictionary, which also consisted of two volumes. Like Honnorat he tried to represent all Occitan dialects and to make visible the linguistic relationship between Occitan and the other Romance languages. The listing of all regional variants was meant to strengthen the role of Occitan internally, that is among its speakers who should recognize their home dialect. The reference to other Romance languages served as an external goal: to prove the equality of Occitan and thus its status as a fully-developed language in its own right. The fact that Mistral, like Avril and Honnorat, chose a bilingual form instead of a monolingual one, was a step in a similar direction: he sought to contrast Occitan and French and to win followers in the north of France where Occitan was only appreciated by a small group of 'émigrés' from the South.

What was different about Mistral's *Tresor* was its character. While Honnorat, as well as Avril, had written a factual introduction "for a better understanding of the dictionary" in which he explained his criteria regarding orthography and the selection of vocabulary,[35] Mistral omitted a formal prologue. Instead, he took an emotional approach by prefacing his dictionary with a sonnet in Occitan which he had composed in Maillane, on 7 October 1878. The poem was entitled 'Au miejour' ('In the South') and can be read as a highly expressive explanation of the dictionary's title (*Tresor*) – as it makes very clear that the revival of Occitan is mainly a matter of the heart. After praising the landscape of the Provence for its abundance of history and agricultural riches, Mistral suddenly turned to its inhabitants:

O pople dóu Miejour, escouto moun arengo: Se vos recouaquista l'empéri de ta lengo, pèr l'arnesqua de nóa, pesco en aquéuo *Tresor*.[36]

[Oh, people of the South, heed my saying: If you wish to win back the empire of your language, equip yourselves anew by drawing upon this *Treasury.*[37]]

Not only is the Occitan language an empire that has to be regained from its conquerors – the French state authorities – but it is also a virtual treasure that completes the cultural and material wealth of the South and is thus an intrinsic part of 'Provençal', that is 'Occitan' in the late-nineteenth-century language, identity.

In retrospect, the way Mistral promoted Occitan culture by combining scientific aspiration with an appeal to emotion was a key element in the success of his dictionary and the Felibrige itself. He and his followers clearly tried to rely on a certain 'emotional repertoire' which they shaped in order to mobilize

speakers of Occitan, as Monique Scheer puts it. The goal of such a 'manip-
ulating' approach was "to evoke feelings where there [were] none [...] or to
change [...] emotions already there".[38] The felibres achieved it mainly by media
'distribution',[39] that is publishing scientific and especially literary texts. This
becomes especially clear when one analyses Mistral's correspondence regarding
the *Tresor*. However, the strategic concentration on emotional aspects also had
a downside that only became visible over time.

The *Tresor* from the subscribers' perspective

Even before the first volume of Mistral's dictionary finally appeared, in 1878,
the first subscribers had already signed up. We know them mostly from their
letters which they sent to Mistral. Since the poet's death in 1914, the correspondence is preserved in his former domicile in Maillane near Avignon.[40]
Including about 230 documents, it forms only a very small part of Mistral's
estate which contains nearly 60,000 letters.[41] They reflect the impressive European network, extending as far as the imperial court in St. Petersburg, that
the writer established by sending his publications abroad and corresponding
about the role and the importance of Occitan.

Among the readers interested in the *Tresor* were government agencies as
well as private individuals. The majority of the subscribers lived in Southern
France, in Paris or abroad, whereas in the Northern part of the country
hardly anyone seemed to be interested in the dictionary. We can therefore
assume that most of them had a personal link to Occitan because they were
either born in Southern France or had been living there for quite a while.
Moreover, the overwhelming majority of private subscribers were obviously
male, although several letters of female readers to Mistral are preserved in
Maillane. As was the case with many other early European linguistic and
national movements, most private subscribers were part of the middle classes
pursuing liberal professions or working as clergymen. Only very few of them
were university-trained experts in the field of linguistics or history, which did
not mean that they were not interested in such questions. On the contrary,
many readers showed great ambition in discussing philological details of the
dictionary, presumably because they supported Mistral's concept of an academic work which could stress the differences between Occitan and French
and claim its linguistic autonomy from a scientific, 'objective' point of view.

According to the letter-writers, providing a basis of comparison for other,
similar academic projects, mainly dictionaries and monographs from the field
of Romance studies, was one of the three main purposes of the *Tresor*. Very
few of them were, however, as familiar with the matter as the Parisian philologist Frédéric Godefroy (1826–1897). Already in 1869, he had approached
Mistral because he had learnt that he was collecting data for an Occitan dictionary.[42] As Godefroy himself was working on an Old-French dictionary,[43]
he wished to include "analogies with ancient and modern Provençal, as well
as analogies with the various neo-Latin languages".[44] Moreover, he asked for

help with some words he did not understand.[45] Although Godefroy had a moderate view on Occitan, which he understood as a separate language, Mistral was not willing to discuss Occitan issues with him, as a letter, written in 1881, proves.[46] Obviously, Mistral was not too pleased to see his research integrated into a French narrative. Besides, he was suspicious about too close cultural and academic ties to the capital since he feared that his ideas could be alienated for political reasons.

Second, the *Tresor* was a valuable tool for those eager to correct and improve their knowledge of Occitan. Thus, in February 1878, the Irish writer and felibre John Duncan Craig explained to Mistral the difficulties he had encountered when he tried to read Occitan literature.[47] Only one month later, a certain Guy Léroix [?] from Nîmes described to the author of the forthcoming dictionary how badly he needed linguistic guidance in order to write properly.[48]

Third – and this was undoubtedly the case with the vast majority of Mistral's correspondents – the dictionary created or met the emotional expectations and needs of its subscribers. This becomes evident when one looks at the language, the vocabulary, and the structure of their letters to Mistral.

Mistral's dictionary and the desire for literary achievement

There are two emotions that clearly dominate the letters to Mistral regarding the *Tresor*: nostalgia and pride, both accompanied by related feelings, such as homesickness, satisfaction, gratitude or joy. They are linked by the desire for the achievement of modern Occitan literature. Strong negative feelings, like anger or shame, occur only randomly.

A lot of Mistral's correspondents used his dictionary as a key to their private past. Some of them had been born in Southern France, but had left the Occitan-speaking part of the country for professional or family reasons. For these 'expats' Occitan represented their home and provided a valuable remedy for homesickness, a gap that French-speaking company apparently could not fill. In the spring of 1879, Lucien Larrey, a native from Languedoc who served as a local government official in French Cochinchina (today's Vietnam), wrote to Mistral "from the depths of the faraway land where my business affairs make me stay".[49] He was happy to learn about the publication of the *Tresor* from a friend and 'compatriote' from the Midi. The fact that Larrey had recently become a member of the Felibrige suggests a general interest in his native region. Mistral's dictionary was one of many options for him to get in touch with the Occitan culture; yet, it did not serve any didactic purpose for him, because it did not help him to improve his practical language skills in his native Occitan and thus had no profound affective meaning for him. A deeper attachment to the *Tresor* itself can be seen from two letters from abroad, which were written by a certain Mr Piat in 1886. Working at the French consulate in Adrianople (Ottoman Empire, today's Edirne/Turkey), he sent two short Occitan poems in a 'Persian' manner to Mistral. They combined his native culture, the Occitan language, with his new living environment by imitating the Ottoman Turkish form and style of poetry. As he explained, writing in Occitan was a pleasant distraction and a way to cope with his life abroad.[50] For Piat, the *Tresor* fulfilled a double emotional function: it was a matter of nostalgic reference to and a self-reassurance of his Occitan identity.

Feelings of longing are also characteristic of those letters that evoke the early childhood of Mistral's correspondents. Occitan is remembered as a part of daily life at one's father's house, something that used to be and now has almost ceased to exist as a mother tongue. In the eyes of his subscribers, it was thanks to Mistral and his *Tresor* that their nostalgic sentiments got a fresh impetus which allowed them to connect past and present. Consequently, the dictionary was also physically precious to its readers. It is therefore no wonder that Guy Léroix not only emphasized that his parents spoke Occitan very well, but at the same time that he wanted to preserve Mistral's dictionary in a jewel case together with those things he really loved.[51]

From Léroix's statement it is only a small step to the second main emotion in the subscribers' letters: pride. Almost every author praised Mistral's literary genius before writing about his (or, rarely, her) personal understanding of the *Tresor*. Given that Mistral had already published several important epic poems in Occitan at that time, this could be read as a simple matter of courtesy, but, obviously, it was more. In fact, Mistral was celebrated because he was able to enhance the prestige of Occitan in two ways. On the one hand, he was a writer who successfully integrated elements of Provençal folklore and history into an Occitan narrative that was both picturesque and artistic at once. On the other hand, his dictionary offered a solid philological basis for the language of his oeuvre which met scientific criteria. Mistral was therefore able to achieve literariness and to raise the status of the often contested 'patois'.

Mr Peyrot, a native from the Midi who was living in Northern France, told Mistral that he had used "the rough and vulgar patois spoken by the Perigordian peasant" as a child, which he had had to forget when entering university.[52] Now, he felt very fortunate because Mistral was composing a dictionary of a language "which he had adopted for his own work in such a wonderful way".[53] The Irish poet and felibre William Bonaparte-Wyse who was a close friend of Mistral went even further when stating that the *Tresor* was Mistral's "arch-epic in prose",[54] thus attributing literary quality to the dictionary. Other correspondents simply glorified the author as a good writer and philologist,[55] praise that was repeated by the Royal Swedish Academy of Sciences when awarding the Nobel Prize in Literature to Mistral in 1904.[56]

A more complex view of the double nature of Mistral's literary production can be seen in a letter by a certain Comte de Beauffort.[57] He not only mentioned Mistral's literary success and his efforts to establish a modern Occitan philology, but also linked Mistral's ability to compile the dictionary to his being a poet. According to de Beauffort this created a huge difference between the *Tresor* and the dictionary of the Académie française. The latter was intellectually overloaded by academics and lacked the simplicity and authenticity of Mistral's oeuvre. By contrasting the *Tresor* and the famous

Dictionnaire de l'Académie française Mistral's correspondent questioned the cultural authority of the dominant French-speaking part of the country and proudly claimed the linguistic superiority of Occitan, which was codified by someone who indeed knew how to write.

Reference to the Académie française was made more than once in the letters to Mistral. Whereas de Beauffort tried to differentiate Occitan from French and had a negative attitude towards Paris, some correspondents wanted Mistral to become a member of the Academy.[58] This can be understood in terms of integrating the Occitan language and literature into French history in order to be respected as a legitimate part of the country's culture: when Mistral's 'Lou pouèmo dóu rose' ('The Song of the Rhône')[59] won one of the Academy's prizes in 1897, the felibre Léopold Constans felt very happy because "it proves that the Academy has ceased to consider brilliant Provençal works foreign matters to the French domain".[60]

The ambivalence of Occitan nationhood

Statements like this raise the question of the significance of nationhood for the subscribers of the *Tresor*. Evidently, Mistral's readership developed a certain sense of Occitan groupness, which it expressed in a highly emotional manner culminating in the desire for literary achievement. Nevertheless, direct manifestations of national feelings occur quite rarely.

Sometimes, the feeling of pride shifted to grandeur; the latter is commonly associated with the images of persistence and eternity that may hint at a regional or national identity. Several correspondents were perfectly satisfied with Mistral having erected a monument to Occitan that would last for future generations. A lawyer from Carros near Grasse thanked Mistral because he had undertaken "the glorious task of codifying our beautiful langue d'oc for future generations".[61] Shortly before the first instalment of the dictionary was to appear, a friend told Mistral to insist on good printing paper. As he explained, this would not have been important if Mistral had written a novel, but given that he had just finished a [linguistic, MN] 'monument', long-term use on a daily basis should be guaranteed.[62] Another correspondent, an employee at the town hall of Marseille called Marius Décard, even described the *Tresor* as "a keystone to the house of Provence", an image that fittingly illustrates the constructive and process-related character of identity building.[63] It is not totally clear how Décard wanted this house to look, when he continued that it was his "heart full of nationality [nationalité, MN]" that made him write to Mistral. What he was truly interested in was literary glory for the Occitan language, because he praised Mistral as the 'immortal' author of 'Mirèio', which suggests that his understanding of belonging was closer to the *petite patrie* than to pure nationalism.

The most explicit proof of an emotive approach to Occitan nationhood is a letter by Antoine Féraud, probably a priest from Grasse, who described a shift of emotional belonging when coming into contact with Mistral's oeuvre: "I was too French and not Provençal enough. I thank you for the beneficial conversion you have effected on me."[64] What triggered the correspondent's conversion was mainly the fact that, previously, he had not been able to appreciate Occitan language and culture from an intellectual point of view. Only Mistral, who had an eye for folkloristic details such as old legends or proverbs, offered him a new perspective.

The ambivalence of Occitan nationhood is nowhere more evident than in the language Mistral's correspondents used in their letters. Though Occitan language, culture, and sometimes even nationhood, were the main topic, Mistral's correspondents only rarely wrote Occitan; most of them chose French. Therefore, the moment when some of them suddenly switched from the standard language to something officially regarded as a corrupted dialect marks a clear wish to distinguish themselves from a homogenous French identity. As Occitan was not taught at school, writing in the language was not a matter of spontaneity, but of careful decision, manifesting a highly personal, conscious act. So, the Occitan phrases and sentences in the letters were often rather short, some of them praising the beauty of the mother tongue or Mistral's work. Another, more complex, example is a letter written by Octave Monier, a native Occitan speaker from Toulon, in 1882.[65] He ended a four-sided letter by writing a full page in Occitan which symbolized his reconciliation with Mistral. Some years earlier, he had heavily criticized the *Tresor* because Mistral had opted for a phonetic and thus French-styled orthography instead of a historic one that revealed the close relationship of Occitan and Latin.[66] Now, Monier stressed that "the language [Occitan, MN] shall be defended against its conquerors". This was probably an allusion to Mistral's sonnet 'Au miejour', in which the poet had reminded his readers of the loss of their language to the French. Thus, Monier had not only changed his view about Mistral, but also clarified his position on the true opponent of his mother tongue: it was not the 'false' orthography promoted by the Felibrige but the French language. This is indeed one of the rare passages in the letters to Mistral that refer to the country's official language and make intense, passionate emotions, as in this case anger, visible.

Emotions and Occitan nationhood: a conclusion

As the letters written to Mistral by subscribers of his dictionary prove, Mistral and his fellow felibres successfully built a certain Occitan groupness which was mainly based on emotional aspects. Readers could identify themselves with Mistral's aim to value the old linguistic tradition of Occitan and its social and cultural polyvalence. By developing strong feelings towards Occitan, mainly nostalgia and pride, they indeed responded to Mistral's emotive appeal at the beginning of the *Tresor*.

It is therefore rather paradoxical that the case of Occitan nationhood remains so precarious until today. Only a few of Mistral's correspondents appreciated the national dimension of his dictionary as a 'monument' – a virtual shrine of Occitan culture and identity. A short notice at the end of Antoine Féraud's letter might allow a better understanding of the problem. Praising the noble muse of the Provence, Féraud complained that farmers in the countryside were not interested in the literary output of the Felibrige and thus used Occitan mainly when singing "immoral and silly songs".[67] Obviously, the highly elitist approach of the Felibrige, which manifested itself among others in the hierarchical order of the movement and in the reference to the tradition of the medieval troubadours, was also typical of the way the felibres tried to 'manage' emotions among their supporters: they mainly attempted to raise strong positive sentiments regarding the glorious past of Occitan and its lexical richness, such as pride or even nostalgia, whereas negative emotions that could affect the present situation and stimulate political change, like fear of linguistic loss or anger about the social status of Occitan, were excluded. This explains also why the authorities had no qualms about buying Mistral's dictionary. For them, it was a mere patriotic act in order to maintain local customs and fully in line with the idea of the *petite patrie*. This can be seen from the fact that the French Ministry of Public Instruction subscribed to fifty copies of the dictionary, which were apparently distributed among various administrative and cultural institutions.[68] Thus, Mistral's *Tresor* was indeed a treasure, but one to be preserved rather than to be retrieved.

Notes

1 Gabrielli, *Manuel*, p. [3]. All translations my own.
2 Today's regions of Auvergne-Rhône-Alpes, Centre-Val de Loire, Nouvelle-Aquitaine, Occitanie, Provence-Alpes-Côte d'Azur. Occitan is also spoken in Monaco, in some valleys in North Western Italy and North Eastern Spain (Catalonia).
3 Gabrielli, *Manuel*, 12. This kind of didactic literature was quite common during the first half of the nineteenth century, see for example N.N., *Grammaire française*; Gary, *Dictionnaire Patois-Français*.
4 Gabrielli, *Manuel*, p. 7.
5 Ibid.
6 In 2008, several languages of France, among them some varieties of Occitan, were recognized as "regional languages" and declared part of French cultural heritage (*Constitution du 4 octobre 1958*, Article 75–1). Nonetheless, France is one of the very few European states that have not yet ratified the European Charter for Regional or Minority Languages. Cf. Council of Europe, *Chart of Signatures and Ratifications of Treaty 148*.
7 Moseley, *Atlas*.
8 Regarding politics, one problem emerges from the fact that Occitan political commitment is often associated with right-wing politics because it is supposed to break with Paris, which symbolizes the democratic ideals of the French Revolution. Cf. Baycroft, *France*, pp. 221–223.
9 Cf. Núñez, 'Historiographical approaches', p. 20.
10 Cf. Van Ginderachter, 'Nationalist versus regionalist?', p. 224.
11 Thiesse, *Ils apprennaient la France*, esp. pp. 7–9.
12 Ford, *Creating the Nation*, p. 19.
13 Brubaker, *Ethnicity without groups*, p. 12.
14 Cf. ibid., p. 12 f.

15 For a history of the Felibrige and the Occitan 'renaissance' see e.g. Calamel and
    Javel, *La langue d'oc pour étendard*; Martel, *Les félibres*; Zantedeschi, *Une langue
    en quête d'une nation*.
16 For a typical example of the self-historicization of the early Felibrige see: Aubanel,
    Brinde de Teodor Aubanel, pp. 6 and 8.
17 Hroch, *Das Europa der Nationen*, pp. 178–180. As Hroch emphasizes, the glor-
    ification of one's mother tongue is a typical phenomenon for the early stages of
    national movements (phases A and B), when the protagonists want to protect their
    language, to praise its beauty (A) and to externally maintain linguistic sovereignty
    (B). However, Hroch takes the important role of 'ethnicity' for the building of the
    modern nation for granted, which can hardly be adapted to the Occitan case.
18 Cf. for example Mistral, *Discours*, p. 6.
19 Cf. Dymond, 'Displaying the Arlésienne'.
20 Cf. La Redacioun, 'Qu'es acò, l'Aiòli?', p. 1.
21 Arouze, *Le museon arlaten*, p. 6.
22 Cf. *Guide sommaire du visiteur*.
23 Lefèvre, *Catalogue félibréen*, pp. 4–6.
24 Mistral, *Mirèio*.
25 Cf. e.g. *Les Fêtes d'Arles*; Ville d'Arles, *Cinquentenaire*.
26 Mistral, *Lou tresor*.
27 Cf. Schnell, *Haben Gefühle eine Geschichte?*, pp. 36–37.
28 Avril, *Dictionnaire Provençal-Français*.
29 Ibid., p. VII.
30 Ibid., p. VI.
31 Ibid.
32 Honnorat, *Dictionnaire provençal-français*.
33 Honnorat, *Vocabulaire français-provençal*. Honnorat's French–Occitan vocabulary
    contained more than 1,050 pages, whereas Avril had published 153 pages.
34 Honnorat, *Dictionnaire provençal-français*, 1846, [p. IV].
35 Ibid. [p. III].
36 Mistral, *Lou tresor*, 1878 [p. V]. Emphasis added.
37 Translation: Downer, *Frédéric Mistral*, p. 93. Emphasis added.
38 Scheer, 'Are emotions a kind of practice', p. 209.
39 Ibid.
40 Musée Frédéric Mistral à Maillane, les Archives (MFMA), Correspondants de Fré-
    déric Mistral 1847–1904 (CFM 1847–1904), Trésor du Félibrige, dossiers 221–224.
41 Cf. the short introduction into the archival holdings at Maillane, available at
    http://museemistral.fr/correspondances (accessed 17 February 2019).
42 MFMA, CFM 1847–1904, dossier 103, 37, Frédéric Godefroy to Mistral, 29.4.1869.
43 It appeared in ten volumes between 1881 and 1902 (Godefroy, *Dictionnaire de
    l'ancienne langue française*).
44 MFMA, CFM 1847–1904, dossier 103, 37.
45 Cf. attached word list, ibid., 37 i.
46 MFMA, CFM 1847–1904, Trésor, dossier 223, 23, Frédéric Godefroy to Mistral,
    18.2.1881.
47 MFMA, CFM 1847–1904, Trésor, dossier 222, 46, John Duncan Craig to Mistral,
    18.2.1878.
48 MFMA, CFM 1847–1904, Trésor, dossier 224,36, Guy Léroix [?] to Mistral,
    8.3.1878.
49 MFMA, CFM 1847–1904, Trésor, dossier 223, 39, Lucien Larrey to Mistral,
    18.3.1879.
50 MFMA, CFM 1847–1904, Trésor, dossier 224, 30 and 31, Ms Piat to Mistral,
    20.8.1886 and 21.10.1886.

51 MFMA, CFM 1847–1904, Trésor, dossier 224, 36, Guy Léroix [?] to Mistral, 8.3.1878.
52 MFMA, CFM 1847–1904, Trésor, dossier 224, 27, Ms Peyrot to Mistral, Le Mans, 4.4.1878.
53 Ibid.
54 MFMA, CFM 1847–1904, Trésor, dossier 222, 16, William Bonaparte-Wyse to Mistral, Manor of St. John's, October 1886.
55 Cf. e.g. MFMA, CFM 1847–1904, Trésor, dossier 222, 22, François de Marin de Carraurais to Mistral, 7 March 1878.
56 Nobelstiftelsen, *Les Prix Nobel en 1904*, p. 81.
57 MFMA, CFM 1847–1904, Trésor, dossier 222, 6, Comte de Beauffort to Mistral, 8.3. [1878?].
58 E.g. MFMA, CFM 1847–1904, Trésor, dossier 222, 42, V. Colomb to Mistral, 9.10.1880[?].
59 Mistral, *Le poème du Rhône*.
60 MFMA, CFM 1847–1904, dossier 62, 72, Léopold Constans to Mistral, 10.6.1897.
61 MFMA, CFM 1847–1904, Trésor, dossier 222, 49, P. E. Clergue to Mistral, 16.3.1878.
62 MFMA, CFM 1847–1904, Trésor, dossier 222, 32, C. Chaves [?] to Mistral, 24.7.1878.
63 MFMA, CFM 1847–1904, Trésor, dossier 223, 6, Marius Décard to Mistral, 23.2.1878.
64 MFMA, CFM 1847–1904, Trésor, dossier 223, 11, Antoine Féraud to Mistral, 1.12.1880.
65 MFMA, CFM 1847–1904, Trésor, dossier 224, Octave Monier to Mistral, 3.1.1882.
66 MFMA, CFM 1847–1904, Trésor, dossier 224, 18/18i, 19, Octave Monier to Mistral, 6.2.1878, 26.2.1878.
67 MFMA, CFM 1847–1904, Trésor, dossier 223, 11.
68 MFMA, CFM 1847–1904, Trésor, dossier 221, 9, Ministère de l'instruction publique, des cultes et des beaux-arts to Mistral, 10 May 1878.

References

Published sources

Arouze, Joseph, *Le museon arlaten en son nouveau local*, Grenoble, Alliers Frères, 1909.
Aubanel, Théodore, *Brinde de Teodor Aubanel sendi de Prouvènco a la taulejado Parisenco de la Cigalo*, Avignon, Fraire Aubanel, 1878.
Avril, J. T., *Dictionnaire Provençal-Français contenant tous les termes insérés et ceux omis dans les dictionnaires provençaux publiés jusqu'à ce jour*, Apt, Edouard Cartier, 1839.
Constitution du 4 octobre 1958, Article 75–71, available at https://www.legifrance.gouv.fr/affichTexte.do?cidTexte=LEGITEXT000006071194 (accessed 23 January 2018).
Council of Europe, Chart of Signatures and Ratifications of Treaty 148, European Charter for Regional or Minority Languages, available at https://www.coe.int/en/web/conventions/full-list/-/conventions/treaty/148/signatures (accessed 23 January 2018).
Downer, Charles Alfred, *Frédéric Mistral: Poet and leader in Provence*, New York, Columbia University Press, 1901.

Gabrielli, C[harles] de, *Manuel du Provençal ou les provençalismes corrigés à l'usage des habitants des départements des Bouches-du-Rhône, du Var, des Basses-Alpes, de Vaucluse et du Gard*, Aix-en-Provence, Aubin, 1836.

Gary, Léger, *Dictionnaire Patois-Français à l'usage du département du Tarn et des départements circonvoisins: Enrichi de quelques observations sur la Grammaire, la synonymie, l'histoire naturelle, etc., et d'un grand nombre de primitifs Latins ou Grecs, d'où dérivent autant de mots patois*, Castres, J.-L. Pujol, 1845.

Godefroy, Frédéric, *Dictionnaire de l'ancienne langue française et de tous ses dialectes du IXe au XVe siècle*, 10 vol., Paris, F. Vieweg, 1881–1902.

Guide sommaire du visiteur au Nouveau Museon Arlaten (Palais du Félibrige), Avignon, J. Roche & Roulliere Frères [1909].

Honnorat, Jude-Simon, *Dictionnaire provençal-français ou dictionnaire de la langue d'oc ancienne et moderne suivi d'un vocabulaire français-provençal*, 2 vol., Digne, Repos, 1846 and 1847.

Honnorat, Jude-Simon, *Vocabulaire français-provençal*, Digne, Repos, 1848.

La Redacioun, 'Qu'es acò, l'Aiòli?', in: *L'Aiòli*, no. 1, 7 January 1891, p. 1.

Lefèvre, Edmond (ed.), *Catalogue félibréen et du Midi de la France (1re année – 1900). Notes et documents sur le félibrige, avec la bibliographie des Majoraux des origines à nos jours (1876–1901): Bibliographie sommaire des œuvres publiées en 1900 concernant le Midi de la France et plus particulièrement la langue d'Oc*, Marseille, Paul Ruat, 1901.

Les Fêtes d'Arles du 10 au 25 Mai 1899: Concours régional, Mireille aux Arènes d'Arles, Frédéric Mistral, Nîmes, Guillot B. [1899].

Mistral, Frederic, *Mirèio: Pouèmo provençau (avec la traduction littérale en regard)*, Avignon, J. Roumanille, 1859.

Mistral, Frédéric, *Discours de Frederi Mistral pèr l'uberturo di Jo Flourau de Mount-Pelié (Santo Estello, 1878)*, Avignon, Gros frères, 1878.

Mistral, Frédéric, *Le poème du Rhône en XII chants: Texte provençal et traduction française*, Paris, Alphonse Lemerre, 1897.

Mistral, Frédéric, *Lou tresor dóu felibrige ou dictionnaire provençal-français embrassant les divers dialectes de la langue d'Oc moderne*, 2 vol., Aix-en-Provence, Remondet-Aubin, 1878 and 1886.

N.N., *Grammaire française expliquée au moyen de la langue provençale, ou nouvelle méthode avec laquelle un provençal qui sait lire, peut, sans maître, apprendre en peu de temps à parler et à écrire correctement le français*, Marseille, Camoin, 1826.

Nobelstiftelsen (Hg.), *Les Prix Nobel en 1904*, Stockholm, Imprimerie royale P.A. Nordstedt & Söner, 1907.

Ville d'Arles (ed.), *Cinquantenaire de Mireille: Jubilé de F. Mistral. Programme Officiel des Fêtes. 29, 30, 31 Mai 1909*, Marseille, Imprimerie régionale, 1909.

Literature

Brubaker, Rogers, *Ethnicity without groups*, Cambridge MA, Harvard University Press, 2004.

Calamel, Simon and Javel, Dominique, *La langue d'oc pour étendard. Les félibres (1854–2002)*, Toulouse, Éditions Privat, 2002.

Dymond, Anne, 'Displaying the Arlésienne: Museums, folklife and regional identity in France', in: Baycroft, Timothy and Hopkin, David (eds.), *Folklore and nationalism in Europe during the long nineteenth century*, Leiden, Boston, Brill, 2012, pp. 137–159.

Ford, Caroline, *Creating the nation in provincial France. Religion and political identity in Brittany*, Princeton NJ, Princeton University Press, 1993.

Hroch, Miroslav, *Das Europa der Nationen: Die moderne Nationsbildung im europäischen Vergleich*, Göttingen, Vandenhoeck & Ruprecht, 2005.

Martel, Philippe, *Les félibres et leur temps. Renaissance d'oc et opinion (1850–1914)*, Pessac, Presses Université de Bordeaux, 2010.

Moseley, Christopher (ed.), *Atlas of the world's languages in danger*, Paris, UNESCO Publishing, 3rd edition, 2010, available at http://www.unesco.org/culture/en/enda ngeredlanguages/atlas (accessed 18 January 2018).

Núñez, Xosé-Manoel, 'Historiographical approaches to sub-national identities in Europe: A reappraisal and some suggestions', in: Augusteijn, Joost and Storm, Eric (eds.), *Region and state in nineteenth-century Europe. Nation-building, regional identities and separatism*, London, Palgrave Macmillan, 2012, pp. 13–35.

Scheer, Monique, 'Are emotions a kind of practice (and is that what makes them have a history)? A Bourdieuan approach to understanding emotion', in: *History and Theory*, vol. 51, no. 2, 2012, pp. 193–220.

Schnell, Rüdiger, *Haben Gefühle eine Geschichte? Aporie einer History of emotions?*, Göttingen, Vandenhoeck & Ruprecht, 2015.

Thiesse, Anne-Marie, *Ils apprennaient la France. L'éxaltation des régions dans le discours patriotique*, Paris, Éditions de la Maison des sciences de l'homme, 1997.

Van Ginderachter, Maarten, 'Nationalist versus regionalist? The Flemish and Walloon movements in Belle Époque Belgium', in Augusteijn, Joost and Storm, Eric (eds.), *Region and state in nineteenth-century Europe. Nation-building, regional identities and separatism*, London, Palgrave Macmillan, 2012, pp. 209–226.

Zantedeschi, Francesca, *Une langue en quête d'une nation. La Société pour l'étude des langues romanes et la langue d'oc (1869–1890)* [Puylaurens], Institut d'Estudis Occitans, 2013.

4 Learning to love

Embodied practices of patriotism in the Belgian nineteenth-century classroom (and beyond)

Josephine Hoegaerts

In 1857, head teacher J. Steyaert published a book entitled *A Leisurely Trip through Belgium*.[1] Featuring two kindly fictional gentlemen, Mr Goodheart and Mr Lovesyouth, the book represented an attempt to inspire more patriotism in its readers. It was, as the author noted, intended mainly for pupils of colleges and atheneums; but also for "all our compatriots who have not gotten to know our country sufficiently, and therefore cannot love it sufficiently".[2] Love for the fatherland was, according to Steyaert, a primordial condition for the creation of good citizens, but also for the "good of the children". And because knowledge of the fatherland necessarily preceded love for it, the book presented a fictional trip through Belgium, that could not only be used as a practical guidebook (pointing out important destinations and sights), but also a moral and emotional one. The trip described in the book was undertaken by five distinct characters, two adults and three children, after which different readers could model their behaviour and reactions. M. Lovesyouth, a teacher, largely led the trip, and was accompanied by M. Goodheart, a former military man who "lived comfortably" in Brussels with his family and his two sons Jantje and Adolf. Also joining them was Lovesyouth's own son Ernest, who had been given "a civilised education, but also proper for his station".

The inclusion of both well-off and lower middle-class characters reflects the book's aim to reach a wide audience, and its contention that knowing and loving the fatherland was of importance for all children (or at least all future citizens – women and girls are conspicuously absent from the narrative). And Steyaert was clearly not alone among teachers to think that love of the fatherland was an important matter, and a matter of education. In the second half of the nineteenth century, travelling through the nation became a part of children's education: on top of their conventional geography classes, some pupils would get a chance to experience different parts of their country first hand.[3] For the children described in *A Leisurely Trip through Belgium*, as for the children whose experiences will be at issue in this chapter, that country was Belgium. Or rather, it was 'Belgium' as it was imagined in the northern, Flemish part of the country, by participants in state-organized education.[4] Belgium may very well have looked and felt different for the many children who received their education in catholic schools, for the French-speaking population in the south or for those who had been privileged enough to be educated at home (or were so lacking in privilege that they received no education at all, although this was increasingly rare). The classic fissures in modern Belgian society (liberal/humanist or catholic, north or south, Francophone or Flemish, middle and working class) have been researched thoroughly, and their wide-reaching effects have their consequences for the story to be told here.[5] Below, I analyse documents produced in an institutional context saturated with these modes of segregation (and they therefore represent only a very particular part of what could be termed 'Belgian' education). Nevertheless, the experience of state-educated Flemish children did not occur in a vacuum either, and the documents they produced give us a particular insight in patriotic performances that are above all particular to children, which is the issue at hand. In this chapter, I base my analysis of children's education towards love for the fatherland for a large part on the practice of taking children on 'excursions'. The Antwerp City Archives contain the correspondence about these trips (by teachers and city officials), as well as reports written about them (by schoolchildren).[6] Together, these documents provide an insight into the practice of learning to know and love the fatherland. Like their subjects (the trips were organized by educational establishments, but outside its walls), the documents hover on the borders between normative discourse and daily practice, between educational discipline and youngsters' agency and occasional rebellion. They reflect a path towards patriotism and knowledge riddled with tensions and contradictions and above all show how slippery the concept of 'love for the fatherland' could become in the hands of the children who were supposed to acquire it.

In the next few pages, I will analyse the process of arousing, acquiring and mobilizing the love for the fatherland as an emotional practice shared by children and adults. First, I will explore the discursive use of the phrase 'love for the fatherland', and its place in nineteenth-century sentimental and educational contexts. Second, I examine the practices associated with this process of acquiring cognitive, moral and emotional skills during the excursions organized by the Antwerp city schools at the end of the nineteenth century. Third, and finally, I look at how embodied practices of patriotism were transposed according to the different identities of the historical actors involved. Age – and the notion of childhood – will serve as a central category for this analysis, but cannot be considered on its own. As Steyaert's insistence on class differences in his strictly male party of travellers shows, not every child learned, practised or 'felt' their attachment to the fatherland in the same way.

What is love?

Considering the history of patriotism as an emotional practice in which children were engaged through numerous (educational) activities, this chapter rests on the assumption that emotions are a kind of practice that can (and should) be historicized.[7] Nevertheless, it seems necessary to first create some conceptual clarity. What is patriotism (or what was it, in the nineteenth century)? It seems obvious that patriotism was indeed 'felt', but upon closer inspection it quickly becomes obvious that patriotism can contain a confusing conglomerate of different emotions. For the nineteenth century, historians have connected it to feelings of honour, duty, pride and loyalty, to a sense of belonging and to notions of obligation.[8] It was also often connected to 'love', an emotion that is perhaps particularly multi-faceted as it shifts shape according to its object, but that is of particular importance for this analysis. The most common Dutch iteration of patriotism (and the one used in the educational texts used in the Antwerp primary schools) was *vaderlandsliefde*.[9] Literally, this translates as love for the fatherland, which – according to the historical dictionary – also included the "willingness to sacrifice one's self-interest for the sake of the nation".[10] This tallied with the definition the dictionary gave of 'love', which included "concern for the happiness and wellbeing of its object" as well as "longing to be together with the object". The readiness to sacrifice oneself for the sake of the fatherland also echoed another type of love: that of mothers for their children which was defined as the "paragon of self-sacrificing love".

More than to romantic love, patriotic love was compared to family-based models of affection. Love for the fatherland implied a filial relation to one's country, and motherly love could therefore very well serve as a 'paragon' for it, much in the same way as it was a point of reference for affective practices within families.[11] And much like family love, love of the fatherland was a generational practice, passed on from one generation to the next and therefore as open to change as it was rooted in history and tradition. As Susan Miller notes in 'Feeling like a citizen', patriotism, while it passes through families and generations, is not 'naturally inherited' but rather repeatedly instilled in young members of the nation. When researching the cultivation of love of the fatherland, these moments of generational transition must be taken into account. Or, as Miller frames it, "the history of political emotions read in conjunction with the history of youth requires us to examine both the emotional valance of patriotic bonds and the means by which they are transmitted to the next generation".[12] Because of this key role of children in the inter-generational transmission (i.e. historical trajectory) of patriotism, I will be conceptualizing love of the fatherland not as a building block of an emotional community or regime (although both have been proven to be valuable perspectives),[13] but rather as the object of an emotional frontier.

I am borrowing this notion of the emotional frontier from Karen Vallgårda, Kristine Alexander and Stephanie Olsen, who define it as "a boundary between different emotional formations". They note that "many children share the experience of having to traverse various emotional frontiers" and "are especially charged with such a role".[14] As representatives of the 'next' generation, responsible for the 'future' of a community, children do indeed seem to be charged more than adults with the cultural work of social and cultural change – which includes changing modes of emotion and affect.[15] In the case of an education towards love of the fatherland, too, "children were taught habits of feeling derived from an emotional formation in contrast to the one according to which they were raised". This process of emotional management and education consisted of crossing 'emotional frontiers' chronologically: during their lives, children moved from older imaginations of the fatherland and their presumed feelings for it to newer ones as the character of both the nation and of the educational system changed over time. More importantly, however, children constantly crossed the border between emotional formations attached to their experiences of home and family life, and the habits of feeling they developed in school, where notions of love and domesticity may well have been quite different. In the public institution of the primary school, children were taught to redirect the affection they had been raised to practise in the context of the nuclear family to the much more abstract object of the father-land. The discursive overlap between these two kinds of 'love' provided a con-tact zone that made the frontier easier to navigate, but the transition nevertheless necessitated considerable emotional and educational work.

The centrality of children to transitions and 'frontiers' in emotional reper-toires echoes, to some extent, the centrality they were given in nineteenth-century discourses on patriotism and the fatherland. Children, and especially boys, were represented as future members and defenders of the fatherland. They were therefore not only supposed to be particularly suited to an educa-tion in love for the (new and modern) nation, their education towards affec-tion for it was of particular importance. These sentiments were implicit in Steyaert's educational trips in Belgium, which started with the assertion that "every good book written for youth" would have the same goal:

> Love for the Fatherland, my dear friends, is such love, such noble affec-tion for the welfare of one's birthplace, which has been planted in man's heart by Faith. [...] Whether a man's home is in the cold North or the fiery South, he feels his heart beat for his birthplace: he cares for his Fatherland. But when this man does everything in his power to further the welfare of his fellow countrymen, and to raise the honour and growth of his Fatherland, then he shows true love for the fatherland, and he deserves the honourable name of a patriotic (vaderlandslievend) man.[16]

Love for the fatherland, it transpired, was not (just) a matter of feeling, but one of hard work: the patriotic citizen was recognizable by his deeds, more than by his beating heart. Showing love for the fatherland could therefore only be achieved by displaying other virtues. And the Belgians, Steyaert asserted, did this in exemplary fashion.

> Such noble people can be found anywhere, but they are more generally found amongst the Belgians. They have always excelled in devotion, charity, courage and bravery, genius and industriousness, and many vir-tues. Our forefathers were famous for it, our contemporaries are no less

appreciated and admired among all peoples for their consummated skill and excellent behaviour.[17]

Given the presumed natural aptitude of the Belgians for patriotic love, it is almost surprising there would be anything left for them to learn, but the intimate connection Steyaert assumed between knowledge and love demanded that, to love the whole fatherland, one had to know all about it. The question of whether patriotism could be learned through such an education appeared as a rhetorical one. The epitaph to Steyaert's book reads "Faire connaître la patrie, c'est la faire aimer", describing a love that could be consciously taught, or even extracted from pupils. Closer to practice, an author in teacher journal *Ons Woord* articulated similar goals and means:

> The government DEMANDS that we teach, or rather pour in, love for the fatherland. One should start by showing the child his country of birth. This necessitates travel – free of expenses – in the canton, the province, the country [...]. And then, let them admire our beautiful Belgium from North to South.[18]

This notion was stated with great certainty, and was indeed hardly questioned – despite the cost of these excursions.

As they were organized by public schools, it was the mayoral office that sponsored the outings that would turn their young townsmen into model citizens. Like the rest of the education offered within public schools, they were free of charge for the pupils. They thus offered an opportunity for education and leisure that most of the travellers otherwise would not have access to – and this was reflected in the report pupils wrote after returning from their trip. Nevertheless, the excursions were not a free for all: only those pupils who had shown exemplary behaviour and proven to be excellent students were selected to join the excursions. Lists of the actual participants are very incomplete and contain little more than the travellers' names and study year, but some of the pupils whose reports were eventually sent to the mayoral office and archived can be identified as relatives of local teachers, composers and authors – members of the (lower) middle class rather than the city's poorest (who were probably less likely to have an exemplary scholarly or behavioural record). Nevertheless, even for these children the trips offered considerable excitement, as is obvious, for example, from their enthusiasm, about travelling by train.

The excursions certainly seemed to incite feelings of joy. Whether they could also elicit love is a question for the next section. But the basic premise of the school excursion certainly resonated with the dictionary definition of love: it promoted proximity to the nation (answering "the longing to be close" to an object of love) and it was supported by (metaphoric) kinship ties promoting filial education. As Steyaert, and a number of geography manuals as well as school songs, asserted, love for the fatherland was imagined as an extension of love for one's family. Children were therefore encouraged to 'love your country like you love your mother'.[19] Physically leaving the family home and coming into contact with the national extended family was therefore primordial in confronting the emotional frontier one needed to cross in order to attain this other kind of love.[20]

A sense of nation

So what happened during these school trips? To a large extent, the practice of travelling seems to have resembled the imaginary trips described by Steyaert. Destinations were carefully chosen for their historical, economic or cultural importance to the nation. Children and teachers travelled to these destinations by public transport, and then proceeded to visit the local sights – often with the help of a local guide. After returning from their trip, children were expected to write a report. Their reports were quite substantial: over several pages, they described the modes of transport they used, the natural and cultural sites they had visited, the explanations their teachers and guides had provided, and what they themselves had 'done' on the trip (in many cases, they engaged in activities such as hiking, singing or swimming). In many ways, the reports were a matter of educational discipline. Writing them was obligatory, and the uniformity across the reports suggests that teachers put considerable effort into shaping and correcting them. Moreover, of all the reports written, every Antwerp school selected only its 'best' reports to be sent to the city council, where they have been preserved in the archives. The documents I have been able to use had been selected as exemplary instances of a practice that was only open to a select group of pupils to begin with. Taken as a representation of children's experiences of education and its emotional world, they proved a very particular window into a very limited group.

Nevertheless, it is precisely their exemplary and formulaic character that makes these reports a useful source to study children's expressions of emotions towards the nation. The 'formula' according to which they were to shape their reports was one of autobiography. Children were clearly encouraged to write as if they were telling 'their' story of the trip to a friend – and most reports were written as long letters (addressed to a 'dear friend' or to the alderman of education). This did nothing to lessen the pressure to conform to educational norms, of course, and the reports bear all the hallmarks of an imagined ideal of learning, but through their autobiographical slant the reports do show children's attempts to grapple with the emotional habits they were supposed to acquire and the behaviour they were expected to exhibit. In these reports we see the normative discourse of education being transliterated (often with considerable virtuosity) by children who were forging the image of 'the schoolchild' through various educational practices such as travelling, remembering and writing. Crucially, as very few planning notes or teachers' reports have been preserved, the reports written by children are our only source of information. They are a very rich source, though, reflecting both the educational norms and expectations imposed on the young travellers and moments of friction and what seem to be recollections of genuine (emotional) experience. The norm-conformity is perhaps most obvious when pupils were recalling the cognitive aspects of the trips. Teachers were encouraged to "be watchful and concerned for the children in their care and during the travel to show and explain anything noteworthy".[21] Upon arrival at their destination, a local municipal official generally guided the groups around their towns, and children – who had been encouraged to take notes – diligently reported having listened carefully and learned a lot. Apart from numerous details about the places they visited (the height of bell-towers, cost of recent restorations, number of soldiers involved in battles), they also seem to have picked up on sources of local pride, which were then swiftly translated into elements of national pride. When visiting Ghent or Liège, for example, the cities' industrial activities were not only reported as impressive, but also as an element of the greatness of the nation as a whole. With cities like Ghent ("the Manchester of Belgium") and Seraing (home to the Cockerill factory, which left a great impression on the students), the pupils could indeed, like Steyaert, "take great national pride in the knowledge that our fatherland is, in this regard, not inferior to England".[22]

Pupils' enthusiasm over, for example, the industrial prowess of Liège, was also the result of careful in-class preparation. When one pupil reported on the trip to the city, he mainly recalled the many stories he had already heard about it in class:

> What joy, what happiness filled our hearts when hearing this: throughout the year we had heard so much about the industry and beauty of Liège, about the arms factories and the furnaces. How could we not be overjoyed to find ourselves to have the opportunity to visit this industrious city.[23]

Overall, the excursion reports are peppered with references to knowledge previously acquired in history and geography teaching. When visiting Bruges in 1883, for example, one of the boys described the city's former, medieval glory in excruciating detail.

> It is no longer the Bruges of the 12th, 14th, 15th century, which was one of the most thriving cities in the world, and the general staple of the trade in the North as much as in the South. Her fame was so great that she was called the Venice of the north. Merchants from almost all nations then crossed her crowded streets, while everywhere rose those beautiful buildings that are still admired. And now? These warehouses do not contain any untold wealth today; the splendor of its women has disappeared, the splendor that once made Queen Joan of Navarre exclaim: "I alone thought to be a queen here, yet I see hundreds!" [...] Who could have thought that one day that fame, that wealth, that magnificence would disappear.[24]

It seems plausible that pupils were not only prepared for their trips, but that they also consulted their manuals again upon return, thus once again strengthening the link between travelling through, learning about and feeling affection (or in this case nostalgia) for the nation. The excursions also repeated other aspects of geographical and historical education towards nationhood. In the classroom, belonging to the nation, and loving it, was explained with imagery of expanding circles. The love of one's home could be extended to the home town, home province and ultimately home country. Likewise, history classes taught pupils that the love for their parents could extend to their grandparents and then the 'forefathers'. School excursions mimicked these circles by introducing pupils first to their own city (in Antwerp by trips to the local zoo, for example), and then to towns further afield, but also by drawing attention to the forefathers. In Ghent, for example, the travellers admired the statue of the medieval hero Jacob van Artevelde, who had "538 years ago called his fellow townsmen to arms to defend the dear Fatherland".[25]

The visit to Artevelde's statue was not just a matter of conveying information, or even of creating a more tangible bond with a historical figure. Pupils were also told they now shared the place where the hero had been active: they stood where he had been and therefore had access to a physical experience of a (historically) important part of the national landscape. This possibility for direct, and above all *sensory*, experience was the main educational advantage of the school excursion, according to teaching staff versed in the theories of object education. In engaging all the senses, they presented an immersive experience that would not only make the knowledge imparted during the trips more memorable, but also strengthen the bonds between the travellers and the places they visited. The sense of sight is most obviously present in excursion reports, as children were constantly pointed to "bezienswaardigheden" (notable sights). The sights they recalled in their reports included particular buildings and statues as well as panoramic views. One pupil reported to have been completely overcome by the landscape's beauty when travelling to Seraing over the river Meuse: "This lovely panorama moved us so much that we believed ourselves to be in an earthly paradise."[26] But children also reported on the experience of seeing itself. The train offered particular opportunities to think of the landscape in a new way, and encouraged children to develop new sensory skills. As one pupil noted, seeing landscapes from a train was initially quite difficult and they "did not have eyes to see everything. It is a pity that it all flew by so quickly".[27] The train also gave children an immersive experience of industry and engineering, as they felt it speeding along, mechanically shuddering to a halt, or as it took them through the man-made tunnels of the Ardennes. Likewise, the galleries in Brussels were described in experiential visual terms, making them out as a particularly remarkable spot to 'see'. According to at least one pupil, "the Saint-Hubert Galleries with their electric lights, and all the splendor and fashion you can imagine, were the crowning glory".[28]

Other sensory experiences were perhaps less frequently described, but with no less enthusiasm or sense of detail. According to a reigning hierarchy of the senses, smell, touch, sound and taste were less rational means of observation, and were therefore more direct and thus carried greater emotional impact.[29] The most immersive of all, perhaps, was the sense of touch. Excursions allowed pupils a kind of physical interaction with the nation, and a heightened awareness of that close interaction, that was otherwise largely unavailable to them. Hiking the country's roads, climbing its hills and exploring its fields were a unique experience for urban children, and central to these trips. On a trip to Ostend, pupils were even given the chance to get up close and personal with the North Sea. One of the girls taking part recalled:

> We could take a bath, were given a bathing suit, got into a little cart in which we got changed and that was led to the sea by a driver and a horse. Every cart had a number, which we had to remember until we would get out of the sea, because our clothes were in there. In the seawater we danced, jumped and sang, and were helped in all this by women who were also wearing bathing suits.[30]

Throughout these bouts of physical exercise and practices of touch, the sense of taste was engaged as well. During their travels, the children were served their meals in local hotels and restaurants. It is perhaps no surprise that, on pupils of rather humble backgrounds, this made a great impression. Meals, and the surroundings in which they were enjoyed, were described in great detail. They were the object of gratitude towards the sponsors of the trips, but also the source of heightened jollity – especially when accompanied by music and beer. As one pupil on a trip to Liège noted, "tongues loosened with the drinking of beer, and the quiet murmur that had been filling the hall soon changed into a lively noise".[31] The meals were mostly described as a time of leisure and joy, but had educational aspects as well. Local delicacies (such as *Dinantse koeken*/cake of Dinant, for example) were savoured as part of the trip, thus adding a gastronomic layer to children's understanding of the national landscape. And, as noted before, mealtimes were often used as a moment to express gratitude to one's host, usually by intoning patriotic songs.

This brings us to yet another sensory experience mobilized during the school trips: that of sounds. Singing was used particularly as a way to connect cognitive, physical and moral practices during the excursions. By singing *about* the nation whilst travelling it, children would experience the kind of unity expected of citizens through rhythmic and melodic unison. The content of some songs, moreover, would remind them of the educational and emotional goal of the trip. The educational value of singing was perhaps most clearly expressed in the popular travelling song *Wij reizen om te leren* (we travel to learn), which had been composed by Antwerp composer Peter Benoit specifically for the school trips and was occasionally referenced in the reports (Figure 4.1). A young Karel De Bom,

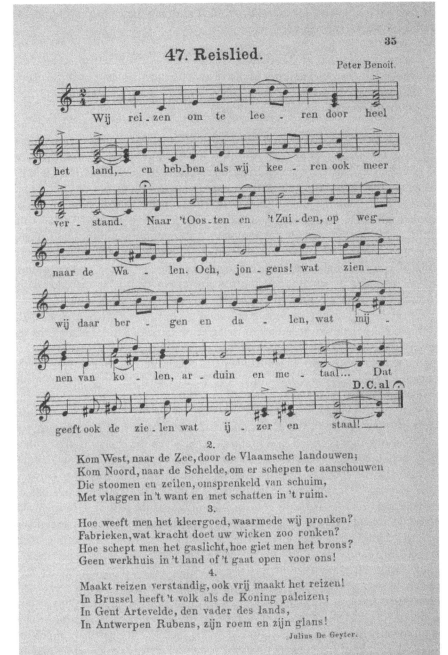

47. Reislied.

Peter Benoit.

Wij rei.zen om te lee . ren door heel het land,— en heb.ben als wij kee . ren ook meer ver . stand. Naar 'tOos.ten en 't Zui.den, op weg— naar de Wa . len. Och, jon . gens! wat zien— wij daar ber . gen en da . len, wat mij . nen van ko . len, ar . duin en me . taal... Dat geeft ook de zie . len wat ij . zer en staal!—

2.
Kom West, naar de Zee, door de Vlaamsche landouwen;
Kom Noord, naar de Schelde, om er schepen te aanschouwen
Die stoomen en zeilen, omsprenkeld van schuim,
Met vlaggen in 't want en met schatten in 't ruim.

3.
Hoe weeft men het kleergoed, waarmede wij pronken?
Fabrieken, wat kracht doet uw wieken zoo ronken?
Hoe schept men het gaslicht, hoe giet men het brons?
Geen werkhuis in 't land of 't gaat open voor ons!

4.
Maakt reizen verstandig, ook vrij maakt het reizen!
In Brussel heeft 't volk als de Koning paleizen;
In Gent Artevelde, den vader des lands,
In Antwerpen Rubens, zijn roem en zijn glans!

Julius De Geyter.

Figure 4.1 A travel song (*Reislied*) for schoolchildren
Source: Joris De Bom, *De kleine zanger en andere kinderliederen*, Antwerp: G. Faes, s.d. p. 2. Available at *Vlaamse Liederendatabank* (http://www.libraryconservatorya ntwerp.be/liederen/kleine_zanger.php).

the later man of letters, for example, recalled intoning these 'deeply felt' phrases during a hike in the vicinity of Namur:

> When we arrived at the bottom of the valley, we struck up a sonorous chorus all together, and one could hear the returning echo of those deeply felt words: We travel throughout the entire country to learn, and have more understanding when we return![32]

The song does indeed circumscribe 'the entire country' in its lyrics, including national landscapes as well as both nostalgic and highly 'modern' sources of national pride (it references illustrious forefathers such as Artevelde, "the father of the fatherland" as well as contemporary industry). With its two-quarter beat, it was particularly well fitted to be sung whilst marching through all these landscapes, and the first verse even musically imitates the landscape it describes (with a rising melody to denote mountains, and then a sinking musical line mimicking the valley). Largely written as a one part song, it is a reasonably easy piece, suited to children's voices and promoting 'unity' amongst its singers, but the rousing major chords at the end of the phrases give the impression of impressive, hymn-like, reverberation.

When they were not singing, children were listening. To their guides, for example, who "spared no effort to make us understand his explanations, he asked two or three times whether we had understood".[33] They also listened to the national soundscape. This included the not entirely foreign sounds of the French language, spoken by members of the extended national family – "our Walloon brothers".[34]

Children articulated a number of emotions in their reports of school trips. Most of those clearly fit the educational and moral norms set by their teachers and sponsors: they declared their gratitude to be given the chance to travel, their excitement (and perhaps some fear) at various technological novelties and natural phenomena and spoke of their joy over some activities. Instances of negative or 'ugly' feelings[35] are almost entirely absent. This is, of course, largely explained by the selection of the participants in these excursions and the reports to be archived. These documents were explicitly designed to underline the value of excursions and to 'thank' their sponsors (encouraging them to keep supporting local schools). We can safely assume that the young travellers would have experienced a whole range of emotions that was deemed improper and therefore was kept hidden from teachers, and from the city council to which the reports were addressed. One boy did manage to express his less than elated feelings upon seeing the city of Dinant, which he claimed they left rather early because "it is a small town, with nothing important except for rocks".[36] Rather than impressed by this example of his country's natural beauty as it was presented to him by educators, this boy seems to have been quite bored. Importantly, however, this particular emotion was not named in the report (which may explain why it passed his teachers' inspection). The selective silence of these reports makes it difficult to gauge the actual emotional effect of the excursions, but at the same time it also shows how adept young writers were at mobilizing the language of emotion they were taught in school. Whereas some feelings were to be expressed openly, others could only be hinted at in educational contexts. And then there were some that were deemed not quite suitable or available before adulthood.

Emotions directly attached to the fatherland were scarcely represented in the reports: the nostalgia for the past glory of Bruges, and pride at the current height of industry were, perhaps, expressions of patriotism, but they certainly do not refer to 'love' of the fatherland. However, the sensory practices described in the reports do echo the longing for proximity that was implied in the discourse of love. If 'love' in a general sense was understood as 'longing to be together with the object' (as noted in the first section of this text), the practice of bringing oneself physically close to different parts of the nation could be read as a similar act of love. Yet, much like children's love for their siblings or parents was seen as somehow 'smaller' than that paragon of intersubjective love (that of a mother for her children), so children's affection for the fatherland appeared as embryonic and not quite complete. It would only become so when it would be accompanied by a 'willingness to sacrifice oneself', again mirroring mothers' assumed willingness to sacrifice themselves for their children. Children's patriotism therefore just appeared, ultimately, as incomplete. Excursions allowed children to confront the emotional frontier between love for one's home and family and love for the fatherland, but they represented just one step on a path that would only be completed later, at the arrival at citizenship. Children seemed to be aware that the trips were part of a long-term educational project. Pupil Gert Verbempt, for example, closed his report by referring to what his abilities in society would be 'later':

> We owe great gratitude to the messrs. mayor and aldermen. They turn us, the Antwerp youth, through the intermission of our teachers, into good citizens, provide us with a thorough education and upbringing so that later we will be able to act in society with a clear and enlightened mind, worthy of an Antwerpian and a Belgian.[37]

Before such time, however, they were in the process of learning. Rather than claiming they felt love for the fatherland, they reported being moved by others' displays of patriotism – displays of flags, or of military service are mentioned as sources of emotion in the reports. Their own feelings of love remained more local, or perhaps 'child-sized', limited to the home-town they had left during the trip.

> Although we had seen such beautiful things, and had enjoyed ourselves so much, we were happy that the time for leaving was near, and we cheerfully jumped on the train that would bring us back to our beloved mothertown Antwerp. Impatiently, we longed for the moment in which we would again set foot on the soil that is more precious to us than that of Liège.[38]

Nevertheless, the lesson that love for the home town would eventually have to be extended to a wider sense of home, seems to echo through the reports as well.

Pint-sized patriots

In a sense, then, love for the fatherland appeared as an 'adult' emotion. Or one that took distinctly different forms according to the patriot's age and his (or her) access to citizenship. The influence of age on feelings and above all practices of love for the fatherland applies to other stages of life as well. Patriotism and its expression would take on very different forms once a young man was drafted into the army, for example, upon gaining the right to vote, or after leaving the workforce. Love for the fatherland would therefore keep shifting throughout one's lifetime, but the step from an infantile to an adult experience of love for the fatherland is arguably a particularly important part of that process, because childhood itself is such a distinctive category. As Karen Sanchez Eppler has noted, "age is inherently transitional" and so the category of childhood itself can never be stable.[39] Children themselves were well aware of the fleeting nature of this aspect of their identity, as is obvious from their references to their future as adults in the travel reports.

It is perhaps this inherent malleability associated with childhood that makes it hard to reconcile with the notion of 'love' (of the fatherland or otherwise) which seems to have been invested with a certainty and finality that did not tolerate fluidity. Willingness to sacrifice oneself, after all, appears as an either/or endeavour. Although children were prepared for this eventual demand (in patriotic songs, for example) they were not yet expected to express their willingness for sacrifice. The love shown to the fatherland is, as displayed in the emotions articulated in the travel reports, connected to joy and gratitude and strengthened by proximity. It is a filial love, mimicking the sense of cheerful obedience (rather than dutiful resignation) that was expected of young children in other educational contexts as well.[40]

Yet even within their own age-group, experiences and expressions of patriotism were expected to vary. Most notably, gender shaped affection towards people as well as the nation in different ways – even though boys and girls went on largely identical trips. Pupils at both boy and girl schools received the same funding for trips, largely their destinations were the same, and the goal of the trips (instilling knowledge and affection for the nation) was formulated in gender-neutral ways, although the stress on future citizenship arguably excluded the girls. Nevertheless, boys and girls were strictly separated for their trips, and were accompanied by teachers of their own gender. At least one result of this separation seems to have been that the adult futures which boys and girls imagined for themselves could be quite different. As noted before, pupils articulated notions of patriotism and national belonging as future identities rather than current ones. For boys, this generally denoted citizenship, but girls – whose connection to the institutions of nationhood would be much looser – aspired to become 'good people' in a more general sense. Concretely, most of the girls selected for the school trips seem to have had ambitions to attend teachers' colleges. For the boys, professional plans are absent from the reports, even though for them, too, the excursion would mark the end of their basic schooling and the start of either working life or professional training. As their path towards patriotic feelings and actions was more clearly defined, however, it was perhaps less necessary for them to articulate the ways in which they would eventually 'serve' the nation as adults.

Despite these differences in educational finality and imagined future selves, boys and girls engaged largely in the same activities: they travelled on the same trains, undertook the same hikes, sang the same songs. Both boys and girls were encouraged to experience proximity to different parts of the nation and develop emotional responses through such proximity. Likewise, boys and girls were expected to engage all their senses to learn and sense the nation. And that is where gendered differences do occasionally emerge in the reports. Although boys and girls were offered the same sights and sounds, they do seem to have seen and heard different things (possibly at the behest of their teachers). Most notably, only in girls' reports are women visible members of the nation. In Seraing for example, the number of women working in the factories "made a great impression" in one of the travelling girls.[41] Similar differences were likely to arise from the practice of singing: (patriotic) school songs were intoned by both genders alike, but often roles were assigned to characters according to their age and gender, which meant that individual singers were likely to remember them differently. Processing sensory experiences in different ways may well have produced different emotions of belonging, and indeed different kinds of love (in which, for example, the notion of sacrifice would shift between future soldiers and future mothers). As the school excursions were only the beginning of a journey towards love of the fatherland, however, these differences were not very pronounced. Less so, in fact, than in most other educational material. The potential future of girls as mothers, for example, is entirely absent from the reports.

Even more subtle are references to class and the ways in which social status or family income could influence experiences of belonging and love for the fatherland. The pupils themselves give no information about their background, apart from the occasional expressions of gratitude for being offered trips and meals their families obviously would not have been able to afford otherwise. Apart from these somewhat cryptic references to the pupils' humble background, the pedagogy and practice of the school trips seem very middle class. Not only do the activities during the trip, and the general focus on a rather lofty sense of culture, remind us of a type of leisure and tourism that was decidedly bourgeois, the ways in which love for the fatherland was discursively represented was modelled on the middle-class norm as well. It was based on the notion of a nuclear family, headed by a (breadwinning and home-owning) father and managed by a mother whose sole responsibility was the household. This representation may well have differed considerably from the children's own experiences: the city schools offered free education to all, and it is unlikely that (even among the 'exemplary' students selected to go on excursion) all these children lived in stable families or in adequate family homes.[42] Nevertheless, this was the imaginary base on which love for the fatherland was to be built.

Conclusion

Children, despite their centrality in narratives on the bright future of the nation or in the imagery of 'the people', have a tendency to disappear in histories of the actual practice of nation-building. Their idealized (or sometimes tragic) representation in stories of national emergence, decay and belonging leaves very little room for any practical or emotional agency of their own. The sources used in the above analysis have severe limits when it comes to children's 'own' narratives as well, despite being written in their hand, but they do underscore at least this important point: that the temporary identities of childhood come with their own distinctive iterations of emotional experience and practice. Love for the fatherland was practised and felt by children in ways that differed from those of the adults these children observed and would later aspire to become. The emotional repertoire mobilized by children during their school trips did not mimic the one associated with adult love of the fatherland, but rather translated the large emotional conglomerate of patriotism into smaller, more child-sized emotions such as joy or gratitude. These were attached to small parts of the nation, to aspects of national belonging and to very concrete sensory experiences during a plunge in the North Sea, whilst intoning a song or raising a glass of beer. Like the nation itself, love for the fatherland was shrunk to a more tangible level. School trips, represented as a way to offer children a broad, panoramic view of the nation, in fact also divided that nation up into smaller vistas. Small regions that could be contained by a train window, taken in by infantile senses, and that could be easily compared to a piece of the nation pupils had already learned how to love: their own home and city. In the eyes of travelling patriots-to-be, the nation came into being gradually, not as a historical process, but as part of their emotional coming-of-age, in which different frontiers had to be overcome before belonging became possible.

Notes

1 Steyaert, *Een speelreisje.*
2 Steyaert, *Een speelreisje.*
3 It also became a literary trope, as stories about children travelling their nation (unaccompanied) were published all over Europe (Nils Holgersson is perhaps the best-known example of a plucky young national traveller). See Cabanel, *Le Tour de la nation.*
4 Education was a contested terrain in nineteenth- and twentieth-century Belgium. In the 1831 constitution, freedom of education was safeguarded by law, as was the provision of an education free of charge by the government. In practice, this resulted in two institutional systems for education, a 'Catholic', private one, and a public one organized by the government and largely supported by Liberals. (For a basic introduction, see e.g. Wynants and Byls, 'Het juridisch en institutioneel kader'.) The situation was further complicated by the bilingual character of the country with Dutch (or Flemish) spoken mostly in the north, and French in the south of the country. Although French remained a dominant language in higher education and administration throughout much of the nineteenth century, primary education was generally offered in the pupils' 'mother tongue'.

5 For an introduction to the notion of 'pillarisation' and other sources of tension and distinction in Belgian (institutional) history, see for example Witte et al. *Political History of Belgium*.

6 Part of the archival research was carried out by Nina Neyrinck, whose MA thesis *Kinderen en natievorming* contains more information about the contents of these archives.

7 Scheer, 'Are emotions a kind of practice?'.

8 E.g. Francois, Siegrist and Vogel, *Nation und Emotion*; Caruso, 'Emotional regimes and school policy'.

9 As mentioned, the focus here is on the public schools in the city of Antwerp, where primary education was organized in Dutch (though no doubt coloured by its local dialect's variations).

10 The historical dictionary of the Dutch language is available on the Internet: http://ivdnt.org/onderzoek-a-onderwijs/lexicologie-a-lexicografie/wnt (accessed 21 October 2019).

11 As Magdalena Beljan and Benno Gammerl have shown in their study of children's literature, models of love within the family were a crucial part of children's introduction to the experiences and practices of love (Beljan and Gammerl, 'Wendy's love').

12 Miller, 'Feeling like a citizen'.

13 Reddy, *The Navigation of Feeling*; Rosenwein, 'Worrying about emotions'.

14 Vallgårda, Alexander and Olsen, 'Emotions and the global politics'.

15 Vallgårda et.al. point to the particular importance of intersecting the history of childhood with the history of emotions, as do Beljan and Gammerl for the particular emotion of love because 'learning to love in a specific way is [...] itself crucial for growing up' (Beljan and Gammerl, 'Wendy's love', p. 116).

16 Steyaert, *Een speelreisje*, 7.

17 Steyaert, *Een speelreisje*, 8.

18 N.N., 'Kan Vaderlandsliefde?'.

19 Moulckers, *Receuil de chants patriotiques*.

20 The conception of the nation as a conglomerate of smaller places to which one could belong has been described extensively for the imagination of the nation for French children by Anne-Marie Thiesse. Her notion of *petites patries* translates very easily to Belgian educational discourses of the nineteenth century in which patriotism is founded on 'the immediate reality of the child. It is about taking the place where the pupil lives as a basis, and developing his love and pride in his petite patrie in order to allow him to then extend these sentiments to the grande patrie' (Thiesse, *Ils apprenaient la France*, p. 8).

21 Antwerp, Felixarchief (hereafter referred to as 'SAA'), MA 223/21 (B), Bericht over de organisatie van de schooluitstapjes van de gemeentescholen naar Brussel, Namen en Dinant.

22 Steyaert, *Een speelreisje*, p. 313.

23 SAA MA 223/21 (A), verslag van de reis naar Luik van Alfons Wuyts, school n° 2, 1881.

24 SAA MA 223/22 (A), verslag van de reis naar Oostende, Brugge en Gent van Hendrik Van Bergen, jongensschool n° 7 Marktgravenlei, 1883.

25 SAA MA 223/22 (A), verslag van Hendrik van Bergen, 1883.

26 SAA MA 223/21 (A), verslag van de reis naar Luik van Hendrik Roose, 1881.

27 SAA MA 223/21 (A), verslag van de reis naar Luik van Karel De Bom, school n° 1, 15.10.1881.

28 SAA MA 223/21 (C), verslag van de reis naar Namen en Dinant van Camille Cuvillier, école communale de garçons n° 1, 1882.

29 The notion of a hierarchy of the senses has been critiqued in histories of the senses, and particularly in histories of sound. However, even though the notion of the nineteenth century as an age of (only) the visual is too limiting, these hierarchies

did hold sway throughout most of the modern age. (Think for example of Proust's madeleine, and the assumption that smell had a more direct impact than sight.) On this hierarchy, see e.g. Sterne, *The Audible Past*; Erlmann, *Reason and Resonance.*

30 SAA MA 223/22 (A), verslag van de reis naar Oostende, Gent en Brugge van Maria Weverbergh, meisjesgemeenteschool n° 6 Abdijstraat, 1883.
31 SAA MA 223/21 (A), verslag van de reis naar Luik van Marie Grimbers, meisjesgemeenteschool n° 7 Biekorfstraat, 24.9.1881.
32 SAA MA 223/21 (C), verslag van de reis naar Namen en Dinant van Karel De Bom, school n° 1, 1882.
33 SAA MA 223/21 (C), verslag van de reis naar Namen en Dinant van Theresia De Meulemeester, Antwerpen, meisjesgemeenteschool n° 3, 30.101882.
34 SAA MA 223/21 (C), verslag van de reis naar Namen en Dinant van Elisa De Hondt, 30.10.1882.
35 Ngai, *Ugly Feelings.*
36 SAA MA 223/21 (C), verslag van de reis naar Namen en Dinant van Martin Preym, 15.10.1882.
37 SAA MA 223/22 (B), verslag van de reis naar Brussel van Gert Verbempt, school n° 11, 1884.
38 SAA MA 223/21 (A), verslag van de reis naar Luik van Alfons Wuyts, jongensschool n° 2, 1881.
39 Sanchez-Eppler, *Dependent States*, p. xxv.
40 Overall, the sentimental imagination of the innocent child went hand in hand with a narrative of the 'vastly educatable' child (Plotz, 'Shut up').
41 SAA MA 223/21 (A), verslag van de reis naar Luik van Alida Goyvaerts, meisjesschool n° 3, 1881.
42 Other contents of the Antwerp city archives betray the constant struggle of many families to afford unemployed children, the long distances children had to travel on foot to reach their schools, and the presence of poor orphans in the schools (recognizable by their blue caps). Even the teachers themselves sometimes struggled to uphold the norms of the nuclear family, as is obvious from a number of letters between the city government and some of the teaching personnel fallen on hard times due to, e.g. post-natal illness of their wives.

References

Beljan, Magdalena and Gammerl, Benno, 'Wendy's love', in: Frevert, Ute *et al.* (eds.), *Learning how to feel. Children's literature and emotional socialization, 1870–1970*, Oxford, Oxford University Press, 2014, pp. 115–132.

Cabanel, Patrick, *Le Tour de la nation par des enfants. Romans scolaires et espaces nationaux (XIXe-XXe siècles)*, Paris, Belin, 2007.

Caruso, Marcelo, 'Emotional regimes and school policy in Colombia, 1800–1835', in: Olsen, Stephanie (ed.), *Childhood, youth and emotions in modern history national, colonial and global perspectives*, London, Palgrave Macmillan, 2015, pp. 139–157.

Erlmann, Veit, *Reason and resonance. A history of modern aurality*, New York, Zone Books, 2010.

Francois, Etienne, Siegrist, Hannes and Vogel, Jakob (eds.), *Nation und emotion: Deutschland und Frankreich im Vergleich: 19. und 20. Jahrhundert*, Göttingen, Vondenhoeck & Ruprecht, 1995.

Miller, Susan A., 'Feeling like a citizen: The American Legion's boys state programme and the promise of Americanism', in: Olsen, Stephanie (ed.), *Childhood, youth and emotions in modern history national, colonial and global perspectives*, London, Palgrave Macmillan, 2015, pp. 158–177.

Moulckers, Jozef, *Receuil de chants patriotiques pour l'école et le foyer des maîtres de l'art musical Belge – Bundel Vaderlandsche zangen van de meesters der Belgische toonkunst voor school en haard*, s.l., 1905.

Ngai, Sianne, *Ugly feelings*, Harvard, Harvard University Press, 2007.

Neyrinck, Nina, *Kinderen en natievorming in België in de negentiende eeuw. De invloed en betekenis van schoolreizen*, MA thesis, University of Leuven, 2014.

N.N., 'Kan Vaderlandsliefde op de lagere school onderwezen worden?' in: *Ons woord*, 1896, pp. 120–121.

Plotz, Judith, 'Shut up, he explained; or, can the young subaltern speak?', in: *Children's Literature Association Quarterly*, vol. 21, no. 3, 1996, pp. 140–142.

Reddy, William, *The navigation of feeling: A framework for the history of emotions*, Cambridge, Cambridge University Press, 2001.

Rosenwein, Barbara, 'Worrying about emotions in history', in: *American Historical Review*, vol. 107, no. 3, 2005, pp. 821–845.

Sanchez-Eppler, Karen, *Dependent states. The child's part in nineteenth-century American culture*, Chicago IL, University of Chicago Press, 2005.

Scheer, Monique, 'Are emotions a kind of practice? (and is that what makes them have a history). A Bourdieuan approach to understanding emotion', in: *History and Theory*, vol. 51, no. 2, 2012, pp. 193–220.

Sterne, Jonathan, *The audible past. Cultural origins of sound reproduction*, Durham, Duke University Press, 2003.

Steyaert, Judocus Johannes, *Een speelreisje in België, Behelzende Schilderachtige En Geschiedkundige Beschryvingen der landstreken en nationale gedenkstukken, zeden, gebruiken en instellingen; levensschetsen van beroemde Belgen, enz*, Gent, Van Doosselaere, 1857.

Thiesse, Anne-Marie, *Ils apprenaient la France. L'exaltation des regions dans le discours patriotique*, Paris, Éditions de la Maison des Sciences et de l'Homme, 1997.

Vallgårda, Karen, Alexander, Kristine and Olsen, Stephanie, 'Emotions and the global politics of childhood', in: Olsen, Stephanie (ed.), *Childhood, youth and emotions in modern history national, colonial and global perspectives*, London, Palgrave Macmillan, 2015, pp. 12–34.

Witte, Els *et al.*, *Political history of Belgium. From 1830 onwards*, Brussels, ASP, 2009.

Wynants, Paul and Byls, Henk, 'Het juridisch en institutioneel kader. Van de vrijheid van onderwijs tot de huidige debatten', in: De Maeyer, Jan and Wynans, Paul (eds.), *Katholiek onderwijs in België. Identiteiten in evolutie 19e-21e eeuw*, Averbode, Halewijn, 2016, pp. 35–64.

5 Performing and remembering personal nationalism among workers in late Russian Poland[1]

Wiktor Marzec

While labour history has long been interested in workers' militant political identities, it has disregarded nationalism. The scholarship on nationalism, in turn, has focused more on the ideological apparatus of the state.[2] Workers were considered important for understanding nationalism, but not much was said about the actual dynamics of the nationalization of labour,[3] which was a crucial factor in establishing the European nation-states of the twentieth century, and their different welfare projects, both in the capitalist 'West' and the socialist 'East'.[4]

In recent years this situation has changed and the nationalization of labour has been tackled by some scholars.[5] This volume addresses the interlocking of emotions and popular nationalism, and offers an excellent opportunity to investigate a crucial, eventful moment when the nationalist labour of Poland asserted itself, and how this moment was later remembered and used as a springboard for nationalist feelings in the interwar period.

This eventful moment was the Revolution of 1905, which brought about the massive political participation of urban workers. The 1905 events demonstrate that for the majority of Polish workers the commitment to the ethnic nation was a contingent event – "something that suddenly crystallizes rather than gradually develops", to use Rogers Brubaker's wording.[6] Against the background of a fractured socialist movement, the National Workers Union (*Narodowy Związek Robotniczy*, hereafter the NZR), was able to mobilize thousands of members after having sided unanimously with the virulently nationalistic National Democracy Party. While factory nationalism was quite widespread before, it was the first time that large groups of workers explicitly and self-consciously joined the nationalist movement. The 1905 Revolution and its aftermath kick-started modern popular nationalism in Poland.

In order to shed light on the down-to-earth dynamic of nationalist mobilization and its emotional background, this chapter examines the link between the language of mass political propaganda and recollections of political mobilization in working-class biographies. I expose the tension between, on the one hand, 'emotives', as William Reddy would call the expression of feelings in a language which circulated in nationalist leaflets, and, on the other hand, the emotions articulated by the workers writing about their pasts several decades later.

My analysis demonstrates how emotives were successfully appropriated in ego-writing to justify a nationalist commitment that went against the mainstream of working-class memory. Emotives were deployed to validate 'fratricidal' practices like strike breaking and antisemitism, while at the same time helping to rewrite the story of nationalist workers as a peculiar part of the main current of Polish nationalism. Feelings of national belonging were expressed through a vernacular primordialism and through family metaphors to buttress the nationalist commitment in the face of intense political headwinds and competing historical narratives.

In the first section of this chapter I revisit the debate on popular nationalism and its rhetorical and biographical dimensions. Subsequently, I construct a virtual biography of a typical novice nationalist militant out of the more fragmentary individual testimonies. I collate the ideological message of the nationalist propaganda with its resonance as remembered and written down in autobiographical materials. In the last section, I focus on working-class nationalist memory within a broader context of contentious legacies of the revolution. How was the nationalist ideological programme approached by its adherents? What did the working-class militants find especially convincing in the nationalism promoted by the National Democracy Party and the NZR? What was the emotional impact of those messages and how were they negotiated, even while generally accepted by the militants?

The corpus my analysis is based on consists of ca. 110 biographical testimonies of different length written by proletarian militants from various political parties in different political circumstances. About twenty were written by NZR members or affiliates. They were published in journals and various anniversary publications in the interwar period as part of the semi-official commemorative effort of this particular political milieu.

The memory of the NZR nationalist workers was pitted against socialism, but also against the main current of Polish nationalism (I get back to this issue in one of the following sections). These biographical testimonies offer an insight into the auto-reflexive constructions of the nationalist self which interweaves memory and experienced emotions of the early twentieth century with the later nationalist memory culture of the interwar period, when these testimonies were created. The discourse of political self-representation in these autobiographies is a highly entangled product of the layering of time. It is produced at the intersection of the synchronous context of a particular utterance, and the diachronic development of a political self.

Thus, facts, experiences and emotions as presented in the biographies are elements of a self that is responsible for producing these biographies in real time. After all, "all autobiographical memory is true. It is up to the interpreter to discover in which sense, where, for which purpose",[7] as one scholar has remarked. Here, they are 'true' as carrying elements of the nationalist discourse and habitus, and as examples of the emotional dispositions acquired earlier through nationalist propaganda and practice of the movement.[8] In order to unwrap these connections I examine the short circuit between the ideological texts of nationalism, the inscriptions of the selves reaffirming the nationalist message, and the respective memory culture, finally unravelling the personal nationalisms of the workers writing these texts post factum.

However, political leaflets stimulating nationalist emotions cannot be interpreted straightaway as inscriptions of sense neither for their authors nor readers. They are 'performative texts' for the author, the audience and their dynamic relationship. By investigating "the intended force with which the utterance is issued"[9] one may examine what writers say in a text, but also shed light on what they are doing with respect to the readers.[10] In turn, the discursive and emotive traces left in biographies may help to shed light on the actual resonance of printed propaganda materials in the long run.

Popular nationalism in late Russian Poland

A theoretical consensus seems to have emerged in nationalism studies. The modus vivendi between constructivist and primordialist approaches delimits the common ground: nations are constructed, but usually this process takes more time than modern state elites had at their disposal. Thus, they built upon stock languages and cultural substances older than the modern state itself.[11] This opened up a new panoply of questions regarding popular nationalism. Meanwhile, the focus on de-reified 'nationness' or 'nationing', relational categories of practice delimiting "visions and divisions" of polity and community,[12] also stimulated research into the personal, emotional and performative dimensions of national belonging.

In such a context, the question posed by Katherine Verdery, namely, "how do people become national?", needs to be investigated in micro-sociological historical sources. The 'sense of self as national' may be theorized as "the homology between the nation and the individual", the former "internalized and assimilated" by the latter.[13] In a similar vein, Jonathan Hearn has probed the relationship between the ideological message of nationalism and its individual appropriation. This message may be successful precisely because of its capacity to accommodate and reinforce individualized 'hidden transcripts' of reception, to aptly interweave the personal and the social dimension of national belonging. These dimensions are neither identical nor even convergent, but the nationalist message offers a sense of self which resonates with certain interests or emotions.[14] In subsequent research more stress has been put on the actual 'popular' base for successful national projects, and corresponding identities among the lower echelons of nationalized societies.

Similarly, in this chapter I study routes of personal nationalization among the popular classes. Polish working-class nationalism in the Russian-controlled 'Polish Kingdom' offers a critical case of entanglement of class and nation, in a highly polarized ideological setting. In Eastern Europe class differentiation partially assumed the older characteristics of status stratification. The reasons were long-upheld regimes of unfree labour, an agrarian-manorial mode of production and large imperial states impeding the emergence of cross-class nationalism. These characteristics rendered emerging identities more complicated, and their class embeddings weightier and more unavoidable.

Status, and later class, were often over-determined by national and ethnic differentiation, making the intersectional identity regimes impossible to disentangle. Even in the cases where the will to change was partially motivated by ethnic or religious factors (as among populist nationalists or Jewish revolutionaries), it was expressed in political languages explicitly addressing the transformation of class structure.[15] These languages were part and parcel of every possible political identity forged in those years. To put it bluntly, every nationalism, regardless of its primordial style, was also a response to rising socialist or populist languages. The Polish case is no different.

After the implosion of the early modern Polish state in the late eighteenth century, its territory was divided over three neighbouring imperial powers. After the Vienna Congress Tsarist Russia took the largest chunk. This was the heartland of the Polish national idea, which was initially nurtured among the noble classes preserving the tradition of a political nation of sorts. The romantic idea of national revival, albeit already idealizing popular cultural lore, was still elitist.

This fact was painfully confirmed by the failures of subsequent national uprisings. Not only did the uprisings come to naught, they also led the Russian administration to abolish the remnants of Polish self-government. This, along with the economic repression of noble-class estates, produced a population of disenfranchised intelligentsia, radicalized by the lack of professional opportunities within the state. Part of this group became professional revolutionaries, others professional nationalists. They already knew, that they needed a new national idea which would include and mobilize 'the people'.

While Polish nationalism's first generation was more focused on a civilizational mission (Polish positivism), it nevertheless laid the cornerstone for an organicist vision of the national body politic.[16] The next generation, not traumatized by the defeat and repressions following the 1863 uprising, was much more radical and ready for a frontal assault on the state. Stemming from a common core of popular radicalism, it soon bifurcated into socialist and nationalist currents.[17] The latter, of interest here, addressed popular grievances but simultaneously transformed itself into a more integral and socially conservative nationalist project. The context of a non-existent state facilitated the ethnic-based nationalism as a vehicle of a modern national project in the late nineteenth century. However, it asserted itself against the backdrop of an older, elite-based political nation of the Polish noble-class republic.[18] The subsequent national upheavals bore the significant imprint of the latter, both as a positive point of reference of tradition, and, negatively, as a spectral threat of the rebirth of an exclusive upper-class nationality.

This elitist context of the early-modern national idea substantially undermined the potential of popular mobilization in the name of the nation, and confused the political leadership of modern nationalist parties. Forging national unity among workers was difficult owing to the historical circumstances that compromised the old national idea among the popular classes. Moreover, the experience of exploitation and long-standing socialist agitation went hand in hand with the effective socialist militancy of the Polish Socialist Party (PPS) against the foreign state, which seized the national emotion as well.[19] While the nationalism of the PPS deserves a separate study in this context, I focus on the integral, ethnic-based nationalism of the National Democracy Party.

National Democracy, a tightly controlled panoply of a nationalist party and various corollary organizations, shifted from popular radicalism to integral nationalism at the turn of the nineteenth and twentieth centuries.[20] While it had previously been more active among peasants, in 1905 it launched a sub-organization dedicated to ideological work among workers, the aforementioned NZR. The nationalists surfed the same wave of mass politics they ardently condemned, fighting the revolutionary upswing through all sorts of accusations. Membership in all parties was rising high, rapidly moving from tiny, cadre grouplets to mass organizations, and with the NZR it was no different.[21] After Russian autocracy yielded in 1905, national democrats became a major contender in the newly established elections to the state Duma.

The National Democrats started an ultimately successful mobilization campaign, intervening in the dynamic field of revolutionary politics.[22] This period epitomizes the nationalization of working-class identities as a rapid, relational process catalysed by an eventful conjuncture. Thus, it allows me to demonstrate the eventful character of 'nationness'. People started to understand themselves and the world around them in national terms under the pressure of circumstances, and militant identities were forged in real time within a dynamic political conflict.[23] The medium of intensive campaigning was political printings: leaflets, proclamations and political journals. The language contained within them was an important tool to explain the rapidly changing reality in nationalist terms.

'Visions and divisions' were defined in a way fostered by the National Democrats. While studying the role of printing in the rise of nationalism, Benedict Anderson has famously remarked that "what the eye is to the lover, language is to the patriot".[24] Printing has often facilitated the emotional exchanges that allow people to envision the invisible bonds of nationhood.[25] The language of nationalist identity brokers was, however, actively re-appropriated and rearticulated by its receivers; that is, by the popular classes.

Among these audiences many personal nationalisms might emerge. As Anthony Cohen notes, "the 'nation' is a grand generalization that does not discriminate among, and says nothing specific about, its individual members".[26] His proposal is to consider nationalized audiences as "listening to leaders' vacuous rhetoric and rendering it meaningful by attributing their own sense to it, so that the sense heard in the words being uttered is their own".[27] This recto-verso dimension of nationalism, which was reinforced by the performative message of printed matter but simultaneously negotiated within the self, may be investigated by the juxtaposition of the printed political propaganda and the biographical testimonies of nationalist militants.

Stories of political commitment

The National Democracy Party and the NZR had to fight an uphill battle. Making national unity meaningful for workers, in the relative absence of pre-existing building blocks, was a process that had to be carried out against the everyday experience of shop floor exploitation, and against the socialist mapping of the social world. One of the nationalist militants remembered that "the workers' movement [...] had a socialist face in the days of its birth",[28] and an official nationalist pamphlet admitted that initially "more vivid and active individuals were under the exclusive spell of international socialism".[29]

Even if the same oppression could very often be coded nationally (Polish worker vs. German foreman in the factory or the exploitation by German/Jewish entrepreneurs), providing meaningful evidence of cross-class national unity was still a challenge. For sure, the national identity of workers was not an artificial invention of the NZR and had some presence before the revolution. Laura Crago has convincingly documented its social and economic background in the preceding years. German cultural hegemony and organizational domination encouraged workers to construct themselves as working-class Poles, striving for recognition of their cultural specificity (language, professional habits) and for the improvement of their job opportunities, mostly, though, against Germans and not Jews.[30] Nonetheless, as a political programme and as an identity explicitly antagonistic to socialist coworkers, nationalism was a result of the revolution and the emergence of the NZR.

What did such a reconstruction of the political field and the political identities of workers look like in detail? Initially, the nationalist political milieus shared the experience of conspiracy with the socialists. In many working-class settings nationalism was a minority position. Even if the seeds of nationalist propaganda were thrown on fertile soil, the national sentiments of the workers might have been focused on cultural, linguistic or professional self-assertion rather than on political campaigning against Jews or socialists.[31] This stimulated a complex process of re-crafting the self in a nationalist manner.

Nationalist publications, which initially came about in a minority context, had to constantly present their position in relation to other, already existing ones. Nationalist texts were designed to undermine the dominant position *gradually*, because a *frontal* attack might discourage potential readers. The arguments they brought to bear had to resonate with the grievances and basic demands of working-class life. For instance, one argument against strikes was that better wages might be acquired through cooperation with Polish factory owners.[32] Once the nationalist message had got some traction, it was possible to go beyond the more gentle suggestion that socialists were mistaken or manipulated. As the balance of power changed, nationalist writers were more explicit in directly insulting their opponents.

In their autobiographical writings workers attempted to reflexively justify their commitments. Some reconstructed their political initiation as stemming from an inner conviction supported by external impulses. In underground conditions, one of the future nationalist militants, Michał Kosiorek, "dreamed about joining the secret patriotic organization because illegal work for Poland excited [him]". Only after a long period of asking around and occasional cooperation in the distribution of printouts was he admitted "to the first secret meeting", where he "was informed about the aims and tasks of the NZR".[33] Another national activist, Jan Posiak, picked up some 'patriotic literature' in the physician's waiting room. Later he "read not only alone, but accompanied by a couple of colleagues. In this way an informal, loose circle of workers was formed, collectively using the doctor's library".[34]

A huge wave of new members entered the movement during the revolution. The NZR was officially founded in June 1905, allowing for mass mobilization. As a result, Michalina Klimkiewiczówna, a female nationalist activist, "joined the organization in 1905, when people massively flocked to political parties – everybody was overtaken by a psychosis of struggle for a better tomorrow and freedom for the country".[35] The political agenda of the NZR was openly hostile to the revolutionary turmoil. Nonetheless, the general turmoil created a tide which lifted many boats, the nationalist one included.

However, other nationalists, in their recollections of their political beginnings, tend to focus on the interplay of the new political agenda with older commitments passed on to them by parents or incidental teachers. The national tradition or spirit was carried forward or revived by the narrator's participation. As one summarized: "The struggle for Poland was in my family, so to speak, traditional. My grandfather was tortured by the Muscovites during the uprising, my uncle was slaughtered on a battlefield."[36] This evokes primordiality of national feeling, thus allowing the narration to smoothly converge with the basic tenets of nationalist commitment. At the same time, nationalist involvement was embedded in a feeling of harm experienced, if not personally, then by previous generations. This offered a sense of participation in a tradition or chain of being. The nationalist involvement was also remembered as a deep emotional experience.

Emotions of nationhood

There is not much evidence in my data of emotional attachments to nationalism beyond the later recollections of memory. There is, however, an interplay between, on the one hand, emotives, as William Reddy would call the expressions of feelings using language, transferred by nationalist propaganda and political culture, and, on the other, feelings expressed by workers writing about their pasts.[37] They explicitly wrote about this interplay and the induction of emotions by written propaganda. A common trope was the emotional attachment triggered directly by the content of nationalist leaflets or journals. One of the narrators recalled:

> When the nationalist proclamations (*odezwy narodowe*) reached our factory, we became interested in their content and I must admit that they appealed to my feeling stronger, with certain sentiment, and they moved my heart; none of the socialist leaflets could do that. All socialist leaflets were based on calculation and materialism, whereas from the nationalist leaflets faith was flowing, heartedness, a burning zeal which took the heart.[38]

Socialist materials indeed presented seemingly rational, economic arguments, like those in favour of an economic strike. By contrast, nationalist pamphlets often called for calm during strikes and had to mobilize different feelings and attachments for the sake of counter-agitation. For such purposes summoning tradition, ethnic bonds or the lore of forefathers might have been helpful.

The overall climate of political mobilization stimulated these processes. As nationalist workers were a minority for a long time, they tended to stress their primary, 'deep' conviction as the reason for their adherence and the loss of their previous, allegedly incidental, socialist fascinations. They considered socialist speeches as "not reaching the soul", "foreign and not creating a collegial warmth between workers [...], an awful cliché, and what is most important, cosmopolitan".[39] Not only were socialists in the majority, Maksymilian Brzezinski admitted that they were also better prepared for political agitation. However, "it was the cause itself, which helped us [nationalists], as it reached the heart of the Polish worker".[40] This clearly indicates the more polemical setting, where equals could have adhered to competing political programmes. Emotives from political propaganda were successfully recirculated in ego-writing to justify the ideological commitment that was initially performed against the grain.

Antisemitism and the rebuilding of political identities

The growth of working-class nationalism was a profound political transformation made through the medium of speech. 'Fighting words' changed the political field.[41] The speed of the process and the step by step reconstitution of meaning given to the surrounding world testify to the powerful role of language in the political realm.

"We, the workers – Poles," announced the proclamation of the NZR, "consider national solidarity as a primary unity welding us together; our holiest obligation is above all to respect this solidarity."[42] That meant abstaining from strikes in the name of national prosperity. "We call You, then, brother-workers to interrupt occupations in factories, to firmly resist the pressure of agitators, to hold back any manifestations, processions and, last but not least, military actions, bearing in mind the calamities it would bring."[43] To ground such a position and make a coherent national identity among workers more feasible, a reference to an outer enemy was of great assistance.

At first sight, a convenient enemy was at hand: Poland was partitioned under three imperial powers against which political energies could be directed in a quest for independence in the long run. Nonetheless, a problem appeared in the very heart of the nationalist attempts at political mobilization: it was impossible to use this framing in the new revolutionary circumstances, as the outer oppressor during the revolutionary unrest was a main addressee of the political contention organized by the socialists.

To establish national unity, National Democrats did not hesitate to clearly exclude Jews, who in their discourse were designated the role of the Other.[44] Earlier intellectual predilections of the National Democrats were combined with a particular conjunctural situation and a residue of pre-modern popular anti-Judaism to create a powerful interpretation of current predicaments and antagonisms. Ceaseless attempts were undertaken to persuade Polish workers that indeed the Jewish proletariat initiated disturbances which negatively influenced the condition of the Polish economy and Polish workers. Moreover, National Democracy discouraged Polish workers from acting in solidarity with Jewish workers or even incited hostility against Jewish colleagues.

During the revolution, the nationalists were increasingly critical of the revolutionary surge, and as the general disorder grew, they further scapegoated 'the Jews' as a foreign element creating chaos for their own profit and gains. Thus, they blamed the revolution on the Jews: "A reason [for a strike] could always be found: [...] unfulfilled Jewish demands or the like," one of the leaflets unambiguously suggested.[45] Pro-Jewish interests were a hidden agenda of socialism, the NZR leaflets and articles insinuated, thus providing a bedrock for the 'racialization' of political difference, instrumentalized on countless occasions later:

> It is high time every worker understood that listening to any orders, without even asking in whose name and to what aim they are given, is an affront for him. Who is ordering us? Who is pretending to be our rulers? Hobbledehoys and noisy Jewish snotnoses [*chłystki i żydziaki krzykliwe*].[46]

Apart from harvesting the gains of the revolution, 'the Jews' could even profit from its failure. That is why they misled the Christian workers in false unity: "Revolution [...] would be profitable for the Jews, who after our weakness and harassment could spread all over the country even more,"[47] one of the leaflets clarified. Polish nationalists suggested that the socialists were affiliated with the Jews, which helped them to discredit political opponents in the eyes of some workers.

It appeared to be a powerful political tool. The initial puzzle of forging a viable identity and redefining the friend–foe distinction was only resolved by an intensified antisemitism, which found resonance among working-class adherents. There must have been a close feedback loop between the ideologues and writers and the assumed and actual audience, as it is highly unlikely that nationalists would have pursued a direction that hindered mass mobilization. Their support grew and their political propaganda started to be more explicitly antisemitic, culminating with the vitriolic campaigns during the third and fourth Duma elections and the boycott of Jewish enterprises in 1912.[48] Antisemitism appeared to be a useful tool to highlight the emerging nationalist identity between the other ideologies on offer.

It is no wonder that later on some nationalist militants were convinced that "a doctrinaire socialist was in most cases a Jew, not knowing the idea of the Fatherland, or a German, who had abandoned his Fatherland beyond the borders of Poland".[49] Polish nationalists built a populist discourse in which they were a singular emanation of the people.[50] The idea of nationalism (and National Democracy) as a natural expression of Polishness was skilfully fanned by nationalist political propaganda. The political identity forged in such a polemical setting bore strong resemblances to a mobilization against an outer enemy. For instance, Józef Drzewiecki (Dejot), a railway worker from the Dąbrowa basin, explained this growing hostility, at the same time giving voice to the major antisemitic *topoi* of the nationalist discourse of those days. This prejudice was fanned even further and reached its pinnacle in the 1930s, when the following narrative was written:

> Naturally, one resisted the socialists [*socjałom* – in Polish a more derogatory expression] at every step by debunking their specious program. The PPS-members attacked our rallies in deranged fury, and at mass meetings and demonstrations they tore up and desecrated the banners with the white eagle [the Polish national emblem], shouting 'Down with the white goose'. [...] Moreover, the ringleted comrades [*pejsaci towarzysze* – euphemism for the Jewish socialists] were numerous and controlled the socialist activists, they contributed significantly to the abomination of Marxist slogans and the jewing [*zażydzenia*] of the PPS ranks with individuals who endlessly, along the Talmudic receipts, called [*podjudzali*] for a struggle against the gentiles.[51]

Such verbatim repetition of explicit clichés from antisemitic propaganda in a memoir is quite rare, however. Overall, former NZR members writing in the 1930s kept some distance from this discourse, even if antisemitism spread beyond what it had been in 1906 or 1907. The reason might have been a political moderation of older activists or a conscious reconstruction of their political lore when facing divergence from the main current of Polish nationalism (see below). Certainly antisemitic sentiments were not the only emotion behind nationalist mobilization.

Citizenship, belonging and self-assertion

A framing more convergent with the socialist programme to improve working conditions also found a place within the nationalist writing. After all, in the multi-ethnic shop floor setting, 'factory nationalism' might convince workers that they "above all needed to gain national freedom, to win the struggle with the capitalist exploitation", as one of the narrators expressed it.[52] Reflecting on their place in the broader class and national community, some of the narrators constructed a certain practical sociology of the movement. They tried to comprehend their own story as part and parcel of a broader social process, which made them feel more important and relieved them from an introspective analysis. What mattered was the expressed "hope for a better future", which gave meaning to the ongoing activities.

> Among workers hopes of a better future had awoken, a social movement developed and coagulated, but maybe what had been happening then should not yet be called a social movement, because so far nothing social had been created yet. Regarding the masses, the workers were only preparing for a struggle for their future rights.[53]

This narrative is an interesting example of the teleological organization of events in a storyline of hidden maturation and politics germinating 'beneath the ground', unavoidably leading to a future upsurge. Its form adheres to a socialist master narrative and indirectly testifies to its influence, reaching beyond the borders of the socialist movement. Strikingly, this is the narrative of a nationalist militant, apparently sharing these premises. Nationalist aspirations were analogously embedded in the working-class milieu and in shop floor experiences. However, for this particular worker the Polish interwar nation-state was already a project putting into practice those 'future rights', which certainly would not have been the case for a left-leaning socialist.

The nationalist ideals gave meaning to positive efforts, but they also helped to make sense in the moment of disillusionment, failure and disappointment: when the revolutionary surge was crushed, and many previously glorious activities turned into anarchic desperation. It is hard to build any source-based phenomenology of failure, but it seems to be an important trigger for the nationalist triumph after the revolutionary heyday. Not only were the nationalists able to give meaning to the perceived anarchy and collapse, which frightened the higher echelons of society, they could also address the grievances of at least part of the dissatisfied and disappointed workers.

For instance, National Democratic labour unions offered perspectives of legal action to people who at one time might have been excited by underground militancy, but were nevertheless unwilling to maintain such a risky life forever – even more so in the days of harsh tsarist repression. Not only did the nationalist discourse give meaning to the revolutionary failure, but it also offered ways to use the moderate gains – e.g. the limited right to participate in labour unions – in a way complicit with the overwhelming feeling of disappointment and fear. The once boosted feeling of workers' dignity was trampled by the post-revolutionary reaction, but moderate forms of politics offered a new channel for these feelings.

This concerned above all the National Democratic politics of the ballot. While the initial project of the Duma did not allow workers to vote and excluded national minorities (Poles and Jews of Russian Poland), the October Manifesto issued under the pressure of the street by Nicholas II in 1905, promised more generous suffrage.[54] Along with this tactical liberalization confirmed by the Duma Decree on 24 December 1905, some parliamentary institutions, albeit often in a caricatural form, were introduced. The voting statute largely disadvantaged the lower classes, allowing only workers from big factories (in the factory curia) or official tenants (in the urban curia) to vote. Moreover, it assigned to these votes only very mediated and limited, if not almost nonexistent, voting power. It nevertheless felt as a significant act of empowerment for many people who had never before been able to participate in electoral politics of any kind.

The very fact of being able to vote, and witnessing an entire electoral campaign with meetings and speeches, provided an unexpected new recognition for workers as political subjects. Even in its meek form the State Duma was soon dissolved. This triggered bitter polemics and limited the belief in any real political leverage of the ballot. Nevertheless, subsequent elections offered workers a certain form of participation and citizenship in the national body politic.

It was the National Democracy Party which used this opportunity to boost its support in a most effective way. From the onset it opted to take part in the election, and soon launched a powerful agitation machine. This was to a significant extent a source of the National Democratic success and its subsequent rise as a significant political player.[55] The electoral agitation instrumentalized antisemitism and antagonized supporters of different political agendas.[56]

The acceptance into a secret and hierarchical order was a significant source of pride benefitting nationalist parties over socialists. Stanisław Parkot-Wójt, many years later, still underlined the emotional impact of the initiation ceremony:

> A celebration of acceptance in the organization and the oath made a huge impression on me. I grew in my own eyes; I felt like a person bearing on his shoulders new obligations about which I had not thought before.[57]

The sense of belonging and self-assertion in the movement was an important factor of emotional attachment. Nationalist circles were more hierarchical and direct recognition of the dignity of a worker was less explicit than in socialist milieus. Nevertheless, it was often the first social context in which people from other social strata addressed the upcoming worker with a basic respect. The importance of such a gesture was also described by narrators.[58] Apparently hierarchy and the possibility to advance within it might have encouraged them to join.

The staged dignity of such procedures could also backfire. One of the socialist 'converts' recollected the rapid switching of sides. After the secret oath of fidelity to the cross (*wierność na krzyż*) the leader tried to convince the novices of the resurrection of the aristocratic Poland (or at least it was perceived and remembered this way). When the listeners objected to this, they were slandered as 'foreign socialists'. The rebellious workers left the meeting and looked for an appropriate organization which would satisfy their patriotic allegiance and reservations against the old class and state privileges (that is, the PPS).[59]

Often the story of political alignment is presented as turbulent and far from obvious, which renders the final choice a well-grounded one. Indeed, the political sphere was highly fractured, which affected the actual paths of narrators. The past experience of plurality urged them even more to present their affiliations as conscious choices. In this vein, the story of initiation often assumes the form of a drama. Narrators write about perils and obstacles, or their own misfortunes and bad decisions, which they had to overcome before reaching the safe haven of their assumed political identity. This drama of unfolding identity did not end with their commitment to the nationalist project, however.

Reclaiming memory and rebuilding personal nationalism

The political biographies of the NZR members were turbulent even if they did not change their affiliation, were not involved in revolutionary politics like the socialists, and usually did not experience spectacular upward social mobility. Their biographies were written as polemical interventions against the dominant memory because "some agents try not to speak about us and remain silent about the fact of our existence".[60] Polish nationalism was not weak (quite the contrary), but the NZR's legacy had been separated from its main current. This rendered the position of former NZR members difficult.

A particular memory culture was fostered by the association of former NZR members, which was busy gathering and publishing memoirs in the 1930s. The first collection was published in the anniversary issue of *Kiliński*, commemorating the foundation of NZR thirty years earlier, in 1905.[61] The name of the journal, now promoted as "the first echo of the NZR past in the independent Poland",[62] had been used before by a discontinued NZR periodical. Subsequent issues of the relaunched edition followed, filled with commemorative articles and autobiographical testimonies written by former members.

The hotbed for nationalist commitment in the pre-1905 period, as Laura Crago has argued, was often a class-based national ethos of the 'Polishness of production'. It was combined with a pride of the craft, a drive to self-assertion as Polish workers, and upward mobility in professional terms, supported also by nationalist trade unions.[63] Nationalist workers' identity, among NZR members and at least some of the right-leaning PPS supporters, was steeped in class *and* national dignity.[64] The National Democracy Party stimulated these emotions to build its working-class constituency in 1905, but to a large extent sidelined both dimensions after the 1905 Revolution.

The party was partially co-opted by the Russian state, seen by party ideologues as a guarantor of order against revolutionary anarchy.[65] As a result the nationalists enjoyed slightly broader margins of legality, and successfully offered to the workers the charms of electoral recognition in the Duma bid. Meanwhile, however, the National Democracy Party abandoned the insurrectionist tradition and lost the urge to fight with 'the Russians' on the state level, and with 'the Germans' on the shop-floor. This was not the only major change within the National Democratic discourse.

In the 1880s, when the National Democracy movement was in its infancy, it was a populist radical party aiming not only at national revival. It also aspired to a social transformation in favour of the popular classes and a much more prominent place in politics for them. However, over time it was not capable of integrating the growing democratic tendencies into its discourse and practice.

Instead it turned towards discipline and an organic political imaginary, and subsequently to a xenophobic, authoritarian and socially conservative nationalistic project. Early proponents of the movement urged 'the people' to become involved in politics and nation building. As soon as 'the people' actually went out onto the streets, however, it appeared that they would not follow the directives of their self-proclaimed nationalist leaders.[66] This completely reversed the attitudes of these leaders.

This shift resonated with the fears of the non-proletarian social strata and simultaneously boosted the support for the nationalists among them, blocking any further development of proletarian constituencies.[67] These tensions led to a split, and in 1908 the NZR parted ways with the National Democracy political camp, which had hegemonized the Polish right in the meantime.

The NZR formally ceased to exist in 1920, when, after a merger with other national workers associations, the National Workers Party was formed. It gained a small parliamentary representation in most of the subsequent elections. The previous patron, the National Democracy Party, was drifting in the direction of the fascist right. The National Democratic political syndicate, however, which mobilized workers along nationalist, anti-minority and anti-Jewish lines, did not support a separate workers' movement. Thus, the NZR memory was orphaned and the association attempted to claim legitimacy amidst the insurrectionist tradition of Polish workers. Therefore, it rivalled the then dominant memory of the right, militarist faction of the PPS, by that time enshrined as a prehistory of the Piłsudski's camp, a secular-centrist authoritarian block which after the coup in 1926 held the political power in the country.[68]

Such a situation nurtured a feeling of abandonment. As one of the militants complained: "There are almost no defenders of the NZR, there are many prosecutors, however."[69] In response, some of the nationalist workers attempted to distance themselves from the contemporary activity of the National Democracy Party in the 1920s and 1930s. Others tried to re-assert their place in the history of the workers' movement, by combining the struggle for the workers' welfare *and* against national oppression. The authors stressed that "the NZR did not come out of the blue", and the background of their activity had been "a noble national longing" rather than a "struggle against socialism".[70] According to the autobiographers, the mobilizing efforts were successful "due to the cause itself, which reached the hearts of the Polish worker".[71] They stressed the military heroism of the fight with the "Muscovite yoke", and a rightful revenge for the "bloody terror and war waged by the Russian bureaucracy to draw in blood the small concessions of 1905".[72] This insurrectionary militancy was intentionally confirmed by reprints of reports issued by the tsarist administration or court proceedings, which for obvious reasons exposed the anti-state radicalism of the nationalists. In the context of the official memory of the movement they yet again created a sense of victimhood.[73]

Not only were the praised values and even wording conspicuously similar to the memory of the right-wing militarist faction of the PPS. This framing explicitly acknowledged the gains of the revolution, and rewarded military struggle. These ideals were almost antipodal to the message and practice of the actual NZR under the auspices of the National Democracy Party between 1905 and 1908.

Simultaneously, the autobiographers bent over backwards to justify their role in the bitter (and often lethal) conflict known as the 'fratricidal' struggles. Nationalist militias confronted socialist ones in 1906 and 1907, which resulted in violence and many casualties.[74] Apart from strategies shifting responsibility onto socialists, the narrators made unambiguous suggestions about "the Semitic leaders of Social Democracy" who "hand controlled the massacres of the Polish workers".[75] A particular 'lieu de mémoire' of these efforts was the so-called 'battle of Zarzew' in Łódź, when socialists allegedly invaded the church during a funeral procession (in the socialist version nationalists shot at the mourners from the bell tower).[76]

The story was repeated in many biographies as almost official memory lore, and probably few of the writers had been actual eyewitnesses of those events.[77] The past struggles were also significantly inscribed into a broader historical process, securing a prominent place of the NZR in the cherished Polish state. As it was announced, "nobody other than the NZR, through stimulating a national spirit among the working class, prevented Bolshevism from chaining the Polish working masses to the chariot of the 'proletarian dictatorship'".[78] The personal nationalism found confirmation of the acquired definition of the self in collective remembering and an officially consecrated historical mission.

Conclusion

The autobiographical writings at the centre of this chapter negotiated variable nationalist identities and their uneasy position within the broader political landscape. As such they offer insight into working-class popular nationalism and its emotional background. I have asked how Polish workers became national and henceforth constructed their sense of working-class nationalist self, how they negotiated conflicted and volatile political identities, and how they recalled conversions of themselves and their colleagues. The historical context renders such choices far from 'natural'.

The nationalist militants had to justify their commitments against the plural, highly antagonistic setting of mobilized labour, find arguments, which would be convincing (also for themselves) and would help them to go against the tide, breaking strikes or waging 'fratricidal' struggles with other workers. Their older cultural identities and present sentiments were not always fully in line with the message of party-sponsored printings. However, political propaganda delivered stock language resources to explain the world and actively participate in it. Autobiographical writers used multiple strategies to reclaim the legitimacy of their commitment and justify their decisions in dialogue with the printed agitation of their former party.

Nationalist writers repeatedly describe the emotional zeal for their community of belonging. The party milieus and nationalist labour unions offered important professional skills and moderate upward social mobility. The nationalist structures provided important leverage for workers' self-assertion. Considering the size of nationalist support in cities, which had a significant inflow of uprooted peasant populations, nationalism appears to be an important vehicle of identity and belonging in the age of dissolution of pre-modern communities, as Ernest Gellner has argued.[79] The path of inclusion was not, however, connected with the state or the liberal parliamentary order, where workers could have fostered their interests. Their commitment was not pitched against a more conservative state nationalism, either.[80] The state structure was unanimously perceived as hostile, and integral nationalism rivalled the right wing of the socialist movement in spurring on working-class resistance against Russian autocracy.

As a result, from the very beginning the securing of national unity required a clear indication of the other. While ethnic conflict had long perpetuated nationalist commitments, the National Democratic propaganda significantly switched its focus. Initially working-class nationalism focused on shop floor issues of hierarchical Polish–German work relations. Due to the National Democratic action on a larger scale, it shifted mainly to Jews, who were perceived as a threat to Polishness.[81] The forceful mobilization along antisemitic lines was able to stir mass support, and resonated with the fear of disorder, hostility to socialism, and family-transferred patriotic sentiments. This allowed the National Democrats to reconfigure the political field thoroughly – from a minority position they successfully turned into the leading force instrumentalizing the disappointment with the revolution.

It was not enough, however, to secure the working-class nationalists' unconditional adherence to the integral, solidarist nationalist project. Nationalism had initially combined conviction about belonging to a true nation, with a strong popular component. This nationalism had been opposed to imperial powers, but also to the elitist noble class national idea of the past. However, after 1908 the National Democracy party openly questioned the class-based values of its militants, and forcefully attempted to subordinate them to the hierarchical order of the nationalist camp. When democratic components had evaporated, working-class nationalism significantly separated from the integral project of the National Democracy Party. This clash demonstrates that, as John Breuilly suggests, the slogans of nationalist parties do not always go hand in hand with the actual ideals of the popular constituencies supporting them.[82] Nonetheless, in the interwar period the party successfully mobilized workers on its own in a much more clearly inter-class nationalist manner. This ultimately blazed a path for the powerful project of the exclusionary, authoritarian Polish right.

Notes

1   I would like to express my gratitude to Holly Case, Maarten Van Ginderachter, Brian Porter-Szűcs and Andreas Stynen for useful remarks and comments on earlier versions of this chapter. The work on the chapter was possible within the project financed by the National Science Centre, Poland, research grant Opus 14, no. 2017/27/B/HS6/00098 realized at the Robert Zajonc Institute for Social Studies, University of Warsaw.
2   Fox and Miller-Idriss, 'Everyday nationhood'.
3   As in Gellner, *Nations and Nationalism*.
4   Berman, *The Primacy of Politics*; Calhoun, *Nations Matter*.
5   Berger and Smith, *Nationalism, Labour and Ethnicity*; Berger, 'In the fangs of social patriotism'; Benes, *Workers and Nationalism*; Van Ginderachter, *The Everyday Nationalism*.
6   Brubaker, *Nationalism Reframed*, p. 19.
7   Passerini, 'Women's personal narratives', p. 197.
8   Heaney, 'Emotions and nationalism'.
9   Skinner, *Visions of Politics*, p. 82.
10 The leaflets in my corpus were issued by major parties in the bigger industrial centres between 1904 and 1908. They were digitized and analysed with the assistance of the QDAMiner software. About one fifth of the collection of around 700 items was issued by the nationalist organizations affiliated with the National Democracy Party.
11 Beyen and Van Ginderachter, 'General introduction'.
12 Brubaker, *Nationalism Reframed*.
13 Verdery, 'Whither "nation" and "nationalism"?', p. 229.
14 Hearn, 'National identity'; Breuilly, 'What does it mean'.
15 Trencsényi *et al.*, *A History of Modern Political Thought*.
16 Modzelewski, *Naród i postęp*; Porter, *When Nationalism Began to Hate*.
17 Mencwel, *Etos lewicy*; Cywiński, *Rodowody niepokornych*.
18 Walicki, *The Enlightenment*; Porter, *When Nationalism Began to Hate*.
19 Snyder, *Nationalism*; Blanc, 'Anti-imperial Marxism borderland socialists'.
20 Porter, *When Nationalism Began to Hate*.
21 By the end of 1906 the three main socialist parties boasted membership numbers as high as 55,000 (PPS), 35,000 (SDKPiL) and 30,000 (Bund), which in total amounted to some 15 per cent of all workers in the Polish Kingdom. In contrast, prior to the Revolution all three parties had no more than 1,500 members. NZR reached about 25,000 members. For aggregated data and a broad political panorama see Blobaum, *Rewolucja*.
22 Scott, *Barricades and Banners*; Marzec, 'Die Revolution 1905 bis 1907'.

23 On the contingent aspect of history and the role of conjunctures see Sahlins, *Historical Metaphors*; Sewell, *Logics of History*; see also Brubaker, *Nationalism Reframed*. An interesting study of a reconfiguring event fostering virulent Polish nationalism is Brykczynski, *Primed for Violence*.
24 Anderson, *Imagined Communities*, p. 154.
25 Eustace, 'Emotion and political change'.
26 Cohen, 'Personal nationalism', p. 802.
27 Quotation modified in order to fit the grammar of the sentence (Ibid., p. 807).
28 Jeremski, Józef, 'Na marginesie walk bratobójczych w Łodzi', in: *Kiliński*, no. 2, 1936, p. 50.
29 *Przez miłość Ojczyzny i walkę do Niepodległości*, in: Kiliński 1935, Anniversary issue (without number), 2.
30 Crago, 'The "Polishness" of Production', pp. 16–41.
31 Ibid., p. 35.
32 This is especially visible in articles in the National Democratic press – *Przegląd Wszechpolski* for the general public and NZR's *Pochodnia* dedicated to workers.
33 Kosiorek, Michal, 'Skład bibuły w Warszawie', in: *Kiliński*, no. 1, 1936, p. 36.
34 Posiak, Jan, 'Dzielnica "Górna" w Łodzi', in: *Kiliński*, no. 3, 1936, p. 108.
35 Klimkiewiczówna, Michalina, 'Praca organizacyjna w Żyrardowie', in: *Kiliński*, no. 3, 1936, p. 134.
36 Rożnowski, Stefan, 'Cmentarzysko społeczne – Przy budowie kolei kaliskiej – Wiec u Henneberga – prowadzenie języka polskiego na kolei W. W. – Praca organizacyjna w gazowni', in: *Kiliński*, no. 2, 1936, p. 60. Other examples see Brzeziński Maksymilian, 'Dzielnica "Zielona" w Łodzi', in: *Kiliński*, no. 1, 1936, p. 17–18; Piskorski, Feliks, 'Z nad dobrzanki', in: *Kiliński*, no. 3, 1936, pp. 102–103; Posiak, Jan, 'Dzielnica "Górna" w Łodzi', in: *Kiliński*, no. 3, 1936, p. 108; Żukowski, Bronisław, 'Pamiętniki bojowca', in: *Niepodległość*, vol. 1, 1929–1930, pp. 115–116.
37 Reddy, *The Navigation of Feeling*.
38 Łączny, Czesław, 'Początki buntu', in: *Kiliński*, no. 1, 1936, p. 24.
39 Rożnowski, Stefan, 'Cmentarzysko społeczne – Przy budowie kolei kaliskiej – Wiec u Henneberga – prowadzenie języka polskiego na kolei W. W. – Praca organizacyjna w gazowni', in: *Kiliński*, no. 2, 1936, p. 60.
40 Brzeziński, Maksymilian, 'Dzielnica "Zielona" w Łodzi', in: *Kiliński*, no. 1, 1936, pp. 17–18.
41 Steinberg, *Fighting Words*.
42 Korzec, *Źródła do dziejów rewolucji*, vol. 2, p. 174.
43 Korzec, *Źródła do dziejów rewolucji 1905–1907*, vol. 1, pp. 205–206, 656.
44 Krzywiec, 'Eliminationist anti-Semitism'.
45 Korzec, *Źródła do dziejów rewolucji 1905–1907*, vol. 1, p. 351.
46 Leaflet of the Central Committee of the NZR, 1 June 1905, APŁ KGP, 390, pp. 382–383.
47 Ibid.
48 On the speeding up of political antisemitism, see Blobaum, 'The politics of antisemitism'; Weeks, *From Assimilation to Antisemitism*; Ury, *Barricades and Banners*.
49 Jeremski, Józef, 'Na marginesie walk bratobójczych w Łodzi', in: *Kiliński*, no. 2, 1936, p. 56.
50 Müller, *What is Populism*.
51 "Jewing" [*zażydzenia*] – the act of making Jewish, contaminated with Jewishness – a derogatory expression with clearly antisemitic undertones. Drzewiecki, Józef (Dejot), 'Okreg w Zagłębiu Narodowego Kola Kolejarzy w 1905 roku', in: *Kiliński*, no. 4, 1937, p. 175.
52 Jeremski, Józef, 'Na marginesie walk bratobójczych w Łodzi', in: *Kiliński*, no. 2, 1936, p. 52.
53 Łączny, Czeslaw, 'Początki buntu', in: *Kiliński*, no. 1, 1936, no. 1, p. 24.

54 On electoral regulations and politics of the ballot see Blobaum, *Rewolucja*; Samuś, *Wasza kartka wyborcza*.
55 See Krzywiec, 'Z taką rewolucją'; Porter, *When Nationalism Began to Hate*.
56 The dark side of National Democratic politics is analysed in Ury, *Barricades and Banners*, ch. 6.
57 Parkot-Wojt, Stanisław, 'W NZR, katordze i na sybirze', in: *Niepodległość*, vol. 12, 1935, p. 222.
58 For a telling example of a socialist worker, see Olbrzymek, *Wspomnienia*, p. 57.
59 Mierzwiński, 'Wspomnienia z czasów', pp. 168–169.
60 Introductory article (untitled), in: *Kiliński*, Anniversary issue (without number), 1935, p. 1.
61 Jan Kiliński (1760–1819) was a shoemaker active as a leader of the Kościuszko's uprising against Russia in 1794, thus he was a venerated figure among nationalist workers.
62 Introductory article (untitled), in: *Kiliński*, Anniversary issue (without number), 1935, p. 1.
63 Crago, *Nationalism*; Idem, 'The "Polishness" of Production'; Karwacki, *Związki zawodowe*.
64 Bereza, F. (full name unknown), 'Wspomnienia z dni rewolucyjnych czyli przebieg rewolucji z roku 1904 i dalej', AAN, Instytut Badania najnowszej historii Polski, Wspomnienia nadesłane do redakcji pisma Niepodległość 1930–1937, syg 357/4, folder 3, p. 34.
65 Monasterska, T., *Narodowy Związek Robotniczy*, p. 43; Marzec, 'Modernizacja mas'.
66 This transformation was analysed by Porter, *When Nationalism Began to Hate*. For more about the early populist writings of the National Democrats, see Kulak, *Jan Ludwik Popławski*; Bończa-Tomaszewski, *Demokratyczna geneza nacjonalizmu*; Marzec, *Rebelia i reakcja*.
67 On the change of social basis of National Democracy see Kozicki, *Historia Ligi Narodowej*, pp. 284–285; Wapiński, *Roman Dmowski*, p. 157. Supportive contemporaries also registered the change, see for instance Skarzyński, Stefan, 'W obronie Narodowej Demokracji', in: *Słowo* 1907, p. 291, quoted in: Kidzińska, *Stronnictwo Polityki Realnej*, p. 118.
68 Plach, *The Clash of Moral Nations*.
69 Jeremski, Józef, 'Na marginesie walk bratobójczych w Łodzi', in: *Kiliński*, no. 2, 1936, p. 54.
70 'Przez miłość Ojczyzny i walkę do Niepodległości', in: *Kiliński*, Anniversary issue (without number), 1935, p. 2.
71 Brzeziński, Maksymilian, 'Dzielnica "Zielona" w Łodzi', in: *Kiliński*, no. 1, 1936, pp. 17–18.
72 Materiały Komisji Odznaczeniowej, AAN, NZR, syg. 41/IV, p. 1.
73 'NZR w oświetleniu wrażej opinii', in: *Kiliński*, Anniversary issue (without number), p. 15; 'Z aktu oskarżenia grupy enzeterowców sądzonych w lutym 1911 w Piotrkowie', in: *Kiliński* 1936, no. 1.
74 Piskorski, Feliks, 'Z nad dobrzanki', in: *Kiliński*, no. 3, 1936, 116; Jeremski, Józef, 'Na marginesie walk bratobójczych w Łodzi', in: *Kiliński* 1936, no. 2, 1936; on "fratricidal" struggles in general see Karwacki, *Łódź w latach rewolucji*.
75 Brzeziński, 'Dzielnica "Zielona" w Łodzi', in: *Kiliński*, no. 1, 1936, p. 21, see also Drzewiecki, Józef (Dejot), 'Okreg w Zagłębiu Narodowego Koła Kolejarzy w 1905 roku', in: *Kiliński*, no. 4, 1937.
76 For instance Posiak, 'Dzielnica "Górna" w Łodzi', in: *Kiliński*, no. 3, 1936, p. 131. Examples of official socialist version may be found in 'Łodzianin' PPS-Lewicy 1907, No. 30, in: Korzec, *Źródła do dziejów rewolucji*, vol. 2, p. 586. The mirror biographical testimonies of the left are gathered in *Kronika ruchu rewolucyjnego*, vol. 4, no. 1, 1938, pp. 2–21.

77 I argue that stressing affinity with important persons or events is a particularity of working-class oral histories or memoirs. The canonization of this story and expectation towards writers to cover "historical events" in their autobiographies further added to this phenomenon. See Portelli, *The death of Luigi Trastulli*, 1991.
78 Jeremski, Józef, 'Na marginesie walk bratobójczych w Łodzi', in: *Kiliński*, no. 2, 1936, p. 58.
79 For data on membership see Monasterska, *Narodowy Związek Robotniczy*; Gellner, *Nations and Nationalism*.
80 For a comparative context see Berger, 'In the fangs of social patriotism'.
81 Marzec, 'What bears witness'.
82 Breuilly, 'What does it mean'.

References

Anderson, Benedict R., *Imagined communities: Reflections on the origin and spread of nationalism*, London – New York, Verso, 2006.

Beneš, Jakub S., *Workers and nationalism: Czech and German Social Democracy in Habsburg Austria, 1890–1918*, Oxford, Oxford University Press, 2016.

Berger, Stefan and Smith, Angel (eds.), *Nationalism, labour and ethnicity, 1870–1939*, Manchester, Manchester University Press, 1999.

Berger, Stefan, 'In the fangs of social patriotism: The construction of nation and class in autobiographies of British and German social democrats in the inter-war period', in: *Archiv für Sozialgeschichte*, no. 40, 2000, pp. 259–287.

Berman, Sheri, *The primacy of politics: social democracy and the making of Europe's twentieth century*, Cambridge – New York, Cambridge University Press, 2006.

Beyen, Marnix and Van Ginderachter, Maarten, 'General introduction: Writing the mass into a mass phenomenon', in: Van Ginderachter, Maarten and Beyen, Marnix (eds.), *Nationhood from below: Europe in the long nineteenth century*, New York, Palgrave Macmillan, 2012.

Blanc, Eric, 'Anti-imperial Marxism Borderland socialists and the evolution of Bolshevism on national liberation', in: *International Socialist Review*, no. 100, 2016, available at http://isreview.org/issue/100/anti-imperial-marxism (accessed 21 October 2019).

Blobaum, Robert, 'The politics of antisemitism in fin-de-siècle Warsaw', in: *The Journal of Modern History*, vol. 73, no. 2, 2001, pp. 275–306.

Blobaum, Robert, *Rewolucja: Russian Poland, 1904–1907*, Ithaca, Cornell University Press, 1995.

Bończa-Tomaszewski, Nikodem, *Demokratyczna geneza nacjonalizmu: intelektualne korzenie ruchu narodowo-demokratycznego*, Warszawa, S.K. Fronda, 2001.

Breuilly, John, 'What does it mean to say that nationalism is "popular"?', in: Van Ginderachter, Maarten and Beyen, Marnix (eds.), *Nationhood from below: Europe in the long nineteenth century*, New York, Palgrave Macmillan, 2012, pp. 23–43.

Brubaker, Rogers, *Nationalism reframed: Nationhood and the national question in the New Europe*, Cambridge – New York, Cambridge University Press, 1996.

Brykczynski, Paul, *Primed for violence: Murder, antisemitism, and democratic politics in interwar Poland*, Madison WI, The University of Wisconsin Press, 2016.

Calhoun, Craig J., *Nations matter: Culture, history, and the cosmopolitan dream*, London – New York, Routledge, 2007.

Cohen, Anthony P., 'Personal nationalism: A Scottish view of some rites, rights, and wrongs', in: *American Ethnologist*, vol. 23, no. 4, 1996, pp. 802–815.

Crago, Laura, 'The "Polishness" of production: Factory politics and the reinvention of working-class national and political identities in Russian Poland's textile industry, 1880–1910', in: *Slavic Review*, vol. 59, no. 1, 2000, pp. 16–41.

Crago, Laura, *Nationalism, religion, citizenship, and work in the development of the Polish working class and the polish trade union movement, 1815–1929. A comparative study of Russian Poland's textile workers and upper Silesian miners and metalworkers*, New Haven, Yale University, 1993.

Cywiński, Bohdan, *Rodowody niepokornych*, Warszawa, Wydawnictwo Naukowe PWN, 2010.

Eustace, Nicole, 'Emotion and political change', in: Matt, Susan Jipson and Stearns, Peter Nathanael (eds.), *Doing emotions history*, Urbana IL, University of Illinois Press, 2014, pp. 104–183.

Fox, Jon E. and Miller-Idriss, Cynthia, 'Everyday nationhood', in: *Ethnicities*, vol. 8, no. 4, 2008, pp. 536–563.

Gellner, Ernest, *Nations and nationalism*, Ithaca NY, Cornell University Press, 2008.

Heaney, Jonathan, 'Emotions and nationalism: A reappraisal', in: Demertzis, Nicolas (ed.), *Emotions in politics*, London, Palgrave Macmillan, 2013, pp. 243–263.

Hearn, Jonathan, 'National identity: Banal, personal and embedded', in: *Nations and Nationalism*, vol. 13, no. 4, 2007, pp. 657–674.

Karwacki, Władysław L., *Łódź w latach rewolucji 1905–1907*, Łódź, Wydawnictwo Łódzkie, 1975.

Karwacki, Władysław L., *Związki zawodowe i stowarzyszenia pracodawców w Łodzi (do roku 1914)*, Wydawnictwo Łódzkie, 1972.

Kidzińska, Agnieszka, *Stronnictwo Polityki Realnej: 1905–1923*, Lublin, Wydawnictwo Uniwersytetu Marii Curie-Skłodowskiej, 2007.

Korzec, Paweł, (ed.), *Źródła do dziejów rewolucji 1905–1907 w okręgu łódzkim*, 2 vol., Warszawa, Książka i Wiedza, 1964.

Kozicki, Stanisław, *Historia Ligi Narodowej: (Okres 1887–1907)*, Londyn, Myśl Polska, 1964.

Krzywiec, Grzegorz, 'Eliminationist anti-Semitism at home and abroad: Polish nationalism, the Jewish question, and Eastern European right-wing mass politics', in: Rosenthal, Lawrence and Rodic, Vesna (eds.), *The new nationalism and the First World War*, New York, Palgrave Macmillan, 2014.

Krzywiec, Grzegorz, 'Z taką rewolucją musimy walczyć na noże: rewolucja 1905 roku z perspektywy polskiej prawicy', in *Rewolucja 1905. Przewodnik*, Warszawa, Wydawnictwo Krytyki Politycznej, 2013, pp. 326–352.

Kulak, Teresa, *Jan Ludwik Popławski: biografia polityczna*, Wrocław, Zakład Narodowy im. Ossolińskich, 1994.

Marzec, Wiktor, 'Die revolution 1905 bis 1907 im Königreich Polen – von der arbeiterrevolte zur nationalen reaktion', in: *Arbeit - Bewegung - Geschichte. Zeitschrift für historischer Studien*, vol. 15, no. 3, 2016, pp. 27–46.

Marzec, Wiktor, 'Modernizacja mas. Moment polityczny i dyskurs endecji w okresie rewolucji 1905–1907', in: *Praktyka Teoretyczna*, no. 3, 2014, pp. 99–132.

Marzec, Wiktor, *Rebelia i reakcja. Rewolucja 1905 roku i plebejskie doświadczenie polityczne*, Kraków – Łódź, Universitas – Wydawnictwo Uniwersytetu Łódzkiego, 2016.

Marzec, Wiktor, 'What bears witness of the failed revolution? The rise of political antisemitism during the 1905–1907 revolution in the Kingdom of Poland', in: *Eastern European Politics and Societies*, vol. 30, no. 1, 2016, pp. 189–213.

Mencwel, Andrzej, *Etos lewicy: esej o narodzinach kulturalizmu polskiego*, Warszawa, Wydawnictwo 'Krytyki Politycznej', 2009.

Mierzwiński, Bolesław, 'Wspomnienia z czasów konspiracyjnej działalności w Łodzi i na wsi', in: *Kronika ruchu rewolucyjnego*', vol. 4, no. 3/15, 1938, pp. 168–169.

Modzelewski, Wojciech, *Naród i postęp: problematyka narodowa w ideologii i myśli społecznej pozytywistów warszawskich*, Warszawa, Państwowe Wydawnictwo Naukowe, 1977.

Monasterska, Teresa, *Narodowy Związek Robotniczy, 1905–1920*, Warszawa, Państwowe Wydawnictwo Naukowe, 1973.

Müller, Jan-Werner, *What is populism*, Philadelphia, University of Pennsylvania Press, 2016.

Olbrzymek, 'Wspomnienia starego robotnika 1893–1918', in: *Z pola walki*, 1927, no. 3.

Parkot-Wojt, Stanisław, 'W NZR, katordze i na sybirze', in: *Niepodległość*, vol. XII, 1935, p. 222.

Passerini, Luisa, 'Women's personal narratives: myths, experiences, and emotions', in: Webster Barbre, Joy *et al.* (eds.), *Interpreting women's lives: Feminist theory and personal narratives*, Bloomington, Indiana University Press, 1989, pp. 189–197.

Plach, Eva, *The clash of moral nations: Cultural politics in Piłsudski's Poland, 1926–1935*, Athens OH, Ohio University Press, 2006.

Portelli, Alessandro, *The death of Luigi Trastulli, and other stories: Form and meaning in oral history*, Albany NY, State University of New York Press, 1991.

Porter, Brian, *When nationalism began to hate: Imagining modern politics in nineteenth century Poland*, New York, Oxford University Press, 2000.

Reddy, William M., *The navigation of feeling: A framework for the history of emotions*, Cambridge – New York, Cambridge University Press, 2001.

Sahlins, Marshall, *Historical metaphors and mythical realities structure in the early history of the Sandwich Islands kingdom*, Ann Arbor, University of Michigan Press, 1981.

Samuś, Paweł, *Wasza kartka wyborcza jest silniejsza niż karabin, niż armata…: z dziejów kultury politycznej na ziemiach polskich pod zaborami*, Łódź, Wydawnictwo Uniwersytetu Łódzkiego, 2013.

Sewell, William, *Logics of history: Social theory and social transformation*, Chicago, University of Chicago Press, 2005.

Skinner, Quentin, *Visions of politics*, Cambridge – New York, Cambridge University Press, 2002.

Snyder, Timothy, *Nationalism, Marxism, and modern Central Europe: A biography of Kazimierz Kelles-Krauz, 1872–1905*, Cambridge MA, Harvard University Press, 1997.

Steinberg, Marc W., *Fighting words: Working-class formation, collective action, and discourse in early nineteenth-century England*, Ithaca NY, Cornell University Press, 1999.

Trencsényi, Balázs *et al.*, *A history of modern political thought in East Central Europe*, Oxford – New York, Oxford University Press, 2016.

Ury, Scott, *Barricades and banners: The Revolution of 1905 and the transformation of Warsaw Jewry*, Stanford, Stanford University Press, 2012.

Van Ginderachter, Maarten, *The everyday nationalism of workers: A social history of modern Belgium*, Stanford, Stanford University Press, 2019.

Verdery, Katherine, 'Whither "nation" and "nationalism"?', in: Balakrishnan, Gopal (ed.), *Mapping the nation*, London – New York, Verso, 1996, pp. 37–46.

Walicki, Andrzej, *The Enlightenment and the birth of modern nationhood: Polish political thought from Noble Republicanism to Tadeusz Kosciuszko*, Notre Dame IN, University of Notre Dame Press, 1989.

Wapiński, Roman, *Roman Dmowski*, Lublin, Wydawnictwo Lubelskie, 1989.

Weeks, Theodore R., *From assimilation to antisemitism: The 'Jewish question' in Poland, 1850–1914*, DeKalb IL, Northern Illinois University Press, 2006.

Żukowski, Bronisław, 'Pamiętniki bojowca', in: *Niepodległość*, vol. 1, 1929–1930, pp. 115–116.

6 In search of the true Italy

Emotional practices and the nation in Fiume 1919/1920

Thomas Blanck

Introduction

On September 12, 1919, the city of Fiume in the Northern Adriatic was occupied by Italian volunteer forces who proclaimed its annexation to Italy. When Mario Carli, a captain of the Italian assault unit *Arditi* ('the audacious ones'), leading futurist and member of the recently founded Roman branch of the Fascists, got notice of the event, he published an article in the Arditi's newspaper.[1] Addressing the latest events, he stated:

> A new roll call sounds for all those who have an Italian liver, heart, and arm. [...] The true Italy, the young Italy, Italy that marches ahead and cuts the diplomatic mazes by a beautiful hit with the dagger, today is in Fiume, either in person or with its soul.

Rome, Carli continued, must learn from the

> agile and graceful young city how to love and how to desire, against any foreign suppression, and how to rule a nation of intelligent heroes. [...] Have in mind that Italy finally is mature for the national revolution. The enterprise of Fiume is the prologue of this revolution.[2]

Three aspects in this short passage are of interest. First, Carli distinguishes clearly between two concepts of the Italian nation. On the one hand, there is the old Italy, governed by lazy Roman bureaucrats and commanded by soldiers who are in the military just to promote their careers. On the other, there is a young, vital nation, led by Arditi and Futurists, who do not serve out of a sense of duty but because the will to fight is an essential part of their selves. Second, Carli makes a strong connection between nation and emotions: since the old Italy in Carli's eyes is apparently not able to evoke or receive feelings, it must learn from the new nation how to love and desire. Third, the nation and its emotional implications are not abstract entities but bound to bodies: it is the Italian livers, hearts and arms Carli is speaking to – not their minds. Carli's peculiar notion of the "Italian liver" refers both to the classical idea of the liver as the physical centre of human emotions and to the Italian expression of being a 'man of the liver', that is, to be daring and audacious.[3] In short, by referring to the notion of a "new Italy" Carli idealizes Fiume as a utopian emotional community; that is, a society with "particular values, modes of feeling, and ways to express those feelings"[4] completely different from those of the old Italy. Furthermore, Carli's imagined patriotic emotional community does not define emotions as open for interpretation but rather as something that exists through its sheer bodily presence "on this side of hermeneutics".[5]

As powerful as this rhetoric was, it raises two questions: first, how did the creation of this emotional community take place on the ground and in everyday life, and second, was it successful? This chapter argues that for roughly half a year up until late 1919, Carli's emotional utopia was in fact partially realized and comparatively stable. Initially, public speeches, rallies and festivities in Fiume successfully aroused shared bodily affects and thereby conveyed the idea of an inclusive emotional community. They created consensus and a sense of belonging through the performance of patriotic love and enthusiasm for the common cause: in Fiume, a legionnaire from Southern Italy could feel 'at home' just like someone born and bred there.[6] From late 1919 onwards, however, the sense of belonging together with the emotional community of the new Italy proved to be short-lived and highly dysfunctional. The reason for this was that those "emotional practices" which initially successfully conveyed the idea of a new nation now turned against their very creators. According to Monique Scheer, emotional practices

> imply 1) that emotions not only follow from things people do, but are themselves a form of practice, because they are an action of a mindful body; 2) that this feeling subject is not prior to but emerges in the doing of emotion; and 3) that a definition of emotion must include the body and its functions, not in the sense of a universal, pristine, biological base, but as a locus for innate and learned capacities deeply shaped by habitual practices.[7]

Emotions, thus, are neither a by-product of certain situations and practices nor do they create them in the first place. Instead, emotions have the power to translate a set of ideas into certain practices, while at the same time the (bodily) practice itself has repercussions on the set of ideas. What happened in Fiume was that emotional practices and bodily affects developed from being an integrating and stabilizing factor to becoming only an end in itself. In other words, love and desire for the nation had become a self-mobilizing emotional practice among large parts of the legionaries. While emotional performances of the nation were first a legitimizing resource of power that reshaped the subjectivity of the legionaries, they later caused a fragmentation of the temporarily stable emotional community. This in turn led to the erosion of discipline, endangered Fiume's institutional framework and resulted in violent conflicts between occupiers and occupied.

To elaborate this argument, I will at first briefly outline the course of the occupation of Fiume. Second, I will concentrate on the first phase of the occupation and highlight the emotional dimension of what has often been described as a 'festivalization' of everyday life in Fiume.[8] Finally, I will show how the appropriation of these emotional practices eventually led to a fragmentation of the emotional community in Fiume. Therefore, I will highlight how the discourse on youth and the renewal of the nation related to the social structure of the legionaries. Subsequently I will explore the subjective monopolization of national emotions in daily life, and examine the role of the body and bodily affects during this process. The investigation will thus start from a macro-perspective and move on towards a more micro-historical approach. The sources used in this chapter stem from research in the State Archive of Rijeka, the Archive of the Vittoriale in Gardone and the Central State Archives in Rome. The source material consists of the daily orders issued by the commanding generals, police records, intelligence reports and personal correspondence. Furthermore, the chapter is based on a critical reading of various newspapers, above all the local *Vedetta d'Italia* and the futurist *Testa di ferro*, as well as unpublished and published ego-documents.

Fiume in the aftermath of the Great War

Fiume, today the Croatian Rijeka, lies in the northern Adriatic. Its history is somewhat typical for a port city amidst the multi-ethnic "shatterzones of empires"[9] in central Europe, up to the present day: a constant stage for ethnic conflicts and agreements, a place of struggles between economic and political interests, a symbol of both freedom and oppression.[10] In 1869, two years after the establishment of the Austro-Hungarian empire, it obtained its status as a separate entity (*corpus separatum*) and depended directly on the Hungarian government. This partial autonomy – the city's inhabitants had "Fiumean" citizenship, not Croatian[11] – benefited the city's economy, based on the port industries and maritime trade, leading to an increase in wealth and population as well as a strong municipal identity.[12] In 1918, around 47,000 people lived in Fiume, 30,000 of whom were Italian-speakers, 10,000 Croatian-speakers, nearly 4,500 Hungarian-speakers and then, among other languages, mostly Slovene- and German-speakers. And yet, these numbers cover a linguistic reality that was far more diverse and complicated, as proven by a sample based on enrolment files of the voluntary army of Fiume from 1919 and 1920: of seventy-two newly enrolled soldiers born in Fiume only five did explicitly *not* speak any other language than Italian. Thirty-six soldiers spoke at least one other language (in most cases Croatian), sometimes even up to five. Of the remaining thirty-one soldiers we have no information concerning their linguistic abilities.[13] Other sources suggest that until 1918 being monolingual in Fiume was an exception and not the rule. The Italian troops arriving in late 1918 were seldom accustomed to and more often overtaxed by the multilingual reality of the city. Especially in confusing or crowded situations, such as bars or restaurants, language deficiencies and the ensuing misunderstandings tended to raise the level of stress.[14]

What would become the 'question of Fiume' in 1918 had not existed before. Unlike Trieste or Trento, Fiume did not lie at the centre of the Italian nationalists' agitation. This changed only after the end of the war. At the beginning of November 1918, after almost three and a half years of bloody warfare, Italy had defeated the Austro-Hungarian Empire. During the conflict, almost six million soldiers had been mobilized, nearly 10 per cent of whom died, over one million had been wounded; due to the unexpected length and intensity of the conflict, the Italian economy was close to a collapse.[15] In late 1918, thus, both the Italian government under Prime Minister Orlando and millions of common Italians who had suffered in the trenches, in the factories or at home, expected to be rewarded for the enormous efforts they had put into the war. The London Agreement, signed in 1915 by Italy and the Entente powers, assured Italy large territorial gains, most importantly South Tyrol and Trieste, both a former part of the Habsburg Empire, but not Fiume. Italy's allies were willing to fulfil the agreement at the Paris Peace Conference, but because of unskilful negotiation on the part of the Italian delegation and pressure by the right-wing and nationalist public, the victorious nation soon felt betrayed by its allies, especially by Woodrow Wilson. Nationalist poet and war veteran Gabriele D'Annunzio, who had rallied vigorously for a war entry in 1915, coined the catchphrase *vittoria mutilata*, the "mutilated victory"[16]: although Italy had suffered as much as the other Great Powers – and it claimed to be one of them – it felt treated as badly as the defeated nations, or even worse.[17]

The political and diplomatic history of Fiume in the aftermath of the First World War can be divided into four phases.[18] The first phase began on October 30, 1918, when a circle of nationalist Italian elites formed a National Council and proclaimed the city's annexation to Italy. Italy sent troops to Fiume and so did the allies, not willing to accept the territorial claims of the Italian part of the population. Until September 1919 the city was governed by an interallied military force under the command of Italian General Pittaluga. Nonetheless, the tension between Italian soldiers and the rest of the allied military forces, especially the French colonial soldiers, remained high and led to severe riots and the subsequent removal of certain, especially intransigent, Italian units in the summer of 1919. To assure the annexation, Fiume's National Council worked on a plan to lead volunteer military forces into the city, collaborating with diverse nationalist associations within the Italian mainland. The only thing missing for such a venture was a highly recognizable representative. Given his reputation as a poet, nationalist agitator and war veteran, Gabriele D'Annunzio was found to be a perfect fit for the operation. He accepted the offer and on September 12, 1919 he led a force of around 1,700 soldiers and volunteers into the city and proclaimed its annexation to Italy.

Now, the *impresa* (enterprise) began: the allied forces left the city, the Italian National Council transferred its powers to D'Annunzio, making him the omnipotent *comandante* of Fiume. Contrary to the hopes of the occupiers, the Italian government under Nitti did not support D'Annunzio's request for an immediate annexation. Instead, fearing the loss of its bargaining power in Paris, it remained hesitant and worked on a compromise that would be acceptable for all parties involved, namely D'Annunzio and his legionaries, the Italian government and the public, and the Entente powers. This compromise, the so-called *modus vivendi*, would make Fiume a Free City and meet the National Council's demands of self-determination. Although the compromise found widespread acclaim among all parties involved, D'Annunzio and his most radical and intransigent followers did not accept it, thereby ignoring both the decision of the National Council and the results of a public referendum.

The rejection by D'Annunzio in mid-December 1919 led to the third phase of the enterprise, when the initial supporters of the occupation distanced themselves from D'Annunzio and increasingly radical forces took over the helm in Fiume. The symbol of this change was the replacement of D'Annunzio's chief of staff, the moderate nationalist Giovanni Giuriati by Alceste De Ambris, a leading representative of the anarcho-syndicalist movement.[19] While the occupation initially had moved mainly within the framework of Italian irredentist claims, De Ambris now tried to transform the occupied city into the birthplace of a worldwide revolutionary movement. Given the city's worsening conditions – due to the naval and terrestrial blockade upheld by the regular Italian army, its economy had collapsed, the supply of food, coal and gas was notoriously bad, money had lost its value, unemployment and crime rates were high[20] – his radical solutions and projects fell on fertile ground. Besides, the rupture between D'Annunzio and both the National Council and the larger part of the population was evident, leaving him no choice but to rely on new projects and allies to retain his grip on the situation. This phase of radicalization reached its climax when D'Annunzio proclaimed the Regency of Carnaro in September 1920 and Fiume became the capital city of an independent republic.

Still, the international community and Italy refused to recognize the new-born state and meanwhile prepared for a territorial agreement with the Kingdom of Serbs, Croats and Slovenes. After the signing of the Treaty of Rapallo, which defined Fiume as a Free City, administrated by the League of Nations, the choice the occupiers had was either to surrender or to await their removal by force. Given the mixture of pride, intransigence and fatalism that characterized this last phase of the occupation, the legionaries chose the latter: on Christmas Eve, 1920, Prime Minister Giolitti ordered a series of naval and terrestrial attacks on the city, and after five days of fighting the self-declared regency surrendered. In the first half of January 1921, D'Annunzio and his followers left the city while the National Council temporarily took over the government and prepared municipal elections.

A patriotic fever: building the emotional community of Fiume

"Fiume lives these days of fighting in a patriotic fever which is impossible to describe, in a romantic atmosphere which seems to come from some old textbook and which brings us back to the times our grandfathers told us about."[21] This depiction of the situation in Fiume from late 1918 is paradigmatic in establishing a connection between the notion of the romantic "patriotic fever" and the myth of recreating the past of the Risorgimento and finally fulfilling its promises. Apparently, the myth of a feverish lifestyle in Fiume, constantly repeated in the press,[22] was highly appealing especially to young men. One of them was Gastone Canziani who ran away from his middle-class home in Trieste at the age of only 15 to join D'Annunzio's troops. In a letter, written some weeks after his arrival in mid-September 1919, he described the atmosphere during a transfer of his unit: everyone was "filled with love and enthusiasm towards the adored Italy, unanimously and enthusiastically from a hundred mouths came the powerful 'yes', a holy oath made to the *olocausta* [sacrifice, i.e. Fiume] in front of its people".[23] Whether "love and enthusiasm" were Canziani's emotions while parading with his comrades in front of the town's population is impossible to determine. What is relevant here is the fact that the young legionnaire *performs* his love for the fatherland publicly by singing with his comrades while later *communicating* it privately in a letter to his family.[24] While Canziani first and foremost stresses the enthusiasm among the volunteers, another letter written at the very beginning of the occupation by Federico Florio, a Tuscan-born lieutenant of the Arditi, to his mother highlights the role the civilian audience played in the performance of patriotic commitment:

[F]or my country I would gladly give my life and more, if I could. [...] Here the enthusiasm is indescribable. You see women, men, children [...] who cry and beg us not to abandon them, to save them. We are determined to everything – we have sworn, and we have all signed this oath. [...] And this I want you to know: you had a son who is crazy but Italian, a true Italian.[25]

It becomes clear that the attraction of performing patriotic love was not only that it guaranteed cohesion among the legionaries, but also that this emotional practice was reciprocal and communicative. Displaying that one was willing to sacrifice one's life resulted in "crying and begging" by the spectators. In other words, the legionaries who performed their love for Italy were instantly rewarded with the admiration and gratitude of the civilian population. Giuseppe Maranini, a 17-year-old legionnaire from Bologna, had the same impression when he wrote to his fiancée. As a volunteer in Fiume he felt like a "superior being" who could get anything he asked for.[26] He as well was struck by the communal nature of performing patriotic emotions which had repercussions both on the legionaries and on the 'Fiumani'. On September 24, 1919 he wrote:

The enthusiasm is great, both among the Fiumeans and among the troops. Every now and then, the whole city moves, descends into the squares, acclaiming regiments, platoons, that come constantly. [...] Really the show [*spettacolo*] of strength, of national conscience that our people has given is beautiful.[27]

And when one evening a group of *Bersaglieri* ('berserks'), next to the Arditi the other famous elite unit present in Fiume, entered the city, Maranini experienced their arrival as a performance of collective "madness" created by the interaction of bodies, sounds and movements that finally affected his own body:

Soldiers, officers, citizens ran like crazy behind the stomping Bersaglieri, contending with the pace, throwing each other on the ground to be faster, like crazy wild. The fanfare, the race, the shaking feathers [of the Bersaglieri's hats]: I too felt how I blushed.

Then the group came to a halt and general Ceccherini spoke to them, his voice "veiled with emotion and a deep tremor took possession of his words little by little. He stopped, panting, moved like all of us". After the ritual exchange of shouts between Ceccherini and the crowd in front of the governor's palace ("Eia, eia, eia – alalà!"), the Bersaglieri's band resumed its "galloping marches" whereupon the crowd started to run as if in a "delirium" – "You cannot imagine what a great thing!"[28]

In his analysis of German soldiers' letters from the First World War, Dieter Langewiesche has shown the discrepancy between the public and private discourse on the nation's emotional appeal, stressing that national emotions are often just a publicly performed rhetoric exercise without any repercussions in private contexts. In our case, though, the testimonies cited above strikingly bridge this gap between private emotions and public emotional performance.[29] The expression of love and enthusiasm for the cause of Fiume by means of songs, flags and parades contributed to an emotional habitus that created cohesion among the legionaries.[30] And by writing about their national emotions, the legionaries justified their presence in Fiume not only to their families, but more importantly, to themselves. In other words, the emotion of patriotic love became, in the words of Scheer, a "practical engagement with the world"[31] the legionaries were living in.

Of course, neither Canziani and Maranini nor Florio belonged to the rank-and-file. While the former two arrived from a middle-class background to Fiume and had not fought in the trenches, the latter was an officer with a different war experience from that of the average infantryman. For those still enrolled in the Army in the Autumn of 1919, deserting to Fiume was a solution to the problem of being stuck in the army, since the disastrous process of demobilization had left hundreds of thousands of Italian soldiers waiting impatiently for their discharge.[32] And yet, it was also a way of finally being acknowledged as a patriotic hero. Armando Diaz, commander of the Italian

Army, clearly saw how attractive the ideal of a patriotic emotional community was for many soldiers. Reporting on the mood of the 8th army, stationed around Fiume, Diaz noted that the Italian soldiers were seeing the nearby city "sheltered from the winds and from the cold, full of lights, parties, dances, [and] they know that the comrades who fled there enjoy double checks, live in abundance and are [...] surrounded by a halo of heroism".[33]

During the war, many soldiers had suffered under the tough disciplinary regime of the Italian army and the, compared with other European armies, extreme measures that had been applied against (suspected) deserters.[34] Now, in Fiume, the significance of being a deserter apparently was turned upside down. Here, those not following the orders of their superiors were soldiers to look up to. They had a deeper and truer understanding of loyalty and duty than their comrades in the regular army. For those still enrolled in the Army the advantages of defecting to D'Annunzio's troops were twofold: not only could one escape the harsh regime of the army, but one could also feel even more devoted to the cause of national greatness than before. When General Pietro Badoglio, until late 1919 extraordinary military commissioner of the occupied province of Julian Venetia, had leaflets distributed above the city that prompted the defectors to leave Fiume and return to their units, D'Annunzio reassured his followers:

> The true Italian Army is here, formed by you, fighters without a stain and without fear. Here the army of victory, without the corrupt and the traitors, comes together again, rises again [...] You preserve faith to Fiume and to the true Italy. The fatherland is here.[35]

And in a speech on September 22, 1919, D'Annunzio addressed the Italian troops outside of Fiume on the question of loyalty. Urging them to remain with their units and to protect the borders – since he was not able to accept any more volunteers in Fiume – he explained what discipline and loyalty meant in Fiume:

> The true discipline is not a dry constraining formula, it is not a severe bodily oppression. For the Latin people [...] discipline means recognizing a sovereign will to which all the other wills converge and limit themselves to be more effective and right.[36]

Thus, loyalty to the nation did not depend on the opinion of the military superior anymore but was a matter of individual commitment; it did not derive from explicit laws and rules enforced by coercion but from the implicit decision of every single soldier to follow his national conscience. This highly individualized understanding of loyalty reconnects to the notion of a 'true Italy' by extending it with a very subjective and emotional dimension. Maranini for instance imagined that his peers at home were speaking about him with the same kind of admiration he had felt for the soldiers who were drafted during the war – only "with a livelier and more profound feeling", as he wrote to his fiancée.[37]

As Diaz correctly observed, this "halo of heroism" created by the public performance of national emotions, paired to an individualized understanding of
loyalty, was a powerful resource when it came to recruiting new volunteers. The
head of the 8th Arditi department, Giuseppe Nunziante, drafted a letter to be
distributed on the Italian mainland, admonishing those who had "the feeling of
the Fatherland and love for her" to enrol in Nunziante's unit. Specifically
addressing young men who left for Fiume against the will of their families,[38] the
commander of the Arditi unit promised them that he would be the "real father of
his legionaries whom he loves like himself; he [Nunziante] will receive them in his
beautiful family of 'Black Flames' [i.e. the Arditi; ...] and he will lead them
towards immortal glory".[39] Nunziante's recruiting strategy is obvious: the love
for the fatherland replaces the love for the family and he as the "real father"
replaces the biological one. Nunziante's propaganda of a patriotic emotional
community in Fiume spread successfully in Italy. A recruiting list from Tuscany
from late 1920 names 94 men with an average age between 19 and 20, 46 of
whom were born as recently as 1902.[40] Although probably only a small portion
of these recruits actually reached Fiume, in these adolescents' imagination the
city *embodied* the ideal of a new Italy in very unclear and yet fascinating manner:
in a letter to the representative of Fiume in Tuscany seized by the Italian
authorities, a 20-year-old justified his wish to become a legionnaire by telling
that he finally wanted to "breathe real Italian air".[41]

Since D'Annunzio could not count on the support of either the National
Council or the local civic bureaucracy; his personal authority and the legitimacy
of the whole enterprise relied solely on these public performances of emotional
commitment. Therefore, in his speeches from the balcony of the Governor's
palace, during demonstrations in the streets, and while gathering with the
legionaries, he constantly appealed to his legionaries' patriotic feelings: their
emotional practices were fundamental to the stability of the regime.[42] Orazio
Pedrazzi, the local correspondent of the *Illustrazione italiana*, called Fiume the

> home of the sounds and the songs. Not without reason a poet is in com-
> mand. And while in the old Italy decrees and laws are published on the
> yellowish paper of the official bulletins [...] we learn the laws and decrees
> through sounding proclamations by D'Annunzio [...] which send electric
> shocks through our veins when we read them.[43]

Here, too, Pedrazzi emphasizes the question of true loyalty and strengthens
the difference between the old and the new Italy by describing the daily
speeches as corporeal experiences: decrees and laws were not intelligible
through a rational act of reading and understanding. Rather, the act of reading itself was an experience of the immediate present. Hence, Pedrazzi
described governing and being governed in Fiume as practices directly connected to the body and its sensations.[44] When nationalist poet Sem Benelli
received the citizenship of Fiume in front of a large crowd, Benelli, according
to Pedrazzi, could not hide his emotions any longer:

When the poet, with tears in his eyes, invited the Fiumans to shout 'long live Italy', the theatre was a single cry and a single flag. From every throat came a sobbing cry of love for the homeland [...] all eyes were coated with tears.[45]

Without a doubt, one must read these sources carefully. Pedrazzi, for instance, was initially a member of D'Annunzio's staff, therefore his articles had clearly propagandistic goals. But the description of everyday life in Fiume as a constant festival also appears in sources by critical observers of the events, such as Giuriati.[46] While in many of these accounts military formations stood at the centre of attention, or were at least an important part of the ceremony,[47] in the following I will look at the festival of Saint Sebastian on January 20, 1920. What set this festival apart from swearing-in rituals or military parades was the active role women played during the ceremonies. As usual, the day began with a procession carrying the statue of the saint through the old town and finally up to the church of Saint Vito, the patron saint of Fiume, where a mass was celebrated.[48] But unlike during previous Saint Sebastian festivals after mass a committee of women donated a silver dagger to D'Annunzio as a votive offering. Already three days before the ceremony, the local newspaper reported on this "pugnale votivo" and asked the women of Fiume for contributions: only those who had donated money would find their name on the parchment that would accompany the dagger offered to D'Annunzio.[49]

The spatial arrangement of the participants reveals how strongly the ceremony was intended to stage the patriotic communion between women and men, soldiers and civilians, secular and clerical authorities[50]: The church of Saint Vito was filled with flowers and the bench where D'Annunzio, and next to him the mayor and the president of the National Council sat was decorated with the Fiumean flag. On the benches alongside the altar the women who were about to offer the dagger were positioned. After celebrating mass, military chaplain Reginaldo Giuliani blessed the dagger. When the liturgical part of the ceremony was over, one of the offering women, Anna Farina, held a speech and presented the "blessed dagger, into which are melted, together with our little silver and gold, our souls and hearts" to D'Annunzio. The dagger, in other words, was not a sign of devotion. Instead, it served as a material manifestation of the emotional, and more importantly, corporeal communion between the women and D'Annunzio. "Religiously," Farina continued "with her voice strangled by crying," they were offering the dagger "so that you finally can scratch the word 'victory' in the living flesh of our enemies": the soul and heart of the women were forged into the dagger which then was destined to inflict harm upon other bodies. According to the *Vedetta*, Farina's speech moved even D'Annunzio and when the dagger was finally handed over and he attached it to his belt, a "moment of general emotion [commozione]" ensued. In his response to Farina's speech, D'Annunzio picked up on the stark notion of embodied emotions. In a sermon-like exegesis of Saint Sebastian's martyrium, he imagined the Saint facing the archers who were about to shoot him and saying: "[H]e who hurts me the most loves me the most." Typical for D'Annunzio's adventurous and volatile appropriation of classical subjects, he then described the dagger as forged by the same "pain" and "passion" that once had made the Roman soldier Sebastian long for his own sacrifice: "Immortality of love! Eternity of sacrifice!" But the coherence of D'Annunzio's speech is not the decisive point here. Rather, the ceremony must be understood as a public performance of patriotic love and passion aimed at guaranteeing stability among the various parts of the population present in the church of San Vito. The central object of this ceremony, the silver dagger, was not only symbolically created out of the bodies of its female donators – it was intended to use the incorporation of patriotic love, achieved by the women's donations, to damage those who did not belong to the emotional community of San Vito.

Etienne François et al. have identified three constitutive aspects for emotionally compelling festivities that aim at constructing a sense of national unity, thus counterbalancing potential differences in terms of class, age, etc.[51] The first is the concrete reality of the person or event that is collectively remembered and/or celebrated – in our case, the poet Sem Benelli or the donation of the dagger. Second, a remote shared past is invoked and at the same time directly connected to current events, for instance in referencing the Risorgimento or, in the case of the festival of Saint Sebastian, the figure of a Roman-Christian martyr who allegorically embodies the "holocaust" of patriotic love and fervour in Fiume. Third, common aims and values are emphasized which are emotionally compelling, exciting and worth imitating and create a sense of belonging – such as unity, the will to sacrifice oneself, the love for the fatherland and the collective desire of annexation to Italy.

And yet, the fundamental precondition for this kind of emotional engagement with the world was hostile emotions towards the 'non-Italian' part of Fiume's population. Constructing the emotional community of the new Italy always meant forcing a monolithic emotional framework upon an ethnically multi-faceted city. This showed already in the way the legionaries imagined the emotional topography of the city. To them, Sušak, a city at Fiume's Eastern border with a predominantly Croatian-speaking population, was not only separated from Fiume by a small river but by a different way of feeling: "Here [in Fiume], one spoke, thought, and loved in an Italian way; there [in Sušak] everything was done in Croatian," as Riccardo Frassetto remembered.[52] Despite the fact that both cities were culturally and economically closely bound together, the bridge to Sušak had become an insurmountable emotional border: even though he actually had never been there, Maranini wrote that it was "really a completely different city. [...] And to think that there are not more than three meters of water from Fiume to Sušak. But there is the old hatred".[53] Eventually it was the combination of these two elements that led to an erosion of the Fiumean emotional community: on the one hand, emotional practices became a means of individualized self-empowerment, thereby undermining the very notion of emotional community time and again emphasized by D'Annunzio. On the other hand, they increasingly relied upon the hatred and exclusion of the 'other'. To develop this argument, I will take a closer look at the legionaries and then ask how the experience of living in Fiume shaped their emotional mindset.

Crazy lovers of the fatherland: self-mobilization and the reshaping of the legionaries' emotions

There is no completely reliable data, but following the estimations of Luigi Emilio Longo, one may assess the total number of soldiers and veterans who arrived with D'Annunzio in September 1919 to be around 1,700.[54] During the good fifteen months of the occupation, another 4,200 to 4,700 men – both defected soldiers and volunteers who had not been enrolled in the Italian army before – joined the occupation forces, although many of them left after a brief time. In December 1920, around 3,600 soldiers were still in Fiume, while another 500 had occupied the islands of Krk, Rab and Sveti Marko, facing the attacks of the regular Italian army. Two statistical facts concerning the generational and hierarchical composition of the legionaries are particularly interesting. First, the average age of the enlisted men and the volunteers was overall around 23 and 24 years, while the average officer in Fiume was around 26 years old.[55] Yet, the special forces (Arditi and Bersaglieri) were on average born around 1900 and therefore almost three years younger than the rest of the legionaries. Second, the number of young non-commissioned officers in Fiume was unusually high. Apparently this imbalance was a consequence of widespread and uncontrolled nepotism among the various units.[56] To sum up, one can say that during the *impresa* the small city of Fiume with its 50,000 inhabitants witnessed an invasion of young men – eventually, they made up more than 10 per cent of the overall population – in the final phase of their adolescence, who had either just returned from the war, belonged mostly to the lower ranks of the military, were recently promoted, or had not participated in the war at all. Nonetheless, they were infected by the thought of a 'mutilated victory'.[57]

The ideal of youth

Against this background it becomes clear why the discourse on youth and the nation, already central for understanding the cultural history of Italy's unification,[58] developed such a mobilizing power in Fiume and therefore was constantly evoked to create coherence among the legionaries. Taking up the question of loyalty to the true nation, D'Annunzio explained his idea of youth as follows: "And today, the victorious soldier is the true conscience of the free nation. And he is not only the conscience of the nation: he is the youth that creates the nation."[59] Hence, the idea of youth had a circular structure, since the nation was shaped by its youthfulness and at the same time the young men in Fiume had the power to create this nation in the first place, as Filippo Tommaso Marinetti explained in front of 300 Arditi: "I am a Futurist, that is, a patriotic revolutionary. [...] Our futurist revolutionary ideal adores Italy so much that it wants to make it young at every cost."[60] And on the day the National Council transferred its powers to D'Annunzio, he addressed the troops: "The ideal youth of Italy cannot have but your face and your gaze. 'Youth' was the motto during the most beautiful Hellenic battle, at Mycale. 'Youth' is the motto of the most beautiful Italian enterprise, at Fiume."[61]

But the power of youthful nationalism was not just a rhetorical figure paradoxically quoted by the leaders of the occupation – in 1919, D'Annunzio was 57 years old – apparently, it was felt among the soldiers as well. Looking back at his time in Fiume, writer Giovanni Comisso stated in his memoirs that his "youth was at its maximum".[62] Being young in Fiume hence did not only mean being a certain age but rather acquiring a certain habitus of youthfulness. Not by chance the signature song of the Arditi was called *Giovinezza* ("Youth").[63] And a few days after the volunteers had entered Fiume, General Badoglio sent a telegram to Prime Minister Nitti and pointed out that "a kind of fever has invaded everyone, especially the young elements who are now the large majority in the Army".[64] The collective habitus of youthfulness was perceived as the very opposite of the old Italy, represented by the government in Rome, by the bureaucrats who unsuccessfully tried to find a diplomatic solution to the question of Fiume, by the world of finance and industry: "These people bury the heroism like an intolerable carrion. And they hide the burial beneath the enormous bureaucratic tar, beneath the pile of promissory notes, bank stocks, market reports."[65]

In sum, Fiume's attraction consisted in the promise that youth was the only prerequisite for displaying one's love for the fatherland. And yet, although D'Annunzio emphasized the habit of youthfulness as the foundation for a true nationalism he underestimated its momentum, since it ultimately led to the constitution of a new emotionally charged subjectivity. Just like in Germany in the aftermath of the war, in Fiume "a space suddenly opened up to unprecedented emotional, physical and verbal acts"[66] which from late 1919 onwards led to an erosion of consensus. Before showing how this reshaping of the emotional subject took place, a brief look back on the war experience is necessary.

The subjective monopolization of national emotions

The emotional and sensorial overload of modern trench warfare has often been described.[67] What distinguished many Italian soldiers' war experiences from those of other armies was that for many of them being drafted was the first contact they had had with the modern state apparatus. Given the illiteracy rates in Italy, the perseverance of local identities, and the shortcomings of inner nation-building before 1915, the war was a giant process of national acculturation.[68] Apart from its administrative side it caused a shift of perceptions, both collectively and individually. Serving as chaplain in the Italian Army, Franciscan friar and psychologist Agostino Gemelli keenly observed the "continuous transformation" of the soldiers' states of mind during the war:

> The psychic physiognomy of the soldier is not something immutable and fixed, because it is not immutable and depends on the life he leads. The war [...] transforms its methods, slowly but continuously, so that the conditions of life of those who fight it change, the stimuli that arouse psychic reactions change.[69]

In his analysis of the Italian war experience, Antonio Gibelli has shown that this transformation must be understood as a rearrangement of the relationship between nation and emotion: in the army, soldiers were exposed to an unknown apparatus of social control and discipline. Overwhelmed by the sensorially induced intensity of fear, anger and sadness, evoking patriotic concepts proved to be an effective coping mechanism for the emotional stress in combat. Or, psychologically speaking, they attributed every kind of arousal to a national emotion.[70] Nationalizing emotions meant giving sense to otherwise incomprehensible events. Therefore, the trench experience deeply inscribed the nexus between nation and emotion into the soldiers' psyche: experiencing emotions and interpreting them in a patriotic framework became a technique of self-control in the face of immediate danger.[71]

The continuity of the same mechanism can be observed in Fiume. When experiencing negative emotions, such as fear, sadness, anxiety or homesickness, one could make sense of them by interpreting them as national. The practice emerges in a letter of Maranini from October 2, 1919. First, he almost dutifully mentions the wildness in the streets, the shouting and the parades. But then he describes his "anxiety" fuelled by the insecurity of the situation and the lack of information, his own and his comrades' homesickness. Finally, technically addressing his fiancée, but in reality speaking to himself, he states: "But let us not be taken away by sadness. Here, one must be joyful and strong."[72] In other words, Maranini knew that in order to belong to Fiume he *had* to feel a particular way; he wrote that he "must" feel patriotic joy. Thus, feeling and performing enthusiasm were an essential part of the "emotional style"[73] expected from him. Already earlier, he had reflected upon the transformative power of the uniform that "crushes and oppresses. Until yesterday, I was a free citizen. I could think and act. Now my movements are automatic and respond to the will of others. I have the impression of not being able to think anymore".[74] Reading these letters, one may conclude that the rhetoric of a true Italy based on the youthful and anti-intellectual expression of patriotism, unrestrained by the rules and laws of the bourgeois society, was in fact successful. Or, as Carli wrote in the futurist newspaper *Testa di ferro* ("iron head"):

Our boys have strong muscles and firm hearts – sweet lips and caressing eyes – terrible in anger. They are the crazy lovers of the fatherland [...] For this love they will leap on the barricade, shirtless and with bombs and daggers to sweep the decay that pollutes the air and suffocates the flowering of the wonderful virtues of a people. Love them – women of Fiume – in the name of their mothers and their distant sisters.[75]

And yet, the relation between this kind of heroic statement and daily life in Fiume is far more complicated. On the one hand, the legionaries were encouraged to be "crazy lovers of the fatherland". On the other hand, from late 1919 onwards precisely this emotional reshaping of the patriotic subject led to unintended consequences and, eventually, undermined the cohesion of the emotional community in Fiume. After some men of the 8th Arditi unit under Giuseppe Nunziante once more had not followed their orders, general Ceccherini described them as a "sample of the most disparate elements, for political view, courage of spirit, disciplinary spirit" who had "their own special psychology". Although this psychology, according to Ceccherini, was based on "unparalleled patriotic sentiment and an exuberant generosity", the Arditi demonstrated a "deviation of the disciplinary sense" since they believed that "the assumed position of 'voluntary' confers special rights of emancipation from the normal disciplinary rules and that an easy contamination of the forms is lawful and better suited to the attitude of the 'voluntary' legionnaire".[76] Time and again, the commanders urged the soldiers to maintain military discipline and not to give in to their emotions. When the news spread on June 10, 1920 that a group of Arditi in Trieste tried to reach Fiume instead of embarking on a ship to Albania, spontaneous demonstrations and declarations of solidarity among the legionaries ensued. In reaction, generals Ceccherini and Tamajo issued an angry order to the division and stressed that the very oath to D'Annunzio came with the duty of acting disciplined.[77] And at the end of May 1920, a group of legionaries spontaneously invaded Fiume's twin town, Sušak. Again, the generals reacted with an irritated order of the day and complained about the soldiers' "grotesque, absurd claim to monopolize the patriotic impulse, which is not the privilege of those who have the loudest voice and stage the most clamorous noises". Instead, they emphasized that the expression of patriotism was the "common spiritual patrimony of the whole Legion". Therefore, these kind of patriotic "manifestations, from the most composed to the most explosive, must be regulated and dosed according to the criteria of choice and form, dictated by him [that is, D'Annunzio]".[78] Even the once successful festivals of patriotism now backfired. For instance, the great commemoration of D'Annunzio's famous flight over Vienna on August 9, 1920 took place in "exceptional disorder and notable confusion" and completely failed to demonstrate discipline, military education, and cohesion of the Fiumean division[79]: the subjective monopolization of patriotic emotions endangered the delicate balance of Fiume's emotional community which was based exactly on this kind of performative declarations of consent.[80]

How dysfunctional the very idea of a true Italy had become was demonstrated once more when the modus vivendi failed in late 1919. After the agreement between Fiume and Rome had become public, a group of "scalmanati [hotheads], excited by passion which did not represent but a negligible minority of the population" – as Giuriati, D'Annunzio's chief of staff at the time, remembered – gathered in front of the governor's palace and made D'Annunzio announce a referendum to finally decide on the acceptance of the agreement. Although a large majority voted for acceptance, the legionaries interfered as much as possible during the elections. By protesting under D'Annunzio's window, a group of legionaries made him change his mind one more time[81]: because he was practically blind he was forced to rely on what he imagined as the will of the crowd in front of his palace.[82] The socialist newspaper *Avanti* later wrote that not even in Central Africa elections were so irregular and fraudulous.[83] D'Annunzio failed to recognize the discrepancy between what he imagined as a manifestation of the true Italy and the situation on the ground. Around Christmas 1919, an intelligence officer of the Italian navy reported from Fiume that after the failure of the modus vivendi three quarters of the population were ready to go out and demonstrate against the occupation: "The population of Fiume today lives in a state of nervousness and huge agitation and is almost unable to bear the situation [...] any longer."[84] Another report by an Italian colonel identified the same kind of emotional exhaustion on the part of the locals: "Assaulted by material difficulties" – above all the rapid inflation, food shortages and bad hygienic conditions – "the Italians have returned to their daily routine, after some ten days of intense life, of emotions [...], of demonstrations".[85] Finally, a report for the Italian government from mid-November 1920 established a general "apathy" among the population and described how during a military ceremony the members of a brigade refused to respond when D'Annunzio asked them to renew their pledge of allegiance. Only some legionaries and women who were not part of the honoured unit responded. And when D'Annunzio came back from the decisive negotiations and had once more refused any compromise, only a small crowd awaited him at the port.[86] Still, D'Annunzio continued to believe in the emotional appeal of his speeches and in his ability to mobilize Fiume's entire population. In May 1920, he mentioned the blatantly exaggerated number of 30,000 people "in front of the balcony" to his new chief of staff, De Ambris, and stated: "I have got the people in my hands and the legionaries never have loved me more."[87]

In fact, quite the contrary happened. While most of the population by the end of 1919 experienced apathy and exhaustion, a minority of intransigent legionaries developed a colonial mentality and behaviour towards the Fiumeans, legitimized by the very idea of a true Italian's emotional superiority. The same commanders who had encouraged this emotional style now were unable to maintain discipline and cohesion among the troops.[88] When travelling by tram, the legionaries acted cheekily and arrogantly; they roamed around the suburbs of Fiume, looting civilian homes and devastating vineyards in search of food.

Again and again, the military authorities made futile attempts to end these incidents: "We are not a corps of occupation in a conquered country; but rather a nucleus of brothers who spontaneously made themselves virtual citizens of Fiume, and we are here, only and exclusively, to do good to them."[89] A criminal incident that took place in the final phase of the occupation illustrates that the opposite was true. Based on various interrogation protocols, the events can be reconstructed as follows.[90] On the evening of October 6, 1920, a group of Arditi and a civilian named Paolo Vertossa, born near Naples and then a resident of Fiume, went to the home of local police officer Erminio Topolsek, after some heavy drinking in a pub. Pretending to be members of the police, they entered his home and tried to arrest him for anti-Italian statements, supposedly on direct orders from D'Annunzio. Topolsek immediately became suspicious, pulled out his gun and tried to force the intruders to leave him and his family alone. The Arditi threatened to use hand grenades, overwhelmed him with brute force,[91] and stole the money he kept at home. While the alleged anti-Italian agitator followed the Arditi outside, his wife managed to send one of her seven children for help. In the meantime, a single Ardito remained with Topolsek's wife and sexually assaulted her while the others escorted Topolsek. When the police arrived to arrest the Arditi, Vertossa responded:

> "What, do you want to kill us? We are true Italians, you are not Italians. [...] I am not scared not even of 100 Fiumans, not even of all Fiumans, you other people are not Italians, I am an Ardito and I am part of the underworld."

Two different things are apparent in this briefly described episode. First, there is a rather prosaic dimension to it since Vertossa was a notorious criminal and had already been under investigation by Topolsek, hence he had an obvious motive for revenge.[92] But, second, the incident is emblematic of the practice of emotional self-empowerment. Vertossa and his friends among the Arditi referred to the 'cause' and the defence of the city's Italian-ness as a pretext for violence against members of what they believed was the Croatian population. To them, the fact that someone reacted unfavourably to the occupation and/or was not Italian, seemed a valuable argument to legitimize violence and pursue personal interests. By claiming to be a member of D'Annunzio's assault troops, Vertossa believed himself to have acquired a certain authority and the power to distinguish between members of the true Italian nation and those who did not belong to it: already, earlier the same evening, the accused had tried to incriminate another man at the pub for allegedly saying: "What do you think that this is Italy, [cursing in Croatian], this is not Italy." In addition, when the brother of the above-mentioned Topolsek arrived at the scene of the crime later that night, Vertossa shouted immediately: "This is a Yugoslav as well!"[93]

What the group of violent young men did may be best described as a practice of emotionally charged othering.[94] Through their words, actions and aggressive behaviour they constructed the abstract entity of a "Yugoslav" population, conceived as emotionally different from and inferior to the Italian occupants: Vertossa shouted explicitly that he, being an Italian, was "not scared" of the local police. Perceiving the police officer and his wife to be part of this potentially hostile "Yugoslav" population made it easier for the Arditi to become violent, since they did not have to engage with the emotions of their victims, especially their fear. Vertossa could ascribe certain features associated with inferiority to the "Croatians" and thereby overwrite the complicated differentiations between Fiume's various and overlapping ethnic communities with an imagined emotional community of true Italians. But even on an administrative level this emotionally charged practice of othering had repercussions. Already on October 16, 1919, D'Annunzio had issued a decree and defined Fiume as a fortress in times of war and ordered the severe prosecution of espionage. Thus, everyone who expressed "hostile feelings against the cause" should be considered an enemy and might face the death penalty.[95]

Look at our chests: emotions and bodily affects

Finally, the deep rupture between the initial and later phase of the occupation caused by the emotional reshaping of the legionaries was reflected in the way they presented their bodies: many started adapting and sometimes exaggerating the clothing style of the Arditi, who were known for their slightly different and less formal uniforms. Even some officers unbuttoned their jackets, put on colourful pants and stopped wearing ties. The soldiers walked around in "baby shirts with collars of excessive size, turned upside down, and with bare chests"; some left their hats at home and stopped saluting their superiors. In short, everyone appeared to be "infected by a whim of originality", as the generals noted indignantly when they reminded their men that a uniform was not just a garment but a symbol of the "national flag which does not bear deformations".[96] Interestingly, this particular association of the body and the nation and Fiume already can be traced back to the months before the Impresa had begun. In his memoirs, D'Annunzio's first chief of staff Giovanni Giuriati remembers the lyrics of a song common among the infantry in Fiume: "If you do not know us / look at our chests: we are deserters, / but not of Caporetto."[97] The song quoted by Giuriati has a semantic layer that goes well beyond the above explained rhetoric of Fiume as a patriotic mutiny: it reverses the meaning of being a defector by explicitly referring to the body, and, more specifically, to the chest. Initially, this reference seems obvious since the chest is usually the part of the uniform to which military decorations are attached. But after 1919, in Fiume the chest was particularly associated with national emotions: after the war had ended, many pro-Italian inhabitants showed their political sympathy for Italy by pinning a ribbon in the colours of the Italian flag and with the slogan "Italy or death" to their jackets. And while the allied powers from November 1918 onwards were fighting a "cold war" to assert their economic and strategic interests in the port city,[98] this geopolitical tension found immediate expression in an endless series of everyday conflicts between supporters and opponents of Fiume's annexation to Italy. One of the most common causes for these quarrels was in fact patriotic ribbons and cockades worn by pro-Italian civilians. For instance, in mid-July 1919, a 50-year-old woman reported to the police that some weeks earlier she had encountered a group of French soldiers of the interallied occupation forces who had just left a restaurant. When the soldiers saw that she was wearing the Italian tricolor and the slogan "Italy or death" they started to provoke her by cheering "Long live France," to which the woman responded with "Long live Italy." The situation escalated when the French soldiers started to swear against Italy and finally one of them opened his pants, showed his genitals to the woman, and shouted: "This is for Italy."[99] Previously, in mid-May, a French soldier had approached a 12-year-old girl wearing the same pin and the slogan "Italia o morte" and asked her: "Why are you wearing this ribbon, you are already dying," whereupon the girl replied: "If I die you will die too."[100] Finally, at the beginning of July, two French soldiers attacked two teenage sisters in the old town because they were wearing patriotic ribbons, and tried to rip them off. Only when some civilians intervened did they let the girls go; and not without insulting and spitting on one of them first.[101]

These incidents show how more than just tense the situation between the Italian-speaking population and the French soldiers was during the period of the interallied occupation. First, they reveal a close link between the individual body and the expression of one's national emotions. By wearing a ribbon and defending it verbally, these women were an "expression of the eternal Italian feminine that makes the fatherland their supreme religion", as the *Illustrazione Italiana* observed: "[A]dorned with their cockades and with the ribbons of the Italian ships on the hat", they "reaffirm the Italianness of Fiume".[102] But second, and most importantly, they highlight the agency of women in trying to assert Fiume's *italianità*: in the first incident described above, the woman was by no means a passive victim, instead of just enduring the provocations she actively responded to them; in the second case, the girl reacted with a mixture of naivety and cleverness to the harassment of the soldier. As seen above in the case of the votive dagger, women were not just spectators but participated actively in emotional practices of nationalism. The decisive point here is that their emotional agency up to some point questioned traditional notions of masculinity, therefore undermining even more the institutional framework and the discipline military leaders like Ceccherini and Tamajo referred to in their daily orders. The *Testa di ferro* in late August 1920 published an article by a certain woman named "Fiammetta" (flame). Although it is not clear who the author is, she loudly voiced a self-empowering form of femininity and mobilized other women against the traditional emotional expression of female patriotism – "[e]xpression organizes the experience", as Scheer has put it.[103] The article read:

> I state that I am not a 'sister of the legionaries'. I am, simply, the lover of an Ardito who is in Fiume. I am young. I smoke a lot of cigarettes. I do not care about the crusade against luxury, and I wear silk petticoats and

thread stockings. And I pay for them. With everyday work. [...] I use the 'Fiumean' perfume from Carlo Erba. I dress elegantly. I love everything that is beautiful. So first, I love the love. Then myself. Then the fatherland. I've been with many men. I confess it without blushing.[104]

Fiammetta's self-description clearly has nothing to do with the notion of a passive, sweet and protective patriotism combined with a high tolerance for suffering. Instead, it symbolizes a mobilized female body that does not care about bourgeois conventions, dress codes or generally any kind of role-specific behaviour; it is an imagined body that represents an extremely subjective and sexually charged emotionality ("I love the love"). And yet, "Fiammetta" attributes all these qualities to Fiume – she is wearing a "Fiumean" perfume and has fallen in love with a nameless Ardito, the most emblematic symbol of Fiume of all.

The habitus of the woman imagined in this article clearly had nothing in common with the devotional, almost submissive emotional style performed by the women who gave D'Annunzio the votive dagger. Their self-mobilization was noted also by the Italian informants who observed Fiume. When reporting on a troop transfer, the "usual women and Arditi" – in this order – were named as the ones who most strongly tried to interfere.[105]

Conclusion

"Every face is peaceful, they smile from an intimate and profound sweetness. Our hearts beat together with the flags that blow gently in the light maritime breeze, full of an ineffable emotion."[106] The contrast between Gino Berri's portrayal of the initial phase of the enterprise and the last months of the occupation could not be clearer. In the second half of 1919, patriotic emotions successfully created a sense of belonging among the newly arrived legionaries and the local population. Performing one's love for the fatherland by wearing patriotic ribbons, cheering the arriving Italian soldiers, and celebrating the newly gained *italianità* were all emotional practices that helped in establishing a cohesive emotional community in Fiume. For the legionaries who either volunteered or deserted from the army the small port city in the Adriatic promised to be the place where just by being and acting youthful they were welcomed as liberators and national heroes. In other words, a legionary could do anything he wanted with his emotions and affected body – always, it was going to be interpreted as a performance of patriotism. In late 1919, though, the modus vivendi and the imagined emotional community of Fiume slowly fell apart. The very emotional practices that once promoted cooperation and were the pillars of the 'true Italy' now led to conflicts. The reason for this was that the leading figures of the enterprise had believed in the stability of a top-down mobilization. Thereby, they fundamentally underestimated the potential that lay within the subjective, bottom-up appropriation of emotional practices by the legionaries themselves: the emotional reshaping of the legionaries resulted in countless acts of indiscipline, violence and, more generally, a colonial mentality that stemmed from the idea of emotional superiority over the non-Italian population. Strikingly, the self-mobilization was not limited to the male section of the legionaries but partially led also to the constitution of a new female subjectivity. Just like the prototypical male legionary, some women developed a new emotional style that relied upon the display of being bodily affected by (patriotic) emotions. But, during the Regency's military failure on "Bloody Christmas" 1920 (when despite D'Annunzio's continuous call for patriotic sacrifice no real resistance on the part of the legionaries followed)[107], it became obvious that not one, but hundreds of emotional sub-communities existed, each of them working against one another.

The question whether the march on Fiume was a precursor to the march on Rome three years later has created an intense debate and cannot be answered in this chapter.[108] Still, what appears from this analysis of emotional practices in everyday Fiume is that unlike D'Annunzio, Mussolini successfully balanced the tension between emotional self-mobilization and disciplinary control – not least because he had the failed example of Fiume right before his eyes.

Notes

1 On the Arditi see Salvante, 'Arditi'; Cordova, *Arditi*; Rochat, *Gli arditi*.
2 Quoted in Carli, *Con D'Annunzio*, pp. 45–46. All translations by the author.
3 D'Annunzio as well picked up on the notion of the liver. In a speech written for his campaign in support of Fiume's annexation, he begins as follows: "I have come to feel your pulse beating, to hear the sound of your hearts, to feel what your liver does" (D'Annunzio, *La penultima ventura*, p. 83).
4 Rosenwein, *Generations*, p. 3.
5 Gumbrecht, *Diesseits der Hermeneutik*.
6 Antonsich, 'Searching for belonging'.
7 See Scheer, 'Are emotions a kind of practice', p. 220.
8 Salaris, *Alla festa della rivoluzione*.
9 See Bartov and Weitz, *Shatterzone*.
10 Stelli, *Storia di Fiume*; Fried, *Fiume*.
11 Longo, *L'esercito italiano*, p. 9.
12 See on Fiume generally Ercolani, *Da Fiume a Rijeka*; then D'Annunzio, *La penultima ventura*, p. XXXVI; Ledeen, *D'Annunzio*, p. 37.
13 The sample is based on a total of 129 enrolment files: *Archivio del Vittoriale, Archivio Fiumano (AF)*, Militare, c. 178, 186/1, 186/2.
14 See for example the case in *State Archive of Rijeka (SAR)*, DAR 53, Nr. 154: 1983/1919.
15 Gibelli, 'Italy'; Rochat, 'The Italian Front'; Rochat and Massobrio, *Breve storia*.
16 'Vittoria nostra, non sarai mutilata', in: *Corriere della sera*, 24.10.1918.
17 See Lunzer, 'Making Sense'; Melchionni, *La vittoria mutilata*.
18 See generally Pupo and Todero, *Fiume*; De Felice, *D'Annunzio*, pp. 3–104; Ledeen, *D'Annunzio*.
19 Serventi Longhi, *Alceste De Ambris*; De Felice, *Sindacalismo rivoluzionario*.
20 Parlato, *Mezzo secolo di Fiume*, pp. 45–141.
21 *L'Illustrazione Italiana*, 29.12.1918.

22 See for example *La Nazione*, 1.11.1918; *La Tribuna*, 16.9.1919; *Il secolo illustrato*, 1.10.1919.
23 Canziani, *A Fiume*, p. 38. In Italy, 'olocausto' was part of the educated classes' vocabulary. Even before the First World War the term was used in the sense of 'sacrifice'. From 1918 onwards, it became associated with the claims of irredentism. D'Annunzio's article 'Italy's Pentecost' (*Il Giornale di Venezia*, 8.6. 1919) read: "Thus Fiume today appears to be the only living city, the only burning city, the only city of soul, all breath and fire, all pain and fury, all purification and consumption: a holocaust, the most beautiful holocaust that has ever been offered for centuries on an insensible altar. Indeed, the right name of the city is not Fiume but Olocausta: perfectly and entirely consumed by the fire." And a headline in the Arditi's newspaper from 1920 read: "From the Olocausta we expect the regenerating spark" (*L'Ardito. Giornale dell'arditismo*, 11.4.1920). See also Afflerbach, 'vani e terribili olocausti'.
24 Klimó and Rolf, 'Rausch und Diktatur', p. 21; Scheer, *Emotions*, pp. 214–215.
25 *Archivio centrale dello Stato (ACS)*, Mostra della rivoluzione fascista, b. 117, f. 19, Letter of Florio Federico to his mother, 16.9.1919.
26 Maranini, *Lettere*, p. 49.
27 Maranini, *Lettere*, p. 42
28 Maranini, *Lettere*, pp. 95–96.
29 Langewiesche, 'Gefühlsraum Nation'.
30 For another example see the account of Botti, *Natale di Sangue*, pp. 71–72: "The volunteers crossed Piazza Dante in their entire war outfit, [...] The Fiumeans watched them with admiration and from their eyelashes came tears of intimate and frank emotion."
31 Scheer, *Emotions*, p. 194.
32 Rochat, *L'esercito italiano*, pp. 5–113.
33 *ACS*, PCM, Guerra Europea, b. 161, f. 19.15.7/1 (1921), Diaz to Presidenza del consiglio dei ministri (PCM), 21.11.1918.
34 Wilcox, *Morale and the Italian Army*, pp. 65–84; Guerrini, 'Obbligare e punire'.
35 D'Annunzio, *La penultima ventura*, p. 128.
36 D'Annunzio, *La penultima ventura*, p. 135.
37 Maranini, *Lettere*, p. 118.
38 *ACS*, MdI, DGPS, Agitazione pro Fiume e Dalmazia, b. 4, f. 18/2, Questura di Roma to Procura del Re, 17.9.1920.
39 *AF*, Corrispondenza fiumana 3666, d. 73, Nunziante, Draft of a leaflet, mid-August 1920.
40 *ACS* MdI, DGPS, Agitazione pro Fiume e Dalmazia, b. 6, f. 42, List of volunteers, November 1920 (?).
41 *ACS*, MdI, DGPS, Agitazione pro Fiume e Dalmazia, b. 6, f. 42, Letter to Umberto Calosci, 3.11.1920.
42 See generally Skradol, 'Carnival of Exception'; Jesné, 'Fiume/Rijeka 1919'; Mosse, *Masses and Man*, pp. 87–103; D'Annunzio's speeches can be found in *La penultima ventura*. For an account of D'Annunzios rhetoric see Kochnitzky, *La Quinta stagione*, pp. 85–86.
43 *L'Illustrazione Italiana*, 19.10.1919.
44 For the same argument in the context of the German workers' movement in the Weimar Republic see Warstat, *Theatrale Gemeinschaften*.
45 *L'Illustrazione Italiana*, 19.10.1919.
46 Giuriati mentions a 'frenzy of passion' ('*delirio di passione*') during D'Annunzio's arrival in town (Giuriati, *Con D'Annunzio*, p. 21).
47 See for instance the mass celebrated in honour of the Italian sailors killed in Split (*SAR*, Z2, Nr. 18/19, f. 4, Ordine di presidio, 13.7.1920).
48 Gerra, *L'impresa*, pp. 237, I.

49 *Vedetta d'Italia*, 17.1.1920; 18.1.1920.
50 For the following *Vedetta d'Italia*, 21.1.1920.
51 François, Siegrist and Vogel, 'Die Nation', pp. 26–27.
52 Frassetto, *I desertori di Ronchi*. Frassetto was one of the initiators of the march on Fiume, the so-called 'sworn-ins [*giurati*] of Ronchi'.
53 Maranini, *Lettere*, p. 65.
54 For the numbers see Longo, *L'esercito italiano*, especially pp. 568–570 as well as the complete list of legionaries in N.N., 'Elenco ufficiale'.
55 The following refers to a calculation by the author, based on N.N., 'Elenco ufficiale' (N=7,161). Still, the exact numbers are hard to determine. In late 1919, the Italian Army estimated a total of 1,086 officers and 8,160 enlisted men. On August 31, 1920, the commanders named a total of 4,463 men (*ACS*, PCM Guerra Europea, f. 19.15.7/1 (1921); Ordine di divisione Nr. 354, 31.8.1920, *SAR*, Z2 18/19 f. 4, Badoglio to PCM, 6.12.1919).
56 *SAR*, Z 2 Nr. 18/19, f. 4, Ordine di divisione Nr. 247, 17.5.1920.
57 See Gibelli, *Il popolo bambino*, p. 179.
58 Riall, *Risorgimento*; Griffin, *The Nature of Fascism*, pp. 38–39; for the fascist period see Ledeen, 'Italian Fascism'.
59 D'Annunzio, *La penultima ventura*, p. 136.
60 Filippo Tommaso Marinetti, *Discorso improvvisato da Marinetti a Riese a 300 ufficiali Arditi (ottobre 1918)*, quoted in Cordova, *Arditi*, pp. 245–248, here p. 245.
61 D'Annunzio, *La penultima ventura*, p. 131.
62 Comisso, *Le mie stagioni*, p. 1123.
63 Salvante, 'Arditi'.
64 Badoglio, *Rivelazioni*, p. 172.
65 D'Annunzio, *La penultima ventura*, p. 85.
66 Föllmer, 'The unscripted revolution', p. 189.
67 Volmar, 'In storms of steel'; Encke, *Augenblicke der Gefahr*; Gibelli, *L'officina*, pp. 164–209.
68 Gibelli, *La Grande Guerra*; Lanaro, 'Da contadini a italiani'.
69 Gemelli, *Il nostro Soldato*, p. 6.
70 Aronson, Wilson and Akert, *Social Psychology*, p. 113.
71 Gibelli, *L'officina*, pp. 101–102.
72 Maranini, *Lettere*, p. 70. Homesickness and a lack of commitment on part of the legionaries were a major problem especially in the later phases of the occupation, when it proved to be difficult to keep the legionaries attached to their units (*AF*, Corrispondenza fiumana 3666, d. 47, Nunziante to D'Anunnzio, 14.6.1919). The homesickness often paired with boredom and a general feeling of delusion, due to the scarcity of food and the overall deteriorating material conditions in Fiume. A letter from Canziani in May 1920 read: "It is not that fantastic cave of pirate, the hiding place of bandits and assassins, it is that boring and annoyed Fiume I was talking about" (Canziani, *A Fiume*, p. 64).
73 Scheer, *Emotions*, pp. 216–217.
74 Maranini, *Lettere*, p. 42.
75 *Testa di Ferro*, 26.2.1920.
76 *AF*, Corrispondenza fiumana 3666, d. 66–67, Ceccherini to Nunziante, 4.8.1920.
77 *SAR*, Z2, Nr. 18/19, f. 4, Ordine di divisione 280, 18.6.1920.
78 *SAR*, Z2, Nr. 18/19, f. 4, Ordine di divisione, undated [end of May 1920].
79 *SAR*, Z2, Nr. 18/19, f. 4, Ordine di divisione Nr. 335, 12.8.1920.
80 De Felice, *D'Annunzio*, p. 57.
81 Giuriati, *Con D'Annunzio*, pp. 113–116.
82 *L'Idea nazionale*, 28.12.1919.
83 *Avanti*, 25.12.1919.

84   *ACS*, PCM Guerra Europea, b. 161, f. 19.15.7/1 (1921), Report by Denti, 22.12.1919.
85   *ACS*, PCM, Guerra Europea, b. 161, f. 19.15.7/1 (1921), Vigevano to Supreme Command, 4.12.1919.
86   *ACS*, PCM Guerra Europea, b. 161, f. 19.15.7/(1920–22), Notiziario fiumano, 16.11.1920.
87   *ACS*, Alceste De Ambris, b. 4, f. 1, D'Annunzio to De Ambris, 30.5.1920.
88   *AF*, Corrispondenza fiumana 3666, d. 80–82, Memorandum by Nunziante, 17.9.1920.
89   *SAR*, Z2, Nr. 18/19, f. 4, Ordine di divisione Nr. 294, 2.7.1920. Further examples of colonial behaviour: Ordine di divisione Nr. 286, 24.6.1920; Nr. 336, 13.8.1920; Nr. 347, 24.8.1920; Nr. 351, 28.8.1920, ibid.; see also *AF*, Corrispondenza fiumana 1811, d. 5,6 for the complaining letters to D'Annunzio (6.1.1920, 7.1.1920).
90   For the following, see *SAR*, Regia Questura di Fiume, Protocollo, 8.10.1920.
91   See *SAR*, Regia Questura di Fiume, medical record.
92   This interpretation is strengthened by the fact that already at Easter 1920, Vertossa had accused Topolsek of insulting Italy and being dangerous to the "cause", apparently trying to malign him. This interpretation was later adopted by the authorities of Fiume who arrested the intruders and charged them with armed robbery.
93   Nr. 1041/1920: Verbale, Questura di Fiume; *SAR*, JU-26 158.
94   Said, *Orientalism*.
95   See Giuriati, *Con D'Annunzio*, p. 50; Jesné, 'Fiume/Rijeka 1919', pp. 92–94.
96   *SAR*, Z2, Nr. 18/19, f.4, Ordine di divisione Nr. 317, 25.7.1920.
97   Giuriati, *Con D'Annunzio*, p. 34. The battle of Caporetto in 1917 had resulted in a terrible defeat of the Italian army against the Austrian and German troops, thereby almost putting an end to the Italian war campaign. Although it was caused by poor strategic planning on behalf of the army leaders, the nationalist myth had it that a mass mutiny had caused the defeat.
98   Ledeen, *D'Annunzio*, pp. 31–35; Alatri, *Nitti*, pp. 46–59.
99   *SAR*, JU-DARI 1108 1918–1924, Questura di Fiume, Verbale, 18.7.1919.
100   *SAR*, JU-DARI 1108 1918–1924, Questura di Fiume, Verbale, 11.7.1919.
101   *SAR*, JU-DARI 1108 1918–1924, Questura di Fiume, Verbale, 14.7.1919. See also *ACS*, PCM, Gabinetto AAGG, 1940–43, b. 2650.
102   *L'Illustrazione italiana*, 29.12.1918.
103   Scheer, *Emotions*, pp. 212–214.
104   *Testa di ferro*, 29.8.1920.
105   *ACS*, PCM Guerra Europea, b. 243, f. 1, Telegram Nunes to PCM, 16.2.1920.
106   Berri, *La gesta di Fiume*, p. 96.
107   Simonelli, *La costruzione*, pp. 275–286; Gerra, *L'impresa*, vol. 2, pp. 275–295.
108   On the vast discussion see Gentile, *Le origini*; De Felice, *D'Annunzio*, pp. VII–XV.

References

Afflerbach, Holger, '"…vani e terribili olocausti di vite umane…" Luigi Bongiovannis Warnungen vor dem Kriegseintritt Italiens im Jahre 1915', in Hürter, Johannes and Rusconi, Gian Enrico (eds.), *Der Kriegseintritt Italiens im Mai 1915*, München, Oldenbourg, 2007, pp. 85–98.

Alatri, Paolo, *Nitti, D'Annunzio e la Questione Adriatica (1919–1920)*, Milano, Feltrinelli, 1959.

Antonsich, Marco, 'Searching for belonging. An analytical framework', in: *Geography Compass*, vol. 4, no. 6, 2010, pp. 644–659.

Aronson, Elliot, Wilson, Timothy D. and Akert, Robin M., *Social psychology*, Boston et al., Pearson, 2013.

Badoglio, Pietro, *Rivelazioni su Fiume*, Rome, Donatello De Luigi, 1946.

Bartov, Omer and Weitz, Eric D. (eds.), *Shatterzone of empires. Coexistence and violence in the German, Habsburg, Russian, and Ottoman borderlands*, Bloomington, Indiana University Press, 2013.

Berri, Gino, *La gesta di Fiume. Storia di una passione inesausta*, Florence, R. Bemporad e figlio, 1920.

Botti, Federico, *Natale di Sangue. Memorie di un legionario fiumano*, Udine, Editore Federico Botti, 1921.

Canziani, Gastone, *A Fiume con D'Annunzio. Lettere 1919–1920*, Ravenna, Longo, 2008.

Carli, Mario, *Con D'Annunzio a Fiume*, Milan, Facchi, 1920.

Comisso, Giovanni, *Le mie stagioni*, Milan, Longanesi, 1985 [1951].

Cordova, Ferdinando, *Arditi e legionari dannunziani*, Rome, Manifestolibri, 2007 [1969].

D'Annunzio, Gabriele, *La penultima ventura. Scritti e discorsi fiumani*, Milan, Mondadori, 1974.

De Felice, Renzo, *D'Annunzio politico 1918–1933*, Rome – Bari, Laterza, 1978.

De Felice, Renzo, *Sindacalismo rivoluzionario e fiumanesimo nel carteggio De Ambris-D'Annunzio 1919–1922*, Brescia, Morcelliana, 1966.

Encke, Julia, *Augenblicke der Gefahr. Der Krieg und die Sinne*, Munich, Wilhelm Fink, 2006.

Ercolani, Antonella, *Da Fiume a Rijeka. Profilo storico-politico dal 1918 al 1947*, Soveria Mannelli, Rubbettino, 2009 [2007].

Föllmer, Moritz, 'The unscripted revolution. Male subjectivities in Germany 1918–1919', in: *Past and Present*, no. 240, 2018, pp. 161–192.

François, Etienne, Siegrist, Hannes and Vogel, Jakob, 'Die Nation. Vorstellungen, Inszenierungen, Emotionen', in: François, Etienne, Siegrist, Hannes and Vogel, Jakob (eds.), *Nation und emotion. Deutschland und Frankreich im Vergleich. 19. und 20. Jahrhundert*, Göttingen, Vandenhoeck & Ruprecht, 1995, pp. 13–35.

Frassetto, Riccardo, *I desertori di Ronchi. L'organizzazione della marcia su Fiume, la diserzione dei granatieri, lo stato libero del Carnaro, il Natale di sangue*, Milan, Carnaro, 1927 [1926].

Fried, Ilona, *Fiume. Città della memoria 1868–1945*, Udine, Del Bianco, 2005.

Gemelli, Agostino, *Il nostro Soldato. Saggi di psicologia militare*, Milan, Fratelli Treves, 1918.

Gentile, Emilio, *Le origini dell'ideologia fascista (1918–1925)*, Bologna, Il Mulino, 1996.

Gerra, Ferdinando, *L'impresa di Fiume*, 2 vol., Milan, Longanesi, 1966.

Gibelli, Antonio, *Il popolo bambino. Infanzia e nazione dalla Grande Guerra a Salò*, Turin, Einaudi, 2005.

Gibelli, Antonio, 'Italy', in: Horne, John (ed.), *A companion to World War I*, London, Wiley-Blackwell, 2010, pp. 464–478.

Gibelli, Antonio, *La Grande Guerra degli italiani. Come la Prima guerra mondiale ha unito la nazione*, Milan, BUR, 2013 [1998].

Gibelli, Antonio, *L'officina della guerra. La Grande Guerra e le trasformazioni del mondo mentale*, Turin, Bollati Boringhieri, 2009 [1991].

Giuriati, Giovanni, *Con D'Annunzio e Millo in difesa dell'Adriatico*, Florence, G.C. Sansoni, 1954.

Griffin, Roger, *The nature of fascism*, London – New York, Routledge, 2006 [1991].

Guerrini, Irene, 'Obbligare e punire. La giustizia militare', in: Isnenghi, Mario and Ceschin, Daniele (eds.), *La Grande Guerra. Dall'Intervento alla "vittoria mutilata"*, Turin, Utet, 2008.

Gumbrecht, Hans Ulrich, *Diesseits der Hermeneutik. Die Produktion von Präsenz*, Frankfurt a. M., Suhrkamp, 2004.

Jesné, Fabrice, 'Fiume/Rijeka 1919. Question nationale, expérimentations politiques et contrôle social dans un cadre urbain', in: *Cahiers de la Méditerranée*, vol. 86, 2013, pp. 85–96.

Klimó, Árpád von and Rolf, Malte, 'Rausch und Diktatur. Emotionen, Erfahrungen und Inszenierungen totalitärer Herrschaft', in: Klimó, Árpád von and Rolf, Malte (eds.), *Rausch und Diktatur. Inszenierung, Mobilisierung und Kontrolle in totalitären Systemen*, Frankfurt a. M. – New York, Campus, 2006, pp. 11–43.

Kochnitzky, Léon, *La Quinta Stagione o I centauri di Fiume*, transl. Alberto Luchini. Bologna, Nicola Zanichelli, 1922.

Lanaro, Silvio, 'Da contadini a italiani', in: Bevilacqua, Piero (ed.), *Mercati e*, Venice, Marsilio, 1991, pp. 937–968.

Langewiesche, Dieter, 'Gefühlsraum Nation. Eine Emotionsgeschichte der Nation, die Grenzen zwischen öffentlichem und privatem Gefühlsraum nicht einebnet', in: *Zeitschrift für Erziehungswissenschaften*, vol. 15, 2012, pp. 195–215.

Ledeen, Michael A., 'Italian fascism and youth', in: *Journal of Contemporary History*, vol. 4, no. 3, 1969, pp. 137–154.

Ledeen, Michael A., *D'Annunzio. The first duce*, New Brunswick, Transaction Publishers, 2002 [1977, Ital. 1975].

Longo, Luigi Emilio, *L'esercito italiano e la questione fiumana (1918–1921)*, vol. 1, Rome, Stilgrafica, 1996.

Lunzer, Renate, 'Making sense of the war (Italy)', in: Daniel, Ute *et al.* (eds.), *1914–1918 online. International encyclopedia of the First World War*, available at http://dx.doi.org/10.15463/ie1418.10632 (accessed 28 August 2015).

Maranini, Giuseppe, *Lettere da Fiume alla fidanzata*, ed. Elda Bossi, Mailand, Pan Editore, 1973.

Melchionni, Maria Grazia, *La vittoria mutilata. Problemi ed incertezze della politica estera italiana sul finire della grande guerra (ottobre 1918-gennaio 1919)*, Rome, Edizioni di storia e letteratura, 1981.

Mosse, George L., *Masses and man. Nationalist and fascist perceptions of reality*, New York, Howard Fertig, 1980.

N.N., 'Elenco ufficiale dei legionari fiumani depositato presso la fondazione del Vittoriale degli italiani in data 24/6/1939', in: *Archivio-Museo Storico di Fiume*, Rome, Tipolitografia Spoletini, s.d., pp. 31–128.

Parlato, Giuseppe, *Mezzo secolo di Fiume. Economia e società a Fiume nella prima metà del Novecento*, Siena, Edizioni Cantagalli, 2009.

Pupo, Raoul and Todero, Fabio, *Fiume, D'Annunzio e la crisi dello Stato liberale in Italia*, Trieste, Istituto regionale per la storia del movimento di liberazione, 2010.

Riall, Lucy, *Risorgimento. The history of Italy from Napoleon to nation state*, Basingstoke, Palgrave Macmillan, 2009.

Rochat, Giorgio and Massobrio, Giulio, *Breve storia dell'esercito italiano dal 1861 al 1943*, Turin, Einaudi, 1978.

Rochat, Giorgio, *Gli arditi della Grande Guerra*, Gorizia, Le Guerre, 5th edition, 2006 [1981].

Rochat, Giorgio, *L'esercito italiano da Vittorio Veneto a Mussolini 1919–1925*, Rome – Bari, Laterza, 2006.

Rochat, Giorgio, 'The Italian Front 1915–18', in: Horne, John (ed.), *A companion to World War I*, London, Wiley-Blackwell, 2010, pp. 82–96.

Rosenwein, Barbara H., *Generations of feeling. A history of emotions, 600–1700*, Cambridge, Cambridge University Press, 2016.

Said, Edward W., *Orientalism*, New York, Pantheon Books, 1978.

Salaris, Claudia, *Alla festa della rivoluzione. Artisti e libertari con D'Annunzio a Fiume*, Bologna, Il Mulino, 2002.

Salvante, Martina, 'Arditi', in: Daniel, Ute *et al.* (eds.), *1914–1918 online. International encyclopedia of the First World War*, available at http://dx.doi.org/10.15463/ie1418.10840 (accessed 19 May 2016).

Scheer, Monique, 'Are emotions a kind of practice (and is that what makes them have a history)?', in: *History and Theory*, vol. 51, no. 2, 2012, pp. 193–220.

Serventi Longhi, Enrico, *Alceste De Ambris. L'utopia concreta di un rivoluzionario sindacalista*, Milan, FrancoAngeli, 2011.

Simonelli, Federico Carlo, *La costruzione di un mito. Rituali, simboli e narrazioni dell'impresa di Fiume (1919–1921)*, diss., Università degli studi di Urbino Carlo Bo, 2015.

Skradol, Natalia, 'Carnival of exception. Gabriele D'Annunzio's "Dialogues with the Crowd"', in: *Rhetorica. A Journal of the History of Rhetoric*, vol. 30, no. 1, 2012, pp. 74–93.

Stelli, Giovanni, *Storia di Fiume. Dalle origini ai giorni nostri*, Pordenone, Edizioni Biblioteca dell'Immagine, 2017.

Volmar, Axel, 'In storms of steel. The soundscape of World War I and its impact on auditory media culture during the Weimar period', in: Morat, Daniel (ed.), *Sounds of modern history. Auditory cultures in 19th- and 20th-century Europe*, New York – Oxford, Berghahn, 2014, pp. 227–255.

Warstat, Matthias, *Theatrale Gemeinschaften. Zur Festkultur der Arbeiterbewegung 1918–33*, Tübingen – Basel, A. Francke, 2005.

Wilcox, Vanda, *Morale and the Italian army during the First World War*, Cambridge, Cambridge University Press, 2016.

7 Bringing out the dead

Mass funerals, cult of death and the emotional dimension of nationhood in Romanian interwar fascism

Raul Cârstocea

When the 'Legion of the Archangel Michael' (also known as the 'Iron Guard') came to power in September 1940, as the only fascist movement outside Italy and Germany to do so without support from either of these two established fascist regimes,[1] the National Legionary State it proclaimed came to be nicknamed the 'National Funerary State'.[2] This was due to the ubiquity of legionary public funerals during the movement's short time in power, and their prominence as the preferred form of mass demonstrations the Legion organized. This feature was by no means limited to the movement's time in power. It was consistently deployed as a mass mobilization tool also during the time that the legionary movement was out of power, opposed to and by the state authorities.

This chapter reads the public funeral ceremonies as an attempt to render salient an emotional dimension of nationhood to a Romanian people that was profoundly marked by the experience of World War I. In doing so, the chapter seeks to provide an answer to the still open question of how an anti-establishment movement, whose members were systematically persecuted by the state authorities, achieved a spectacular growth in popularity despite very limited resources by successfully using nationalist appeals to mobilize popular support against the state.[3] I also aim to dispel the extraordinary, even bizarre, aura that still surrounds the legionary cult of death,[4] identified in a recent article as an expression of "thanatic nationalism".[5] By placing it in the broader context of the considerably expanded post-World War I Romanian state and its aggressive nationalizing project to which – paradoxically – the Legion stood in stark opposition, I argue instead that this "unique death cult, unusually morbid even for a fascist movement"[6] represented a fine-tuned and skilfully employed tool of mass mobilization that resonated profoundly with popular emotional experiences of interwar Romania.

My argument focuses on the funeral of Ion I. Moța and Vasile Marin, two of the movement's prominent members who were killed in combat fighting as volunteers in the Spanish Civil War. The funeral took place in Bucharest on February 13, 1937. The scale and grandeur of this public mourning ritual impressed even the sceptics in Romanian politics who thought of the movement as a fringe group with no real bid for political power. This is all the more remarkable since the funeral was not sanctioned by the state authorities, and thus participants to it could legitimately expect reprisals, which were frequent at legionary events. The present chapter analyses the symbolic importance of this funeral for legionary propaganda, arguing that the emotional mobilization developed before and during the event itself, as well as the rhetoric of 'sacrifice for the nation' employed in its aftermath, played a significant role in the movement's electoral success in the elections of December 1937. It shows that an instance of heart-breaking mourning that was purposely coded as 'apolitical' by those staging it could activate feelings of belonging to the nation among a population for which religion remained an important identifier, perhaps one that still trumped the national one. As such, the simultaneous drawing on religious rites and 'traditional' funeral customs rendered the funeral ceremonies more meaningful to "the anonymous crowds" than the state's nationalizing project, which failed to mobilize precisely the emotional and personal dimension of nationalism that the legionary movement successfully appealed to.

This chapter also engages a well-known debate in studies of nationalism, between Jon Fox and Cynthia Miller-Idriss on one side, and Anthony D. Smith on the other, concerning "everyday nationhood"[7] and its "limits".[8] The debate hinged on the importance of studying the everyday manifestations of nationhood among non-elites, the "ordinary people" who, as Eric Hobsbawm put it, "are not necessarily national and still less nationalist".[9] To Fox and Miller-Idriss' call for studying nationalism 'from below', Smith responded with a corrective emphasizing both the historical dimension of nationalism, which was largely absent or obscured in their project, as well as the importance of the interaction between elites and non-elites in the (re)production of the nation. Of the four modalities of everyday nationalism identified by Fox and Miller-Idriss – "talking the nation", "choosing the nation", "performing the nation", "consuming the nation"[10] – this chapter is concerned mostly with the third, i.e. "the production of national sensibilities through the ritual enactment of symbols".[11] By showing how the accomplishment of this event was equally dependent on staging by elites and essential contributions from non-elites, the present argument situates itself in this debate and advocates the complementarity of the study of nationalism 'from above' and 'from below'.[12] Moreover, by focusing on a case study where the elites and non-elites alike were non-state actors, and where the former were acting in the name of a nation-state but outside the remit of its institutions, the chapter zooms in on one of the sensitive aspects of this debate, i.e. Smith's charge that the model of 'everyday nationhood' proposed by Fox and Miller-Idriss tends to be state-centric even while trying to undermine such a perspective.[13] As such, the argument is that, in this case, the messages conveyed did not become 'mixed' at the interface between elites and non-elites,[14] but that the legionary movement created a new code of emotional expression that purposely blended the national with the religious, the public with the personal, and the movement's commitment to a fascist 'regeneration of Romania' with its claim to be the nation's only authentic representative.

Greater Romania and its discontents

Romania came out of World War I as a country that benefited significantly from the post-war peace agreement. Both its territory and its population doubled, and the new state incorporated provinces (Transylvania, Banat and Bucovina from the Austro-Hungarian Empire, Bessarabia from the Russian Empire, Southern Dobrogea from Bulgaria) that were culturally and politically distinct from the ones making up the Old Kingdom of Romania.[15] Moreover, 'Greater Romania' (as the interwar Romanian state is commonly referred to in the historiography) was an ethnically heterogeneous state, much more so than the Old Kingdom before. The proportion of ethnic minorities within the population increased almost fourfold, from 7.9 per cent in 1899 to 28.1 per cent in 1930.[16] As can be inferred from this significant increase, most of the ethnic minority groups lived in the new provinces, the largest groups having occupied elite positions prior to their incorporation into the enlarged Romanian state (e.g. Hungarians in Transylvania, Germans in Bucovina, Russians in Bessarabia).

If the dreams of nineteenth-century Romanian nationalists of the unity of all Romanians in one state were fulfilled in 1918, Greater Romania also faced significant economic problems, of which the bleak situation of the peasantry was the most salient.[17] With 79.8 per cent of the population involved in agriculture in 1930,[18] and ethnic Romanians making up the bulk of the rural population while often in a minority in urban areas, turning 'peasants into Romanians' was effectively the most important challenge for the new state. Coupled with the revisionist claims of both the Soviet Union and Hungary, this situation ensured a nationalist consensus as the dominant ideology in interwar Romania among parties both on the left and right of the political spectrum. The state embarked upon an extensive nationalizing project, which, typical of the patterns identified by Ernest Gellner,[19] Benedict Anderson[20] and Anthony D. Smith,[21] focused primarily on education, in an attempt to create a homogeneous and centralized national culture. Accompanying the drive to provide primary education in Romanian to a considerably larger population was also the one to educate a national elite that would replace the former imperial ones in the recently acquired territories. In practical terms, this translated into "an unprecedented expansion in educational facilities [that] increased the number of students to a record level".[22] The total number of students enrolled in Romanian universities almost tripled, from 8,632 in 1913–1914 to 22,379 in 1924–1925.[23]

Such a rapid increase of the student population soon went against the limits of the state education system. "The number of places in dormitories was limited, rents were high, and government scholarships few."[24] The state's capacity of absorption of new graduates into bureaucratic jobs was also limited, leading to high intellectual unemployment and increasing levels of frustration. In the last country in Europe to emancipate its Jewish minority (formalized in the Constitution of 1923), such frustration was often channelled towards Jews, a group that was generally much more urban than ethnic Romanians, better educated, and, as a result, over-represented in universities. As a result, the urban environment of the universities, which many Romanian students of rural origin came to perceive as alienating and hostile, provided an excellent breeding ground for the proliferation of anti-Semitic nationalist organizations, from which the legionary movement developed.[25] This is reminiscent of Gellner's argument regarding the effects of rapid change on the identity of migrants from rural areas to an urban environment, with a nationalist identity becoming more salient with the disappearance of traditional ties.[26] It was indeed in such contexts that the more radical nationalist organizations in interwar Romania developed, and while the students who created them could on the one hand present themselves as an alternative to the corrupt ruling political elites, their ties to the countryside rendered them more attuned to the peasants' emotional and personal experiences of nationhood.

The latter were simultaneously marked by several contrasting experiences. An important one was the wartime trauma, where according to figures of the US War Department the losses (combining dead, wounded and missing) suffered by the Romanian Army reached 71.4 per cent of the total 750,000 mobilized men. Civilian casualties were the highest proportionally of all countries participating in the war.[27] It is also important to note that these losses occurred in the context of the first general mobilization in Romania's history, and that peasants made up the bulk of the armed forces. At the end of the war, the trauma was contrasted by the elation associated with the fulfilment of the national ideal through the proclaimed 'Union of all Romanians', doubled by a land reform which was presented as a comprehensive resolution of the country's main social problem, the condition of "neo-serfdom" that the peasantry experienced.[28] Long debated and overdue, the agrarian reform involved one of the most extensive land redistributions in Central and Eastern Europe, and was initially extremely popular with the peasantry. The first half of the 1920s was a time of general optimism about the future, if not quite prosperity, on the back of post-war economic growth prompted by the acquiring, together with the province of Transylvania, of considerable industrial infrastructure that the Old Kingdom of Romania had badly lacked. By contrast, the end of the decade brought about stagnation and disillusionment, deepened by the effects of the global economic crisis. The persistence of all the socio-economic and political problems (from severe poverty and endemic corruption to ever-deepening inequality) characteristic of pre-war Romania was exacerbated by a dependence on foreign capital that rendered the much-cherished independence of the country all but illusory in practical terms.[29] Consequently, a national and nationalizing state that had been positively perceived by the 'masses' doubly empowered by land reform and universal male suffrage increasingly came under attack as the economic crisis affected both the majority of the peasantry, who continued to live at the limit of subsistence, and the urban poor. In such a context, the targeting of 'foreigners' (a term which was often used as a code word for 'Jews') – associated with the former imperial elites and conflated with the importance of foreign capital for Romania's economy – represented important political capital that was indeed employed by most political parties.

From local student group to nation-wide mass movement – the Legion of the Archangel Michael

Founded on June 24, 1927 by a group of five students, the 'Legion of the Archangel Michael' (also known from 1930 as the 'Iron Guard') developed in the course of a decade into a nation-wide mass movement and the third largest fascist organization in Europe.[30] The 'All for the Country' party, the political arm of the movement after its initial designations were repeatedly made illegal in the 1930s, came third in the 1937 elections, with 15.58 per cent of the votes.[31] Moreover, unpublished police reports, as well as contemporary comments of democratic politicians neutral to the movement indicate it as the favourite for winning the scheduled 1938 elections, which were subsequently cancelled for this very reason.[32]

As most authors writing on the subject acknowledge, the legionary movement was no imitation of Italian or German fascism.[33] While acknowledging the Legion's affinity to movements of "national regeneration", Corneliu Zelea Codreanu – founder and undisputed leader of the organization until his death in 1938 – was also keen to distinguish it from the Italian and German variants, and proclaim "the superiority of the legionary idea over fascism and national-socialism".[34] The peculiarity of the Legion within the fascist 'party family' was noted already by Ernst Nolte in 1966, in one of the first studies attempting a definition of generic fascism, and the organization was identified by the author as "the most interesting and the most complex fascist movement".[35] Although Nolte's argument has been extensively disputed, similar conclusions are to be found in more recent studies on fascism, such as the authoritative history of the phenomenon by Stanley Payne, who includes the Legion among the four main variants of fascism and characterizes it as "arguably the most unique of the entire genus, except for the German Nazis".[36]

While the limited scope of the present chapter does not allow elaboration on any of these features, a brief enumeration of the peculiarities of the legionary movement appears necessary: the distinctive organizational structure of the movement in 'nests' of three to thirteen members capable of acting autonomously from the centre, and with a leader meant to 'emerge spontaneously' rather than being elected or appointed; the active role reserved for women within the movement – unlike in other fascist organizations, legionary women were to undergo similar training and preparation for combat as men; the rigorous selection (a three year process) and limitation of membership numbers; the constructive voluntary work projects undertaken by the movement, involving grassroots mobilization and the cross-class solidarity of intellectuals, workers and peasants; the organization's professed religiosity, strictly observed by leaders in their daily lives and proclaimed as the main guiding principle in its ideology; and, finally, the "genuine cult of death" omnipresent in their rhetoric,[37] which led Stanley Payne to argue that "in the Legion, martyrdom was virtually required".[38]

Following an initial period of stagnation, caused by a dire lack of funds and support from traditional elites, as well as by the competition for the extreme nationalist and anti-Semitic vote from the much better established League of National-Christian Defense (*Liga Apărării Naţional-Creştine*, LANC), the Legion's first inroads into mass popularity began during 1929–1930. These were partly explained by the aforementioned political and economic context, favourable to a contestation of the state institutions by an anti-establishment nationalist movement, and partly by a purposeful decision of the legionary leadership to "step out to the masses"[39] – an almost direct translation of the *narodniki*'s slogan "going to the people". Here, the legionaries' familiarity with the countryside proved decisive, and their propaganda strategies, driven as much by necessity (due to a lack of funds for standard electoral propaganda) as by the conscious choices made by legionary leaders (who, coming from a rural background themselves, were aware of the limitations of conventional political propaganda in a predominantly rural country), proved effective. The electoral propaganda strategies employed by the Legion in the countryside involved direct contact of the leadership (especially Codreanu) with the peasants, the recourse to symbolic elements such as wearing the peasant costume, riding white horses, displaying the sign of the cross, etc.[40]

Fusing elements of "popular Orthodoxy"[41] with folklore, and taking stock of local identities and personal experiences, the Legion successfully managed to link such localized experiences to a notion of the 'nation' that had not been sufficiently institutionalized by the state in the countryside, and in a country where significant regional differences persisted throughout the interwar period, despite the state's incessant efforts at cultural homogenization and nationalization. According to Anthony Cohen, "[t]o be successful, the politician must formulate nationalism in terms that enable individuals to reappropriate it for their own requirements and propensities",[42] and it was indeed along these lines that the Legion proved successful, initially in the countryside. As argued in more detail below, the all-important feature of legionary ideology that allowed connecting its ultra-nationalism to peasants' personal and emotional lived experiences of nationhood was religion, articulated as the 'popular Orthodoxy' of the village and espoused through rituals that simultaneously relied on the legitimacy conferred by tradition and corresponded to a distinctly fascist political style. Such a popular version of religion, unfolding around a religious calendar linked to the rhythms of nature, simplified and centred around a dichotomy of good and evil, incorporated elements of folklore and lay tradition, as well as pre-Christian beliefs and practices, accommodating at the same time the (many) deviations from Christian Orthodox dogma that the legionary ideology incorporated.[43] As Gail Kligman notes in her ethnographic study of peasant funerals in a village in north-western Romania, nowhere was this aspect more pronounced than with the "rituals associated with death", which 'more than the other rites associated with important moments in man's life, in our [Romanian] folklore [...] have preserved ancient pre-Christian beliefs and practices' [...]. The village priest concurs with this scholarly appraisal; from his point of view, there are many 'pagan' elements from popular culture bound to religious customs by centuries of practice.[44]

The Legion was not a peasant movement, however, and the 'authentic peasant' that its rhetoric often invoked was merely a model to be employed for populist purposes. If Codreanu and the legionary leadership initially wore the peasant costume on all occasions, even in parliament, they changed to uniforms once the movement established a strong presence in Bucharest. In the industrial capital of Romania, attention turned to the other underprivileged group, the workers, whom left-wing parties had failed to mobilize. Strategies were developed for activating the cross-class solidarity that the movement preached, from the extremely popular voluntary public work projects known as 'work camps'[45] to shops, restaurants and canteens opened particularly in working-class neighbourhoods, providing goods below the market price as part of a project of legionary commerce, viewed as a form of principled, "Christian" trade, guided "not by the lust for profit" but "the joy of providing a service to those around us". All of these were based on voluntary work, brought together intellectuals, workers and peasants working side by side, and were re-coded back into legionary rhetoric as exemplary practices for a voluntaristic, activist ideology that was perceived as rendering the movement distinct from all other political organizations in interwar Romania. At the same time, every minor legionary achievement was consistently juxtaposed to the failure of the government to address a certain issue, and the construction of a 'new' Romania in accordance with fascist principles was permanently contrasted with the corrupt state of Romanian democracy. Through this permanent dichotomy, the Legion established itself as the (ultra-) nationalist competitor to the Romanian state's nationalizing project, a competitor that kept increasing in importance as the latter plunged into ever deeper crisis.

The legionary team in the Spanish Civil War

Somewhat paradoxically, the year when the Legion reached the height of its popularity also saw the death of one of its most valuable leaders, Ion I. Moța. One of the original five founders of the movement, and second-in-command to 'Captain' Codreanu, Moța was generally perceived by neutral observers as "the most intelligent of the leaders of the Iron Guard". A doctor in law with a thesis on 'Juridical Security in the League of Nations' (arguing against the principle of collective security), he was also the Romanian translator of the 'Protocols of the Elders of Zion' and a more rabid anti-Semite than Codreanu himself.[46] In 1937, it was his death in the Spanish Civil War, interpreted as 'martyrdom' in legionary rhetoric, and especially the public funeral that ensued, that was to propel the movement to an unprecedented popularity. The other legionary 'martyr', Vasile Marin, was also a doctor in law (with a thesis entitled 'Fascism'). He had joined the Legion in 1932, in the 'first wave' of legionary intellectuals. Both were very prominent in the legionary leadership as well as part of Codreanu's personal entourage.

On November 25, 1936, a delegation of legionary leaders, led by General Gheorghe Cantacuzino, left for Spain to deliver the honorary gift of a sword to General José Moscardó, the defender of the Alcázar of Toledo against Republican forces.[47] While Moța had apparently been one of the initiators of this trip, Marin added his presence to the original seven members at the last minute, allegedly stating: "you have decided to bring seven coffins back from Spain. I would like mine to be the eighth".[48] This statement was not exactly corresponding to the mission of the delegation, which was initially meant to be purely symbolic. Codreanu gave specific orders to the team not to exceed the term of one month and to return on January 1, 1937, and also not to engage in active combat and put their lives at risk.[49]

Once in Spain, the legionaries were all given officer ranks, in line with their corresponding ranks in the Romanian army, as they were all university graduates. However, soon the notorious arrogance of General Cantacuzino – a Romanian war hero in World War I – led him to demand the command of a brigade, and the rudeness of his insistence eventually got the legionaries demoted to common soldiers.[50] The general returned in fury to Romania, leaving the command of the team to Ion Moța. Presented with the opportunity to engage in active combat, Moța, who had left a testament and several letters upon departure indicating his desire to sacrifice his life "for the defence of the Cross"[51] and thus awaited just such an opportunity, led the team into battle.

On January 13, 1937, less than two weeks after their enlistment as regular soldiers in the Spanish Foreign Legion, Ion Moța and Vasile Marin were killed during a Republican attack in Majadahonda. According to Codreanu's first succinct telegram informing legionaries about this, "[t]he heart-rending news came as a lightning bolt on us. It will move every Romanian. We gave to God the best children of our nation".[52] As press articles show, the expectations of the legionary leader were not misplaced – on January 17, 1937, the mainstream daily *Universul* (The Universe) wrote that in Iași, the north-eastern city where the Legion had been established, "the news of the death of legionaries lawyer Ion Moța and Dr. Vasile Marin made a profound impression among the Romanian population of the city", with students deciding to organize a commemorative religious service and initiate a public subscription for the return of their bodies and the funeral. Regarding Moța, the article added that

> his death, as noble as it is through the sacrifice on the front of the defence of the national idea, of Christianity and of civilization, saddened all those who knew him and appreciated him. He leaves behind an inconsolable wife and two small children.[53]

Money donations for the return of the two bodies from Spain reached 170,000 lei on the first day, in the capital alone, and more than 2,000 people visited the Legion's headquarters that day.[54] The loss of the two legionary commanders, and especially of the second-in-command, was compensated by the pageantry of their funeral, the most spectacular public manifestation of the Legion to that date. The entire symbolism of death and resurrection of the Legion's doctrine was deployed for this purpose. The premonitions of Moţa and Marin were presented as "visions" or "divine signs", their death as a wilful "sacrifice" and "martyrdom", and both were virtually sanctified.[55] Even a religious hymn was written invoking the two "saints", their death depicted as "the Annunciation of the Resurrection of the nation".[56] From the point of view of the Orthodox dogma which legionaries claimed to uphold, this was nothing short of blasphemy. This aspect, however, did not prevent more than three hundred priests from attending the funeral.

The transport of the bodies of the two legionaries from Spain by a special train, as well as the funeral itself, was paid for by a nation-wide public subscription. In Berlin, the train was saluted by SS and SA troops, including members of Hitler's personal guard, joined by Italian *squadristi* and Spanish members of the *Falange*.[57] Its entrance in Romania at the station of Grigore Ghica Vodă was greeted by "200 legionaries and 100 others [...], all of them on their knees",[58] and its first major stop, at the station of Cernăuţi, was attended by a huge crowd, kneeling solemnly and reciting prayers at the arrival.[59] The train subsequently followed a route traversing the country, in a symbolic journey "designed to unite every Romanian province in its mourning for the two dead leaders".[60] The numerous stops at railway stations across the country represented also a grandiose parallel to traditional peasant ritual, where the funeral procession stops several times on the way from the house to the cemetery.[61] As Kligman notes,

> the number of times that the cortège is halted, however, depends on the wishes and the purse of the deceased's family; the priest is recompensed for each prayer he performs. There is no mandatory number, but in view of the belief that prayers nourish and comfort the soul as well as reflect beneficially on the living, then the more stops the better.[62]

Police reports followed the train in its journey through Romania, and both the accounts and the photographs taken at railway stations attest to the mass participation at the religious ceremonies officiated at each station where the train stopped, as well as the emotional state of the attending population. "A crowd of over five thousand peasants fell to its knees when the bodies arrived in Paşcani,"[63] another town in north-eastern Romania, and in places like Cuciurul Mare and Dorneşti in Bucovina, Cluj and Orăştie in Transylvania, Piteşti and Titu in Wallachia, the police indicated that the audience was moved to tears during the ceremonies.[64] Even in places where the train did not stop, such as Goleşti, Muscel County,

[a]t its passing the CFR [Romanian Railways] workers and those working to clean the snow from the tracks stood to attention and, uncovering their heads, gave the salute; the legionaries from the train responded by saluting with their arms stretched. At the church in Goleşti the bells were rung.[65]

The profound impression the funeral train made on the population, the solemnity of the ceremonies, the atmosphere of "piety and humility" and the "outstanding order and introspection" of the occasions are all leitmotifs of the police reports from across the country.[66] Reports also mention that "the impressions left by these manifestations were of a sentimental nature",[67] with the emotions highlighted in the otherwise typically unemotional police statements ranging from deep compassion, through piety and "mysticism",[68] to spiritual torment and pain, on the one hand,[69] and admiration and exaltation on the other.[70]

While varying in scope at different locations across the country, both as a function of their respective size and the Legion's popularity, the commemorations unfolded according to a similar pattern: religious services, officiated by priests in vestments, followed by the 'Song of Fallen Legionaries', and an oath that legionaries, and often significant parts of the non-affiliated attendance, took at the end of the ceremony.[71] Written by Codreanu and identified as a "baptism in the legionary faith", the oath made direct reference to the palingenetic component of legionary ideology: "I swear before God, before your holy sacrifice for Christ and the Legion, To tear away from me all earthly joys, To sever myself from humanly love, And for the Resurrection of my nation, at any moment, to stand ready for death".[72] Notably, almost no overtly political speeches were held anywhere along the route, the few exceptions being at the most important stops, such as Orăştie (Moţa's birthplace, where the two coffins were brought to the courtyard of the family home), Cluj and Sibiu, and, in those rare cases, the speeches were mostly delivered by priests and had a primarily religious rather than political character.[73] In fact, police reports note that political speeches and discussions did not take place precisely "because the crowd was not in the emotional disposition to make any comments on legionary principles, but was under the profound impression of the religious service performed in front of the two coffins".[74] Where speeches were held, however, they were rarely explicitly political, and instead appealed directly to the emotions of the participants. In Cluj, bishop Nicolae Colan began his speech by saying "in front of the coffins with the remain so dear to us, our hearts are hard tested", while Tiberiu Vereş, a legionary representative of the 'Petru Maior' student centre, added "our soul is boiling with pain, but their sacrifice will echo across the centuries, that on the brotherly land of Spain some drops of Romanian blood were spilled, washing away the shame of our Nation."[75] In Orăştie, Damian Aron, the director of the local high school, exalted the two dead legionaries as 'saints' in a speech with pronounced emotional overtones that, typically, interpreted their death by emphasising the link between religion and nationalism:

> The emotion that announces the great renewals of the Romanian nation
> is felt more following the sacrifice of the two heroes of Majadahonda, Ion
> I. Mota and Vasile Marin. [...] Let us not cry, but walk the path marked
> by their blood, for on the day of 15 January [sic!] they were summoned as
> Archangels guarding Greater Romania. They are saints, for saints are
> those who die for the nation and for Christ, and the Romanian nation
> has been uplifted through their work and their Sacrifice. [...] It is sublime
> to feel the universal heart of the nation beating in the rhythm of your
> heart, as it beat for the two friends, unseparated in body and soul.[76]

The religious rites, performed according to custom but on a much grander scale,
were almost unanimously highlighted in police reports as the most important
aspect that elicited an emotional response from the audience, which is often
portrayed as "deeply moved".[77] Thus, the synthesis report mentioned that

> the religious ceremonies, which took place in the main railway stations,
> the pomp with which the oath of the legionaries was taken, as well as the
> gravity of the moments – since everything happened in front of the coffins
> draped in Romanian colours – impregnated a note of mysticism on the
> audience, which had the effect of deeply impressing even those who were
> not members of the 'All for the Country' party, prompting part of them
> to also take the oath.[78]

However, the insertion of legionary songs and the oath into an otherwise
traditional funeral ritual, combined with the unmistakable visibility of
legionaries in uniform in all stations and towns where the train stopped,
ensured that the ceremonies were clearly marked as legionary events, and
their purportedly apolitical nature helped render them even more emotionally
powerful for the audience. In their attempt to portray themselves as a movement beyond and opposed to the 'politics as usual' that most of the population had come to resent, the legionaries frequently relied on the religious
character of their ideology, as well as relating to the familiar aspects of
everyday lived experience they incorporated in their rituals. As Roland Clark
notes, "funerals and commemorations [...] helped confuse the family, the
nation, and the church with the Legion, and they provided numerous examples of heroism that legionaries could aspire to".[79] The importance of this
ostensible rejection of politics is duly noted by the synthesis report on the
funeral of Mota and Marin, which states that "the present state of mind in
the country is apolitical, an aspect which favours the legionary movement".[80]

Prominent Romanian intellectuals and politicians, as well as representatives
of various professional associations, paid their homage to the two 'heroes'.
The mass exaltation surrounding the funeral spread even to democratic politicians and some of the reputed enemies of the movement. Nicolae Iorga, the
same man who, as Prime Minister, had wanted to execute the members of the
Iron Guard with machine guns, wrote in an article entitled 'Two brave boys'

about the "precious blood of our youth [...] and their enthusiasm which calls to be led and not stifled".[81] A massive press campaign covered every step of the journey, with right-wing newspapers joined by mainstream ones typically neutral to the movement (*Universul, Tempo, Gazeta, Ordinea, Capitala, Curentul*). The press articles covering the event were atypical both in their number (mainstream publications did not usually cover aspects of the activity of the legionary movement so extensively) and their quality, appearing certainly more positive than was common for otherwise neutral observers or, as in Iorga's case, even former opponents of the movement.

As for the publications that were either issued by the legionary movement or sympathetic to it, the hyperbole knew no boundaries. The first issue of the most important legionary daily, *Buna Vestire* (The Annunciation), opened with an editorial entitled 'The Contemporaries of Jesus...', written by the director of the newspaper, Professor Dragoş Protopopescu. In a profoundly emotional tone, the editorial began as follows:

> We are lucky people. We write on our knees. We write next to the most beautiful dead of today's Romania. We appear in the shadow of two graves whose glory weighs heavy on us and whose suffering shakes us. But whose sacrifice and faith, beyond anything else, binds us.[82]

In the typical legionary style that exalted the movement and poured scorn on its enemies, reproducing the Legion's constant dichotomy between itself and the political establishment, the article continued by expressing the author's wish that his "chest would have today thousands of latitudes, so as to encompass all the exaltation, all the Godly wave that rises up to the heavens the soul of a Romanian nation of millions of people".[83] Complete with comparisons between the "Holy Friday" when Moţa and Marin died with the Friday of Jesus' crucifixion, and incorporating a fragment of the Pascal Troparion, an hymn sung during the Orthodox Easter service, which refers to Jesus "trampling down death by death", the article concluded by announcing the coming 'resurrection' of legionary making. Referred to as "the Dawn" which he faced as he wrote, the author proclaimed the new legionary daily as being "pierced by the bullets of Moţa and Vasile Marin", and published "so that the two Romanian contemporaries of Jesus may read and approve us from the grave".[84]

An article written by Mihail Manoilescu compared Ion Moţa to Lord Byron, whose death in 1824 in the Greek War of Independence ennobled even the hated English nation,[85] while another article by the same author, entitled 'Beyond Hero and Superman', expressed his conviction that the death of the two legionaries "is capable of shaking the moral consciousness of the world, as much as there is left of it".[86] The exaltation of the two legionaries culminated in the special issue of *Ideia Românească* (The Romanian Idea) dedicated to them, where they were referred to as "Saints Ion and Vasile"[87] and where the religious hymn composed in their honour saw Moţa depicted as "an angelic hypostasis" and "celestial being".[88] Stepping beyond the revered profiles of the two legionaries, an article by Ion Vial claimed that "the entire country knelt before the sacrifice of the two and exalted their names! All Romanians shed a tear on their fresh grave!"; and that "this lived experience [*trăire*], this participation [in their mourning] is the only valid one for our nation and for the integration of all of Moţa and Marin's contemporaries in the line of the Romanian destiny!".[89] The author concluded the article with a question and an admonishment/exhortation to the members of Moţa's generation, asking

> how can you keep on living your blind lives *now*, when the sun has shown itself and the miracle has happened here, today, in this country, with one of you? When you knew Moţa, you came close to him, you heard his word, you lived next to Him, the Teacher![90]

Electoral mourning: the funeral of Ion Moţa and Vasile Marin and its aftermath

The funeral itself took place in Bucharest on February 13, 1937, on an unprecedented scale even for royal events. After crossing all the regions making up Greater Romania, the funeral train arrived at the Bucharest main station, Gara de Nord, at 11.50. A "synod composed of four bishops, several protopopes, and 180 priests, part of them in vestments, led by the Vicar of the Holy Patriarchy" awaited on the platform.[91] The coffins were brought out of the mortuary car by peasant legionaries and a procession was then formed "in the following order: the flags, the wreaths, the priests, the coffins, then the attending people, who, in deathly silence, went on to the catafalque set up in the station square, where they were laid in state".[92] By the time the procession reached the Green House, the legionary headquarters in the courtyard of which the two were buried, the number of priests had increased to 300, and the two coffins were lowered into the graves to the sound of alpenhorns blown by legionaries in peasant costume.[93]

The orderly character of the funeral procession was ensured by legionaries in uniform, estimates of their numbers varying between 16,000 and 50,000, significantly higher than the 5,000 "legionary police" Codreanu had called for.[94] The legionaries came in numbers from all regions of the country, prompting a massive logistical effort on behalf of the Bucharest chapter of the organization. As most of the legionaries coming from outside Bucharest lacked the money for a hotel, Codreanu gave orders that all members and sympathizers of the Legion from Bucharest should host them overnight.[95] While the staging of the ceremony was itself carefully planned and entrusted to a former actor, Ion Victor Vojen, it must be noted that the event would have been impossible to organize without the support of rank-and-file members, from the financial contributions for the repatriation of the bodies to providing accommodation to visitors from outside Bucharest. As such, this instance of 'collective effervescence' appears as a nationalist commemoration equally dependent on the elite's organization 'from above' and on the enthusiastic participation of ordinary citizens providing their support 'from below'.

The members of the movement were joined in the procession by an immense crowd of non-legionary participants – police estimates mention a total of approximately 200,000 participants[96] – including delegates from all nationalist parties, as well as from some democratic ones. As had occurred at the many stops during the funeral train's journey through Romania, even the bitter rivalry between the Legion and the other radical right party, the National Christian Party (a successor of LANC following its fusion with the Agrarian Party), was laid aside for the occasion, with a delegation of 'lancers' paying their homage to the two legionary leaders.[97] The participation of four foreign ambassadors (Germany, Italy, Spain and Portugal) to the funeral prompted a diplomatic crisis, with deputies of the democratic parties in Romania submitting a motion of protest in the Chamber against the involvement of foreign diplomats in the activities of an extremist, officially dissolved political formation.

The accounts of neutral observers present the funeral as "impressive". If the government feared violence and disorder, considering the legionary reputation for such actions, it was eventually the unprecedented order of the ceremony and the "moral discipline of the thousands of young men who paraded" that spread fear in the government and deeply worried King Carol II.[98] The symbolism employed led observers to speak of the "new mysticism, the mysticism of the dead" developed by the movement.[99] The Spanish ambassador read the roll-call of the legionary team, and, when Moța and Marin's names were pronounced, thousands shouted back 'Present!' The ceremony culminated with the taking of the aforementioned oath, distributed among legionaries and published in newspapers in advance, so that the thousands of participants could learn it.

The aftermath of the funeral saw the use of this event as a mobilization tool for political purposes. The selflessness of the two legionaries was exalted, and the idea of 'sacrifice for the nation' became a central feature of the 1937 electoral campaign. Calendars, postcards and stamps with the image of the "heroes of the Cross" were issued, and the names Moța and Marin became virtual synonyms of martyrdom. Moța's testament was published and widely disseminated, and its opening words, "Captain, may you make a country splendid as the holy sun in the sky," were the most common slogan on the electoral posters of 1937.[100] From the peasants to whom the dynamic of sacrifice and resurrection was all too familiar from church sermons to philosopher Nae Ionescu, who wrote of his conviction that "for the salvation of our nation God has to accept Moța's sacrifice just as for the salvation of humanity He accepted the sacrifice of the lamb",[101] Romanians appear to have received this interpretation with enthusiasm. In February 1938, the final words of the oath taken by the participants at the funeral, "ready for death", became the slogan of the 'Moța-Marin Corps', an elite formation of volunteers who took a similar oath of asceticism, chastity and self-renunciation.

Although the number of members of this formation was limited to 10,000, allegedly more than 40,000 legionaries volunteered in the first day registration was opened.[102]

The nationalist display of power at the funeral both impressed and concerned King Carol II. Following a secret audience between the two representatives of the competing nationalist projects in interwar Romania, the state vs. the anti-establishment grassroots one, the king's failed attempt to wrest leadership of the Legion from Codreanu[103] eventually led to his persecution of the movement, carried out from the outset of the royal dictatorship he established in March 1938. Codreanu's arrest and assassination while in prison in November 1938, followed by the legionary assassination of Prime Minister Armand Călinescu – held responsible for Codreanu's death – in 1939 and the reprisals in which 256 legionary leaders were executed, spelled doom for the movement. When it eventually came to power, following the king's compromised position after the loss of the province of Bessarabia to the Soviet Union and of Northern Transylvania to Hungary in 1940, which signalled the end of the interwar 'Greater Romania', its initial leadership was gone, so that the Legion in 1940, as the joke went at the time, was much like a potato: the best part of it was under the ground.[104] This in turn prompted a proliferation of further funeral ceremonies, of exhumations and re-inhumations of the remains of those killed by order of the king, including Codreanu – themselves customary in some regions of Romania, and particularly in Codreanu's native Moldova – this time with the full weight of the resources of the National-Legionary State behind them.

Bringing out the dead: mass funerals, cult of death and the emotional dimension of nationhood

In an attempt to make sense of the importance of this funeral in reproducing national identity, the preparations for the event, as well as its aftermath, appear as equally significant, or even more so, than the event itself, especially since these were reproduced, albeit on a smaller scale, in the numerous other funerals organized by the legionary movement during the interwar period, for the movement's members killed by the authorities.[105] The line of interpretation adopted in the following analysis thus focuses less on the actual funeral that took place on February 13, 1937, and more on its implications for the success of a nationalist project alternative to, and frequently even opposed to the state.

Understanding the 'success' of the funeral of Moța and Marin in mobilizing the general public and creating an unprecedented wave of sympathy around a controversial radical movement can be undertaken along several lines of argument, each of these presenting its own challenges: the importance of the war dead for nationalist rhetoric, as 'heroes' transcending the realm of ordinary politics and providing through their sacrifice a symbolic "defence of the homeland"[106]; the role of a religious interpretation in transforming two random casualties in a distant conflict unrelated to Romania into 'martyrs' for the national cause; the importance of the two dead legionaries for a project of revolutionary regeneration of the nation characteristic of fascist movements,[107] undertaken in the Romanian case along the lines of a primarily 'spiritual revolution'; and, finally, the interaction between elites and non-elites,[108] the complementarity of elite staging 'from above' and essential contributions 'from below'[109] in the success of this event.

As Michael Freeden argues in 'The Politics of Ceremony', "in all cultures, the war dead occupy a particular place": because of the difficulty of rationalizing sacrifice and the inherently altruistic nature of such a gesture, and because of the symbolic protection they provide to the rest of the community.[110] In public funeral ceremonies, the spontaneity of private mourning is trumped by an elaborate political choreography, which attempts to present itself as equally spontaneous.[111] This is because of the insistence on the grassroots level of interaction in such ceremonies, the striving for an 'authenticity' that is believed can only be encountered in spontaneous solidarity, remote from the callous realm of 'official politics'. Yet Freeden is writing about the Wootton Bassett ceremonies of repatriation of British soldiers dead in Afghanistan, in a conflict initiated and carried out by the state. In the case of the two legionaries, the public came to mourn the members of an extremist movement, participating in a conflict to which the Romanian state remained neutral, as part of a team whose mission, even when taking part in active combat, remained purely symbolic. This is yet more striking for other legionary funerals that took place during the interwar period, of members of the movement who had been killed by the authorities, and which commemorated not just members of a non-state group, but nationalists who died in opposition to a nationalizing state.

However, two elements in Freeden's interpretation of the Wootton Bassett ceremonies stand out as possible 'clues' to understanding the wave of sympathy surrounding the funeral of the two legionaries, and, precisely because of the notable differences between the two cases, appear as yet more relevant. The first is related to the grassroots level of mobilization and the assumed 'authenticity' of the nation at this level. Indeed, in the case of the Legion, the success of the legionary voluntary work projects as opposed to the state-funded, much better organized 'royal student teams' doing effectively the same thing, can be understood only along these lines.[112] The movement's popularity was equally dependent, if not more so, on the practical examples of solidarity between intellectuals, workers and peasants visible in the work camps as on a nationalist ideology lacking a clear programme, riddled with contradictions (e.g. strict adherence to Christianity and political violence), and aimed at a vague 'resurrection of Romania'. Grassroots mobilization appears as the key to the understanding of the success of an alternative nationalist project to that of the state, which made the Legion by the late 1930s into an effective "parallel society"[113] or "state within a state".[114] If, following John Breuilly, nationalism is best understood not as a unilateral state project but as an ideology constantly negotiated between competing groups laying claim to national identity,[115] the legionary movement appeared as the 'winner' of this contest in 1930s Romania. Moreover, it did so precisely because of its popularity at the grassroots level, among the 'ordinary people' who, as Eric Hobsbawm put it, "are not necessarily national and still less nationalist".[116]

Such 'ordinary people' were less swayed by grandiose projects announced by politicians, or by state-sponsored nationalist events that took place far away from their everyday reality, in the capital or major cities of Romania, and much more so by the building of a dam or road or church by enthusiastic young people whose efforts were often confronted with police brutality. Although many of the constructions of the legionaries were either destroyed or taken over by the state upon completion of a project, the altruism of the participants was always noted. Also implied in the legionary slogan 'all for the country, nothing for ourselves', this alleged altruism was elevated to the level of the supreme sacrifice with the death of Moţa and Marin. By interpreting their death in a mystical-religious note, as having both national and religious significance, the legionary movement managed to circumvent the blatant evidence that it had actually nothing to do with Romania. The interpretation proved convincing, as the words of philosopher Constantin Noica, one of Romania's future prominent intellectuals who became a sympathizer of the movement after Moţa's death and a committed supporter after Codreanu's, show:

> The Legion did not want to *make* another Romania. It wanted *to be* another Romania. He who does not feel this does not understand why Moţa died, or why the great dedication of the Captain was one of his ways of triumphing and of making the Romanian nation triumph. A foreign rule could also make another country. Two hundred Swiss technicians, whom we would pay to manage us, could make another country. But can't you see this is about something else than roads, drills, and hospitals? Can't you see this is about the Romania of the spirit before all others?[117]

In another article, Noica exalted the "purity" of Moţa, a model for the entire legionary elite, and urged all Romanians to become worthy of his sacrifice, worthy of becoming the "10,001[st] member of the Moţa-Marin elite corps".[118] This aspect is directly related to the second element relevant for understanding the 'success' of legionary funerals as public events, expressed in Freeden's interpretation of ceremonies of mourning for the war dead as

> an ideal of public altruism that is rarely evident in the mundanities of normal political life; that is to say, the political is indirectly elevated to a seemingly pure and unsullied form, a form only attained by blatantly and paradoxically denying its political nature. Suffused with the above is a strong nationalism that is ranked as an unstated superior commitment.[119]

Importantly, as mentioned above, the Legion managed to convey this even for their dead, who did not die fighting for the Romanian state, but sometimes even against it. In doing so, it deepened the rift between the 'official' nationalism of the Romanian state and the anti-establishment radical nationalism it promoted, a split which eventually contributed to the de-legitimization of the very notion of a (at least nominally) democratic form of nationalism, leading to the royal dictatorship which adopted many of the fascist trappings of the legionary movement.

In the case of the Legion, its alleged superior commitment to the nation was wedded to a religious vision proclaiming "the resurrection of the nation in the name of the saviour Jesus Christ".[120] In his analysis of the funeral of Moţa and Marin, Valentin Săndulescu puts forth an interpretation inspired by the concept of "sacralisation of politics" employed by Emilio Gentile for the case of Italian fascism.[121] However, while Săndulescu limits his discussion to observing the similarities between the Romanian and Italian fascist funerary rituals, such as the "political liturgy" involved in staging the funeral, the role of the roll-call as "the supreme rite of fascism", actualizing "the sacred bond between the living and the dead",[122] and the "cult of the fallen" (which is by no means specific to fascist movements and regimes), he fails to account for the notable differences between the two cases. For one, in an Eastern European country with a much more pronounced agrarian character, the process of secularization proceeded at a different pace, and the importance of pre-national religious identities for the popular masses was significantly different from the case of Italy. Moreover, in the territories of Greater Romania that had been part of the Habsburg Empire, religion had effectively overlapped with ethnicity, and belonging to the Orthodox (or Uniate) confession trumped a recent and as-yet incomplete affiliation to the Romanian nation. Beyond the official church hierarchy and its changing political stances, the Orthodox faith was entrenched as the most significant institution at the village level, and the mutation of official dogma into the popular Orthodoxy that incorporated pre- or non-Christian rituals was accompanied by the priests' growing importance as local actors. It was precisely at this level that the Legion's popular religiosity made inroads, among both lower clergy that acted as local elites and in which the movement was much more interested than mainstream political parties, and the population at large.

However, while the lower clergy was attracted to the movement and 33 of the 103 elected members of parliament from the lists of the 'All for the Country' party in 1937 were priests,[123] the higher ranks of the Orthodox hierarchy were frequently opposed to it. This aspect points towards another important distinction, concerning the specificities of Orthodox Christianity and its difference from Catholicism both in terms of dogma, and, particularly, of relationship to the state. While in Germany and Italy, attempts to 'nationalize' the Church often came against the universalism of Catholicism,[124] Orthodox dogma is much more prone to national interpretations,[125] and the Church has strong traditional connections to the state.[126] This is certainly

part of the explanation behind the attitude of the higher ranks of the Orthodox Church towards the Legion, fluctuating across time in a relationship of
dependence to the position of the government with respect to the movement.
Its primary allegiance was to the state, and not to a revolutionary group,
albeit one advocating a 'spiritual' revolution.

Finally, the Italian 'sacralization of politics' identified by Gentile revolved
exclusively around ritual, around the moments of 'collective effervescence' that
were staged according to a veritable political liturgy. The sacralized character of
Italian fascism was limited to spectacle, meant to impress rather than convert,
and the dead, while revered, were not quite sanctified. Hence, the term 'political religion' appears accurate for the case of Italy, while seeming much more
problematic for the Romanian one. For the Legion, religiosity was all-pervad-
ing and fused with nationalism, and the envisaged revolution, while equally
comprehensive in its political aims, was meant to be primarily a spiritual one,
the final victory resulting "from the perfection in the soul of the nation of a
process of human improvement".[127] As Roland Clark notes,

> [l]egionaries not only stated that church and nation were identical com-
> munities that were represented most perfectly by their movement; they
> enacted these relationships by using Orthodox funerary rituals to com-
> memorate legionaries as national heroes. Legionary nationalism did not
> replace religious communities with national communities. Through ritual
> commemorations it reinforced the Orthodox Church as national, and the
> nation as Orthodox.[128]

This complete overlap and mutual reinforcement of the two systems of belief,
Christianity and nationalism, in the movement's rhetoric and particularly in the
case of the funeral of Moța and Marin, aligned with the self-perceptions of the two
dead legionaries,[129] resonated with a religious population more than the secular
nationalism of the Romanian state. This is attested by the reproduction of this
association by many of the participants in the funeral ceremonies held throughout
the country, from the director of the primary school in Cuciurul Mare, Constantin
Ianevschi, who told his pupils that "Moța and Marin sacrificed themselves in Spain
for the cause of Christianity and nationalism"; through the railway workers in
Adjud who claimed that the two "sacrificed their lives for the Christian cause and
the national idea", to Vicar Stan of the Bishopric of Sibiu who told the attending
audience more of the same; and finally to Professor Priest Zaharia Stanciu of
Orăștie, who said that "the Holy Relics of those who enriched the heroic patrimony
of our nation will be a further impetus for the ideal of the accomplishment of a
Christian and National Romania", proceeding even further to state, in direct dialogue with the dead, that "through your deed, you are of the nation, of the country,
of humanity".[130]

The success of the legionary funerals, more than of other public displays of
its 'disciplined troops', thus lay partly with the familiarity on a personal and
emotional level of mourning for the dead (especially in a country that had

experienced staggering casualties during World War I), and partly with the religious nature of the ritual, a spirituality which attracted elites and masses alike to an unprecedented extent. To the peasant masses, it offered a simple, unambiguous version of popular Orthodoxy, complete with legionary 'saints', and a familiar dynamic of sacrifice and resurrection. To the young generation of intellectuals, striving to find a possible synthesis between tradition and progress, and define an 'authentic' Romanian culture that would not be indebted to borrowings from the West,[131] it represented an answer that was in line with contemporary European developments while at the same time distinct from and allegedly superior to it. For the exponents of a minor, late-developing culture "at the edge of Europe",[132] marked by an acute awareness of 'backwardness', experienced simultaneously as a developmental lack and a temporal lag relative to an imagined 'West',[133] this represented a possible 'solution' that repositioned it (centrally) within European culture. In his answer to an enquiry entitled 'Why I believe in the triumph of the legionary movement?' carried out by the most important legionary newspaper before the elections in December 1937, Mircea Eliade, the future internationally renowned historian of religions, wrote:

> Today the entire world stands under the sign of revolution. But while other nations are living this revolution in the name of the class struggle and the primacy of the economic (communism), or of the state (fascism), or of the race (national-socialism) – the Legionary Movement was born under the sign of the Archangel Michael and will triumph through Godly grace. That is why, while all contemporary revolutions are political – the legionary revolution is spiritual and Christian, while all contemporary revolutions have as their purpose the conquest of power by a social class or by a man – the legionary revolution has as its supreme purpose the redemption of the nation, the reconciliation of the Romanian nation with God, as the Captain said. That is why the legionary movement has a different meaning with regard to everything that has been done until now in history, and the legionary triumph will bring with it not only the restoration of the virtues of our nation, a Romania that is worthy, dignified and powerful – but will create a new man, corresponding to a new type of European life.[134]

This aspect brings the present argument to its conclusion, connecting the different threads explored in this chapter, and positioning the case study of the funeral of Ion Moța and Vasile Marin within the discussion between elite and non-elite approaches to nationhood, as well of the competition between various actors, state and non-state, over the prevailing nationalist narrative. Referring back to Săndulescu's article arguing for the applicability of Gentile's concept of 'political religion' for the legionary movement, a final distinction between the Italian and Romanian cases that the author ignores is that the Italian funerary rituals were performed by a fascist regime, and were thus controlled by the state, while the Romanian one under discussion here was the expression of a nationalist project opposed to the one institutionalized by the state. The nationalist project of the Legion grew strong precisely because of being an 'alternative' to the corrupt government, as well as due to the solidarity it managed to create between elites and non-elites. In the emergence of this solidarity, the grassroots mobilization strategies employed by the movement represented a central factor. Once created, the networks connecting elites with 'ordinary people' proved accountable, providing both the funding and the disciplined bodies necessary for public celebrations of the scale of the funeral of Moța and Marin. Without the mass participation of 'ordinary people', the staging of such an event by elites lacking any support from the state would have proved impossible.

As repeatedly emphasized in this chapter, a key factor for producing the aforementioned solidarity between elites and non-elites in the case of the legionary movement was religion. Missing from the account of 'everyday nationhood' put forth by Jon Fox and Cynthia Miller-Idriss, the importance of religion for national identity, "the proximity of the Church in both the eastern and western traditions to the villagers and peasants" is duly noted by Anthony Smith.[135] In the case of the Legion, the bridge between the intricate theological arguments employed by elites in arguing for the religious character of the movement[136] and the popular Orthodoxy which proved so important for securing the allegiance of the peasant masses was represented by the sense of "ethnic election and mission"[137] embodied in the 'martyrdom' that the legionary movement constantly appealed to. The appeal to self-sacrifice for the nation, already employed by the Legion in previous propaganda campaigns, gained considerable weight with the example of the two legionary leaders. The funeral ritual itself, solemn and sober and staged as what was fundamentally a 'peasant funeral' on a gigantic scale, was familiar to elites and non-elites alike, and its salience for the peasant masses can be inferred from their extensive participation in the ceremony.

To conclude, an event such as the funeral of Ion Moța and Vasile Marin analysed in the present chapter, organized with the direct contribution of 'ordinary people', argues for the complementarity of approaches to nationalism focusing on elites and non-elites. Within such a complementary framework, those fleeting moments of collective effervescence when the voices of 'ordinary people' join the grand narrative of 'the nation' represent good vantage points for exploring the interaction of "personal and social identities", as well as the "role of intervening structures and contexts through which these interact".[138] For the Legion, public mass funerals were a preferred stage for inserting their 'martyrs' (even when they had died fighting the Romanian state) into a national narrative that stretched back beyond the limits of historical time, while simultaneously putting them forth as heralds of an impending future of legionary making.

In a mythical vision of the nation comprising, according to Codreanu, "1) All the Romanians presently alive. 2) All the souls of the dead and the graves of the ancestors. 3) All those who will be born Romanians",[139] the dead 'for the nation' were given special consideration, manifested in ubiquitous commemorations of already consecrated past sacrifice and in funerals exploiting the contemporary 'martyrdom' of the many victims from among the movement's own ranks, while constantly seeking to fuse the two. This aspect struck a sensitive chord with many who had recently experienced personal loss of close ones in World War I, and rendered salient an emotional notion of 'nationhood' that resonated with the public more than the state's modernizing project, prompted by notions of accelerated development modelled on Western patterns that remained alien to a predominantly peasant population.

Ultimately, it was this form of nationalism that proved to be persuasive insofar as it reflected people's personal and local experiences.[140] Consequently, reading legionary funerals and the movement's cult of the dead in light of their reception rather than performance, as they have been studied so far, goes a long way towards not only 'normalizing' practices that may appear bizarre only when considered outside their Romanian context and of the elements of popular religiosity that infused them, but also towards explaining the remarkable increase in popularity of a political organization that developed out of a fringe group of five students into the largest mass movement in Romania's modern history and the third largest fascist movement in Europe. Through the spectacle of its mass funerals, and by establishing a tenuous connection between its own 'martyrs' and the 'nation's' dead, an anti-establishment ultranationalist group skilfully enlisted them in its project of violent opposition to its own nationalist and nationalizing state.

Notes

1 Heinen, *Legiunea*, p. 357.
2 Arhiva Consiliului Naţional pentru Studierea Arhivelor Securităţii (henceforth ACNSAS), Bucharest, Romania, Fond Documentar, File 10160, vol. 1, pp. 364–374. All translations in the text are my own, unless specified otherwise.
3 Breuilly, *Nationalism*.
4 See Payne, *A History of Fascism*; Griffin, 'Shattering crystals'.
5 Rusu, 'The Sacralization'.
6 Payne, *A History of Fascism*, pp. 280–281.
7 Fox and Miller-Idriss, 'Everyday nationhood'.
8 Smith, 'The limits'. See also the response of Jon Fox and Cynthia Miller-Idriss, 'The "here and now"'.
9 Hobsbawm, *Nations and Nationalism*, p. 10.
10 Fox and Miller-Idriss, 'Everyday nationhood', pp. 537–538.
11 Ibid, p. 538.
12 See Van Ginderachter and Beyen, *Nationhood from Below*.
13 Smith, 'The limits', pp. 567–568.
14 Fox and Miller-Idriss, 'Everyday nationhood', pp. 546–548.
15 See Jowitt, *Social Change*; Georgescu, *The Romanians*.
16 Colescu, *Analiza*, p. 85; Manuilă, 'Recensământul general'.
17 Roberts, *Rumani*.
18 Livezeanu, *Cultural Politics*, p. 9.

19 Gellner, *Thought and Change*; Gellner, *Nations and Nationalism*.
20 Anderson, *Imagined Communities*.
21 Smith, *The Ethnic Origins*.
22 Iordachi, 'Charisma, religion, and ideology', p. 22.
23 Livezeanu, *Cultural Politics*, p. 234.
24 Yavetz, 'An eyewitness note', p. 599.
25 Cârstocea, 'Students don the green shirt'.
26 Gellner, *Thought and Change*, pp. 147–178.
27 Veiga, *Istoria Gărzii de Fier*, p. 19. Estimates for civilian casualties range from a minimum of 275,000 to a maximum of 430,000. See Prost, 'War losses'. According to Keith Hitchins, combining military and civilian deaths, Romania "is estimated to have lost one-tenth of her pre-war population" (Hitchins, *Rumania*, p. 291).
28 Dobrogeanu-Gherea, *Neoiobăgia*.
29 Hitchins, *Rumania*, p. 368.
30 Heinen, *Legiunea*, p. 357; Payne, *A History of Fascism*, pp. 275–277.
31 *Monitorul Oficial*, December 30, 1937.
32 ACNSAS, Fond Penal (henceforth Fund P), File 11784, vol. 12; Argetoianu, *Însemnări zilnice*, vol. 4, pp. 105–106.
33 Veiga, *Istoria*; Heinen, *Legiunea*; Clark, *Holy Legionary Youth*.
34 ACNSAS, File P 11784, vol. 6, pp. 152–153.
35 Nolte, *Die Krise des liberalen Systems*, p. 227.
36 Payne, *A History of Fascism*, p. 136.
37 Griffin, 'Shattering crystals', p. 80.
38 Payne, *A History of Fascism*, p. 280.
39 Zelea Codreanu, *Pentru legionari*, p. 364.
40 ACNSAS, File P 11784, vol. 2, p. 94.
41 Haynes, 'The Romanian legionary movement', pp. 113–125.
42 Cohen, 'Personal nationalism', p. 805.
43 Kligman, *The Wedding of the Dead*. At the time of her fieldwork in 1985, after almost forty years of rule of an allegedly 'atheist' and 'totalitarian' regime, Kligman could still note that "the church calendar broadly dictates the rhythm of activity that binds Ieudeni [villagers of Ieud] to one another" (p. 264).
44 Ibid. It is important to note that one cannot speak of 'Romanian' funeral rites, as there are considerable regional variations within the country, with regards to the objects and practices employed, the sequence of the funeral, the participation of family members, etc. The classic study on this subject for the period under consideration in this chapter remains Florea Marian, *Înmormîntarea la Români*. Another important study is the regional one carried out by the ethnographer Ernest Bernea in 1934 in North Gorj, a county in south-western Romania. While both the time of publication and the fact that Bernea was a legionary sympathizer who authored numerous publications in support of the movement render this ethnographic study important, it is itself heavily reliant on Marian's earlier work and, for the most part, describes very similar practices (see Bernea, 'La mort et l'enterrement').
45 See Haynes, 'Work camps'; Săndulescu, 'Taming the body'; Cârstocea, 'Building a fascist Romania'.
46 Nagy-Talavera, *The Green Shirts*, p. 262.
47 Marin, 'Note'.
48 Săndulescu, 'Sacralised politics', p. 268.
49 ACNSAS, File P 11784, vol. 11, p. 251.
50 ACNSAS, File P 11784, vol. 8, pp. 19, 50–53.
51 Moța, 'La Nașterea Domnului'.

52 Arhivele Naţionale Istorice Centrale (henceforth ANIC), Bucharest, Romania, Fond Ministerul de Interne, Diverse (Fund Ministry of the Interior, Varia), File 12/1937, p. 48.

53 N.N., 'Legionarii Ion Moţa şi Vasile Marin'. This juxtaposition, of the personal dimension of the death of the two legionaries and its 'higher meaning' in the national context, was consistently reproduced in speeches and other press articles, inscribing a personal connotation to the events. The religious service officiated in the courtyard of Moţa's family home in Orăştie was particularly emotional in this respect, and earth from the garden of his native house was consecrated by five priests, to be transported and entered in Bucharest together with his remains. ANIC, Fund MI, File 4/1937, p. 190. While files of the Ministry of the Interior at the National Central Historical Archives of Romania do not normally have titles, only numbers, this one is an exception, and is entitled (in large bold capital letters on the cover of the file) "The solemnity of the inhumation of legionaries I. Moţa and V. Marin". It appears that the funeral procession and the funeral itself impressed even the police, gendarmerie and *Siguranţa* (secret police) organs mobilized for the event.

54 ANIC, Fund MI, File 12/1937, p. 55.

55 See *Ideia Românească*, vol. 2, no. 1, 1937, special issue dedicated to the death of Moţa and Marin. The publication opened with an image of Moţa with angel wings, and with the following text written by Codreanu: "I have but one comfort: I entrust myself to what He saw in his immense sacrifice… I believe in what his soul saw, something which we are only beginning to glimpse." In spite of the capitalization, the 'He' referred to Moţa and not to Jesus.

56 Stamatu, 'Acatistul Moţa-Marin'.

57 See *Libertatea*, March 11, 18, 25, 1937.

58 ANIC, MI, File 4/1937, p. 127.

59 Argetoianu, *Însemnări zilnice*, vol. 2, p. 60.

60 Săndulescu, 'Sacralised politics', p. 263.

61 Florea Marian, *Înmormîntarea la Români*, pp. 286–307; Bernea, 'La mort', pp. 32–34. Mihai Stelian Rusu mentions two further sources of inspiration for the funeral train: "The 12 November 1936 state funerals of Wilhelm Gusthoff, the Nazi leader of Switzerland, assassinated in his home in Davos" and the 1923 reburial of the Romanian Unknown Soldier, where a randomly selected coffin "traveled in a funerary train that stopped at every station from Mărăşeşti to its final burial place in Bucharest" (Rusu, 'The sacralization of martyric death', pp. 18–19).

62 Kligman, *The Wedding of the Dead*, p. 196.

63 Clark, *Holy Legionary Youth*, p. 206. Other mentions of participants to the ceremonies kneeling solemnly as the train approached are provided in ANIC, MI, File 4/1937, pp. 70 (Râmnicu Vâlcea), 71 (Slatina), 112 (different locations in the Vâlcea, Romanaţi, Olt and Argeş counties), 133v (Dorneşti), 142 (I.G. Duca), 146 (Dolhasca, Roman, Paşcani), 148 (Galbeni), 165 (Târgu Mureş), 193 (Sibiu), 202v (Piatra Olt), 213 (Costeşti), 215 (Piteşti). It should also be noted that this was taking place in February 1937, and the police reports refer to the very bad weather and significant snowfall, conditions that rendered such emotional public manifestations even more unlikely. Moreover, the train travelled continuously, with only one overnight stop in Moţa's native town of Orăştie, so in many stations it arrived in the middle of the night, an aspect which did not seem to have prevented people from attending the ceremonies.

64 ANIC, MI, File 4/1937, pp. 133v, 139v, 140v, 169, 176, 188v, 215, 220, 229.

65 Ibid, p. 228. While uncovering one's head at the passage of a funeral procession is typical of traditional peasant funerals, the giving of the fascist salute indicates how seamlessly aspects of the legionary ritual blended with traditional ones. See

Bernea, 'La mort', p. 34. If the ringing of church bells is also customary at traditional funerals, the Adjud railway workers provided a modern version of it, blowing the sirens of the railway depot and of all the locomotives in the station. ANIC, Fund MI, File 4/1937, p. 117.

66 Ibid, p. 184. In the village of Adâncata, one of the very rare occasions where 'the approximately 250–300 peasants who were present were not too impressed', the report accounts for this by specifying that "the majority of them being Ukrainians [they are] not interested in the legionary cause" (p. 137v). While it stands to reason that an ultra-nationalist Romanian movement was not too popular among the country's national minorities, this was by no means a foregone conclusion, as demonstrated by the massive participation to the ceremonies of German students in Cernăuți and of Hungarians and Germans in Sibiu (pp. 128, 193).

67 Ibid, p. 144.

68 Ibid, pp. 112–112v.

69 Ibid, pp. 163, 178.

70 Ibid, pp. 179, 184, 213. Following the instructions received from the central command of the gendarmerie, the reports are mostly concerned with names (of prominent people attending the ceremonies, especially army officers, priests and public functionaries) and numbers (of the attending 'crowds', as well as more specific information concerning social class, gender, age, etc.). Consequently, the very fact that they frequently mention the emotional state of the participants is in itself notable.

71 While Roland Clark claims that "[r]ather than collectively chanting the Orthodox liturgy, mourners were expected to repeat words that bound them to the Legion in the same way that they might have bound themselves to God in a different context" (Clark, *Holy Legionary Youth*, p. 209), abundant evidence shows that they did *both*: religious and lay choirs provided the answers customary in the Orthodox liturgy during the funeral ceremonies held along the route of the train. ANIC, Fund MI, File 4/1937, pp. 18, 155v, 176, 188.

72 ANIC, Fund MI, File 4/1937, p. 157.

73 Ibid, pp. 169, 176, 190–193. Notably, in Cluj, Father Ioan Agârbiceanu paid the respects of the Greek-Catholic (Uniate) Church to the two legionaries. The participation of representatives of 'the minority cults in the locality' in officiating the religious service was also noted in Moța's native Orăștie.

74 Ibid, p. 193.

75 Ibid, pp. 176–177.

76 Ibid, p. 190.

77 Ibid, p. 215.

78 Ibid, p. 15.

79 Clark, *Holy Legionary Youth*, p. 198.

80 ANIC, Fund MI, File 4/1937, p. 27.

81 Iorga, 'Doi băieți viteji'.

82 Protopopescu, 'Contemporarii lui Iisus…'.

83 Ibid.

84 Ibid.

85 Manoilescu, 'Dela Lord Byron la Ion Moța'.

86 Manoilescu, 'Dincolo de erou și supraom'.

87 Deleanu, 'Buna Vestire', p. 3.

88 Stamatu, 'Acatistul', p. 7.

89 Vial, 'Iar generația lui Moța?'.

90 Ibid.

91 ANIC, Fund MI, File 4/1937, p. 14. In Christian Orthodoxy, a protopope is a priest of higher rank, the equivalent of a dean in Catholicism.

92   Ibid. The order of the procession paralleled the one at traditional peasant funerals. The religious banners customary at such funerals were accompanied by Romanian flags.

93   Ibid, p. 93. Simion Florea Marian notes that the playing of alpenhorns is a funeral custom from Moldova. While this was Codreanu's native region, neither of the two deceased came from it: Moța was from Transylvania, while Marin was from Bucharest. The colour of the two coffins was the typical legionary green, also diverging from tradition: in traditional funerals, coffins are either unpainted or painted in black, red, blue or brown. Finally, the use of fir tree branches, with which the coffins were covered, is reserved in peasant funerals for unmarried dead, whereas both Moța and Marin were married. Florea Marian, *Înmormîntarea la Români*, pp. 195, 237, 251. Roland Clark notes a similar issue concerning the regional variations of funeral rites with regards to the people responsible for digging the grave, which was also resolved in this case by asserting the primacy of the Legion over tradition and "the two men's families" (Clark, *Holy Legionary Youth*, p. 209).

94   N.N, 'Ion Moța și Vasile Marin'.

95   ACNSAS, File P 11784, vol. 8, p. 21.

96   Sandache, *Îngerii căzuți*, p. 180.

97   ANIC, Fund MI, File 12/1937, p. 12; ANIC, Fund MI, File 4/1937, pp. 112, 150.

98   Argetoianu, *Însemnări zilnice*, vol. 2, pp. 68–77.

99   Ibid, pp. 68–69.

100 ANIC, Fund MI, File 5/1933, pp. 178–180.

101 Ionescu, 'Prefață'.

102 Argetoianu, *Însemnări zilnice*, vol. 4, p. 58.

103 Boilă, *Amintiri și considerații*, pp. 51–55; Interview with Serban Milcoveanu, February 12, 2008, București. Șerban Milcoveanu was Codreanu's personal secretary at the time of the events discussed in the chapter.

104 Interview with Serban Milcoveanu, Șerban, February 15, 2008, București.

105 See Clark, *Holy Legionary Youth* for an example of a legionary funeral held for a 16-year-old schoolgirl, Maria Cristescu, who had joined the Legion four months prior to dying of a sudden illness. According to Clark, "[t]he theatricality, religiosity, and community spirit displayed at Maria Cristescu's funeral hint at how fascism transformed the lives of rank-and-file legionaries" (pp. 1–2, here p. 2).

106 Freeden, 'The politics of ceremony'.

107 Griffin, *The Nature of Fascism*; Griffin, *International Fascism*.

108 Smith, 'The limits of everyday nationhood'.

109 Hobsbawm, *Nations and Nationalism*; Fox and Miller-Idriss, 'Everyday nationhood'; Van Ginderachter and Beyen, *Nationhood from Below*.

110 Freeden, 'The politics of ceremony', p. 2.

111 Ibid, p. 8.

112 Cârstocea, 'Building a fascist Romania', pp. 189–190.

113 Haynes, 'Work camps', p. 943.

114 Argetoianu, *Însemnări zilnice*, vol. 4, p. 92.

115 Breuilly, *Nationalism and the State*.

116 Hobsbawm, *Nations and Nationalism since 1780*, p. 10.

117 Noica, 'Fiți înfricoșători de buni'.

118 Noica, '10,001'.

119 Freeden, 'The politics of ceremony', p. 9.

120 Zelea Codreanu, *Pentru legionari*, p. 425.

121 Săndulescu, 'Sacralised politics'; Gentile, *The Sacralization of Politics*.

122 Gentile, *The Sacralization of Politics*, p. 27.

123   Ioanid, 'The Sacralised Politics', p. 436.
124   See Gentile, *Il culto del littorio*; Steigmann-Gall, *'The Holy Reich'*.
125   See Stăniloae, *Naţiune şi Creştinism*.
126   Stan and Turcescu, *Religion and Politics*; Bănică, *Biserica Ortodoxă Română*, pp. 132–135.
127   Zelea Codreanu, *Circulări şi manifeste*, p. 273.
128   Clark, *Holy Legionary Youth*, p. 209.
129   These were expressed in letters written by the two while in Spain, subsequently published as articles in the nationalist newspaper ran by Moţa's father, *Libertatea*. See Cârstocea, 'Native fascists, transnational anti-Semites', pp. 231–233.
130   ANIC, Fund MI, File 4/1937, pp. 135, 156, 190, 193.
131   Hitchins, *'Gîndirea'*.
132   Nolte, *Three Faces of Fascism*, p. 462.
133   Todorova, 'The trap of backwardness', p. 145.
134   Eliade, 'De ce cred în biruinţa mişcării legionare'.
135   Smith, 'The limits of everyday nationhood', p. 571.
136   See e.g. Racoveanu, *Mişcarea Legionară şi Biserica*.
137   Smith, 'The limits of everyday nationhood', p. 571.
138   Hearn, 'National identity', p. 659.
139   Zelea Codreanu, *Pentru legionari*, p. 423.
140   Cohen, 'Personal nationalism', p. 810.

References

Anderson, Benedict, *Imagined communities: Reflections on the origin and spread of nationalism*, London, Verso, 1983.

Argetoianu, Constantin, *Însemnări zilnice*, 10 vol., Bucureşti, Editura Machiavelli, 1998–2009 [1935–1944].

Bănică, Mirel, *Biserica Ortodoxă Română: stat şi societate în anii '30*, Iaşi, Polirom, 2007.

Bernea, Ernest, 'La mort et l'enterrement dans le Gorj du Nord', in: *Martor: Revue D'Anthropologie du Musée du Paysan Roumain*, vol. 3, 1998 [1934], supplement.

Boilă, Zaharia, *Amintiri şi consideraţii asupra mişcării legionare*, Cluj-Napoca, Biblioteca Apostrof, 2002.

Breuilly, John, *Nationalism and the state*, Chicago, University of Chicago Press, 1985.

Cârstocea, Raul, 'Building a fascist Romania: Voluntary work camps as a propaganda strategy of the legionary movement in interwar Romania', in: *Fascism*, vol. 6, no. 2, 2017, pp. 163–195.

Cârstocea, Raul, 'Native fascists, transnational anti-Semites: The international activity of legionary leader Ion I. Moţa', in: Bauerkämper, Arnd and Rossoliński-Liebe, Grzegorz (eds.), *Fascism without borders: Connections and cooperation between movements and regimes in Europe from 1918 to 1945*, New York, Berghahn Books, 2017, pp. 216–242.

Cârstocea, Raul, 'Students don the green shirt. The roots of Romanian fascism in the anti-Semitic student movements of the 1920s', in: Fritz, Regina, Rossoliński-Liebe, Grzegorz, and Starek, Jana (eds.), *Alma Mater Antisemitica. Akademisches Milieu, Juden und Antisemitismus an den Universitäten Europas zwischen 1918 und 1939*, Vienna, New Academic Press, 2016, pp. 39–66.

Clark, Roland, *Holy legionary youth: Fascist activism in interwar Romania*, Ithaca, Cornell University Press, 2015.

Cohen, Anthony P., 'Personal nationalism: A Scottish view of some rites, rights, and wrongs', in: *American Ethnologist* vol. 23, no. 4, 1996, pp. 802–815.

Colescu, Leonida, *Analiza rezultatelor recensământului general al populaţiei României din 1899*, Bucureşti, Institutul Central de Statistică, 1944.

Deleanu, Pavel Costin, 'Buna vestire', in: *Ideia Românească*, vol. 2, no. 1, 1937, pp. 3–6.

Dobrogeanu-Gherea, Constantin, *Neoiobăgia. Studiu economico-sociologic al problemei noastre agrare*, Bucureşti, Editura Librăriei Socec, 1910.

Eliade, Mircea, 'De ce cred în biruinţa mişcării legionare', in: *Buna Vestire*, 17 December 1937.

Florea Marian, Simion, *Înmormîntarea la Români. Studiu Etnograficu*, Bucureşti: Litotipografia Carol Göbl, 1892.

Fox, Jon and Miller-Idriss, Cynthia, 'The "here and now" of everyday nationhood', in: *Ethnicities*, vol. 8, no. 4, 2008, pp. 573–576.

Fox, Jon E. and Miller-Idriss, Cynthia, 'Everyday nationhood', in: *Ethnicities*, vol. 8, no. 4, 2008, pp. 536–563.

Freeden, Michael, 'The politics of ceremony: The Wootton Bassett phenomenon', in: *Journal of Political Ideologies*, vol. 16, no. 1, 2011, pp. 1–10.

Gellner, Ernest, *Nations and nationalism*, Ithaca, Cornell University Press, 1983.

Gellner, Ernest, *Thought and change*, London, Weidenfeld and Nicolson, 1964.

Gentile, Emilio, *Il culto del littorio: la sacralizzazione della politica nell'Italia fascista*, Roma, Laterza, 1993.

Gentile, Emilio, *The sacralization of politics in fascist Italy*, trans. Keith Botsford, Cambridge MA: Harvard University Press, 1996.

Griffin, Roger (ed.), *International fascism: Theories, causes and the new consensus*, London, Arnold, 1998.

Griffin, Roger, '"Shattering crystals": The role of "dream-time" in extreme right-wing political violence', in: *Terrorism and Political Violence*, vol. 15, no. 1, 2003, pp. 57–96.

Griffin, Roger, *The nature of fascism*, London, Routledge, 1993.

Haynes, Rebecca, 'The Romanian legionary movement, popular orthodoxy and the cult of death', in: Anton, Mioara, Anghel, Florin and Popa, Cosmin (eds.), *Hegemoniile trecutului: evoluţii româneşti şi europene: profesorului Ioan Chiper la 70 de ani*, Bucureşti, Curtea Veche, 2006, pp.113–125.

Haynes, Rebecca, 'Work camps, commerce and the education of the "new man" in the Romanian legionary movement', in: *The Historical Journal*, vol. 51, no. 4, 2008, pp. 943–967.

Hearn, Jonathan, 'National identity: Banal, personal and embedded', in: *Nations and Nationalism*, vol. 13, no. 4, 2007, pp. 657–674.

Heinen, Armin, *Legiunea 'Arhanghelul Mihail': o contribuţie la problema fascismului international*, Bucureşti, Humanitas, 2nd edition, 2006.

Hitchins, Keith, 'Gîndirea: Nationalism in a spiritual guise', in Jowitt, Kenneth (ed.), *Social change in Romania, 1860–1940. A debate on development in a European nation*, Berkeley, University of California, 1978, pp. 140–174.

Hitchins, Keith, *Rumania: 1866–1947*, Oxford, Clarendon Press, 1994.

Hobsbawm, Eric J., *Nations and nationalism since 1780: Programme, myth, reality*, Cambridge, Cambridge University Press, 1991.

Hobsbawm, Eric, *Nations and nationalism since 1780: Programme, myth, reality*, Cambridge, Cambridge University Press, 1991.

Ioanid, Radu, 'The sacralised politics of the Romanian iron guard', in: *Totalitarian Movements and Political Religions*, vol. 5, no. 3, 2004, pp. 419–453.

Ionescu, Nae, 'Prefaţă', in Marin, Vasile, *Crez de generaţie*, Bucureşti, Editura Majadahonda, 5th edition, 1997 [1937], p. 14.

Iordachi, Constantin, 'Charisma, religion, and ideology: Romania's interwar legion of the archangel Michael', in: Lampe, John and Mazower, Mark (eds.), *Ideologies and national identities: The case of twentieth-century Southeastern Europe*, Budapest, Central European University Press, 2003, pp. 19–53.

Iorga, Nicolae, 'Doi băieţi viteji: Moţa şi Marin', in: *Neamul Românesc*, 19 January 1937.

Jowitt, Kenneth (ed.), *Social change in Romania, 1860–1940. A debate on development in a European nation*, Berkeley, Institute of International Studies, University of California, 1978.

Georgescu, Vlad, *The Romanians: A history*, ed. Matei Călinescu, trans. Alexandra Bley-Vroman, Columbus, Ohio State University Press, 1991.

Kligman, Gail, *The wedding of the dead: Ritual, poetics, and popular culture in Transylvania*, Berkeley, University of California Press, 1988.

Livezeanu, Irina, *Cultural politics in Greater Romania: Regionalism, nation-building, and ethnic struggle, 1918–1930*, Ithaca, Cornell University Press, 1995.

Manoilescu, Mihail, 'Dela Lord Byron la Ion Moţa', in: *Buna Vestire*, 24 February 1937.

Manoilescu, Mihail, 'Dincolo de erou şi supraom', in: *Ideea Naţională*, 22 February 1937.

Manuilă, Sabin (ed.), 'Recensământul general al populaţiei României din 29 decemvrie 1930', in: *Anuarul Statistic al României. 1939 şi 1940*, Bucureşti, Ministerul Industriei şi Comerţului, 1940, pp. 58–75.

Marin, Vasile, 'Note din drumul spre frontul spaniol', in: *Porunca Vremii*, 12 December 1936.

Moţa, Ion I., 'La Naşterea Domnului', in: *Libertatea* (Freedom), 25 December 1936.

N.N., 'Legionarii Ion Moţa şi Vasile Marin au căzut în luptele din jurul Madridului', in: *Universul*, 17 January 1937.

N.N., 'Ion Moţa şi Vasile Marin', in: *Frontul*, 12 February 1937.

Nagy-Talavera, Nicholas, *The green shirts and the others – a history of fascism in Hungary and Romania*, Stanford: Hoover Institution Press, 1970.

Noica, Constantin, '10,001', in: *Buna Vestire*, 20 September 1940.

Noica, Constantin, 'Fiţi înfricoşători de buni', in: *Buna Vestire*, 10 September 1940.

Nolte, Ernst, *Die Krise des liberalen Systems und die faschistischen Bewegungen*, München, Deutscher Taschenbuch Verlag, 1966.

Nolte, Ernst, *Three faces of fascism: Action Française, Italian fascism, National Socialism*, trans. Leila Vennewitz, New York, Holt, Rinehart and Winston, 1966.

Payne, Stanley G., *A history of fascism, 1914–1945*, Madison, University of Wisconsin Press, 1995.

Prost, Antoine, 'War losses', in: Daniel, Ute *et al.* (eds.), *1914–1918-online. International encyclopedia of the First World War*, Berlin, Freie Universität Berlin, 2014, available at https://encyclopedia.1914-1918-online.net/article/war_losses (accessed 26 January 2019).

Protopopescu, Dragoş, 'Contemporarii lui Iisus...', in: *Buna Vestire*, 22 February 1937.

Racoveanu, Gheorghe, *Mişcarea Legionară şi Biserica*, Rome, Armatolii, 1973 [1943].

Roberts, Henry L., *Rumania: Political problems of an agrarian state*, New Haven, Yale University Press, 1951.

Rusu, Mihai Stelian, 'The sacralization of martyric death in Romanian legionary movement: Self-sacrificial patriotism, vicarious atonement, and thanatic nationalism', in: *Politics, Religion and Ideology*, vol. 17, nos. 2–3, 2016, pp. 249–273.

Sandache, Cristian, *Îngerii căzuţi. O istorie a extremei drepte din România*, Bucureşti, Corint, 2010.

Săndulescu, Valentin, '"Taming the body": Preliminary considerations concerning the legionary work camps system (1933–1937)', in: *Historical Yearbook*, vol. 5, 2008, pp. 85–94.

Săndulescu, Valentin, 'Sacralised politics in action: The February 1937 burial of the Romanian legionary leaders Ion Moța and Vasile Marin', in: *Totalitarian Movements and Political Religions*, vol. 8, no. 2, 2007, pp. 259–269.

Smith, Anthony D., 'The limits of everyday nationhood', in: *Ethnicities*, vol. 8, no. 4, pp. 563–573.

Smith, Anthony D., *The ethnic origins of nations*, Oxford, Basil Blackwell, 1986.

Stamatu, Horia, 'Acatistul Moța-Marin', in: *Ideia Românească*, vol. 2, no. 1, 1937, pp. 7–9.

Stan, Lavinia and Turcescu, Lucian, *Religion and politics in post-communist Romania*, Oxford, Oxford University Press, 2007.

Stăniloae, Dumitru, *Națiune și Creștinism*, ed. Virginia Carianopol, București, Editura Elion, 2003.

Steigmann-Gall, Richard, *'The Holy Reich': Nazi conceptions of Christianity, 1919–1945*, Cambridge, Cambridge University Press, 2003.

Todorova, Maria, 'The trap of backwardness: Modernity, temporality, and the study of eastern European nationalism', in: *Slavic Review*, vol. 64, no. 1, 2005, pp. 140–164.

Van Ginderachter, Maarten and Beyen, Marnix (eds.), *Nationhood from below: Europe in the long nineteenth century*, New York, Palgrave Macmillan, 2012.

Veiga, Francisco, *Istoria Gărzii de Fier 1919–1941: Mistica ultranaționalismului*, trans. Marian Ștefănescu, București, Humanitas, 1993.

Vial, Ion, 'Iar generația lui Moța?', in: *Buna Vestire*, 26 February 1937.

Yavetz, Zvi, 'An eyewitness note: Reflections on the Rumanian Iron Guard', in: *Journal of Contemporary History* vol. 26, nos. 3/4, 1991, pp. 597–610.

Zelea Codreanu, Corneliu, *Circulări și manifeste*, Madrid, Colecția Omul Nou, 1951.

Zelea Codreanu, Corneliu, *Pentru legionari*, Sibiu, Editura Totul Pentru Țară, 1936.

8 Feeling the fatherland

Finnish soldiers' lyrical attachments to the nation during the Second World War[1]

Ville Kivimäki

Introduction: patriotism revisited

The ability of nationalism to foster wilful sacrifice on behalf of the community is one of the peculiar features that separates national belonging from many other identities. To understand this willingness has motivated some of the key works in nationalism studies, from Benedict Anderson's *Imagined Communities* to Michael Billig's *Banal Nationalism*[2]; yet the issue remains open for new interpretations. The present chapter will, for its small part, search for answers to this same question by looking at the Finnish soldiers of the Second World War as 'artisans' of nationalism – i.e. as active participants in 'doing the nation'. It seems evident to me that to explain soldiers' suffering and dying for the nation requires paying attention to the emotional dimension of how the nation was experienced. Therefore, my focus will be on the soldiers' attachments in relation to national belonging.

Finnish participation in the Second World War can be divided into five distinctive phases. First, in the Winter War from November 30, 1939 until March 13, 1940, Finland faced the Soviet Union's unprovoked aggression, which tended to bring people together, level earlier social and political schisms, and ease the traumatic memory of the fratricidal Civil War in 1918 – at least momentarily. The peace terms of March 1940 were consequently experienced as utterly unjust, causing widespread bitterness and revanchism.[3] These emotions peaked in June 1941, when Finland joined Operation Barbarossa in the so-called Continuation War. The areas lost after the Winter War were recaptured, and the Finnish Army advanced far into Soviet Karelia, which had never been part of Finland. In this second phase of war, from June to December 1941, the Finns seemed to be on the winning side of the now global conflict and thus able to fulfil the old nationalist dream of Greater Finland: the incorporation of large Eastern Karelian and Ingrian territories to Finland proper. These eastern areas had had a key role in the Finnish national romanticism as the cradle of the Finnish 'tribe' and during 1918–1922, Finnish volunteer troops had tried to defeat the new Bolshevik rule in Soviet Karelia. Through the 1920s and 1930s, Greater Finland had remained an object of passionate advocacy by the nationalistic student movement and other right-wing activists.[4]

Third, from the beginning of 1942 until June 1944, Finland remained on the quiet margins of the war in the east. The frontlines remained in place, occupied Soviet Karelia was administered as part of Greater Finland (although not formally annexed to Finland), and as long as Leningrad was under siege, the Finnish heartland was safe from serious threats. Nevertheless, after the German defeat in Stalingrad in January 1943, the Finns started to observe their prospects much more cautiously: in public opinion surveys, the faith in Axis victory collapsed,[5] as did the siege of Leningrad in January 1944. The fourth phase of war – the Soviet offensive against Finland in June–July 1944 – was thus not a total surprise, yet the strength and determination of the attack were a shock both to the Finnish soldiers and to the population at large. Although the Soviet offensive was eventually halted, the summer of 1944 and the ensuing armistice terms in September 1944 were a sobering and demoralizing event for the Finns: the high expectations of 1941 had experienced a definite defeat. In the fifth phase of war, from late September 1944 until April 1945, the Finnish Army fought to drive off the German troops in Northern Finland, an area now devastated by the German scorched earth tactics.[6]

At the end of the Second World War, Finland remained independent and unoccupied and was spared from the most violent hardships experienced in East and Central Europe. Yet the war's outcome proved the moral and political bankruptcy of those passionately nationalistic sentiments that were bound to the ideology of Greater Finland. After the military desertions, the waves of panic, and the near-collapse of the front in the summer of 1944, even the solemn patriotism of the Winter War now seemed partly compromised.[7] In addition, during the long and passive trench warfare period in 1942–44, Finnish officers' views of their soldiers and their motivations had started to change, gradually emphasizing the importance of group dynamics and pragmatic leadership instead of ideological devotion and inherited patriotism.[8] At the same time, similar observations on the nature of soldiers' behaviour were made in the emerging faculty of military sociology and psychology, developed especially inside the US Army. The soldiers' will to fight and to fulfil their duties was no more a simple matter of 'moral fibre' and 'patriotic spirit', but a more complex social psychological and situational phenomenon.[9]

Perceived from this perspective, wartime expressions of patriotic emotions are easily seen as a matter of top-down propaganda and manipulation. In Finland, this view was immortalized in author (and frontline soldier) Väinö Linna's immensely influential war novel *Tuntematon sotilas* (*The Unknown Soldier*, 1954), which cemented the stereotype of Finnish soldiers as a bunch of unruly, grumbling, ironic fellows, who usually did their share but ridiculed anything too high-flown or bombastic. Patriotism as a motivation was put aside; or at least redefined as something much more down-to-earth than the military chaplains' zealous sermons or the educational officers' elevated lectures.[10]

There is much to agree with in the above-mentioned observations of modern military sociology and Väinö Linna alike. In my own readings of both wartime materials and the Finnish soldiers' post-war reminiscences, it is obvious that the frontline soldiers were often averse to any patronizing attempts to promote patriotism from above. It is also clear that the soldiers grew disillusioned with the lofty nationalistic rhetoric during the long war years.[11] But to become disillusioned there must first be something that is consequently exposed as an illusion. This is the topic of this chapter: Finnish soldiers' emotional attachment to the nation *before* the apparent disillusionment; and what this tells us about the power and attraction of nationalism.

Research question and sources: a wartime collection of soldiers' poems

In modern wars of the twentieth century, the soldiers have formed a very distinctive group of a nation-state's citizenry. This was true also in wartime Finland: the soldiers in uniform embodied the collective 'Finnishness' as a national-masculine self-image.[12] Yet the patriotic civic education of the soldiers-to-be had, of course, started already long before the war. In the Finnish public school system and in the various children's and youth organizations (some of them paramilitary), boys were brought up as the future defenders of the fatherland from early on.[13] The pre-war conscription service complemented the training: ideally, a collective spirit of comradeship and patriotism should have been forged among entire age cohorts of young men, overwriting their social and political differences.[14] During the war, the Finnish practice of repatriating all the fallen soldiers to be buried in their home parishes in the so-called 'Hero's Cemeteries' emphasized the emotional link between the war front and the home front and situated the soldiers' sacrifices at the heart of each locality, both physically as well as symbolically.[15] As in Germany and many other war-waging countries – in 1914–18 and again in 1939–45 – there were aspirations in the Finnish wartime rhetoric to import the ideal of frontline comradeship as an overarching ideological model for social relations to civil society at large, thus revitalizing and unifying the Finnish nation. This idea became institutionalized in the Union of Finnish Brothers-in-Arms (*Suomen Aseveljien Liitto*), a soldiers' and veterans' organization founded after the Winter War in 1940 and banned under Soviet pressure in 1945.[16]

The Finnish patriotic civic education of young boys and men was not uniform. There were, for instance, evident differences in its reception according to social class, political affinity and family background.[17] The prime point I want to make here is that there was a strong ideological invitation to the patriotic duty of soldiering, aimed at male citizens who were either about to enter their military conscription or who were already serving in the army. There were distinct cultural roles reserved for the conscript-soldiers in the collective mindset of the nation. As Michael Billig has stressed, those national sentiments that become fervent at the times of crises are created already in peacetime, in the everyday routines and repetitions of banal nationalism.[18] With a view to the wartime manifestations of soldiers' attachments, this background in pre-war civic education is important to keep in mind.

My claim is that – contrary to post-war (and post-defeat) descriptions – the Finnish soldiers were not immune to the nationalistic education so forcefully thrust upon them. The key question is, how did they themselves respond to the call to defend the fatherland and even to die for it? How did the soldiers describe their affection for the nation and relate it to other attachment relations? What does this tell us about the personal experience of nationalism and the phenomenon of national belonging as 'emotional practice'? Although this chapter is empirical in nature, I will back my findings by drawing ideas from the existing research on the affective dimension of nationalism and from the history of emotions.

In order to answer the above-mentioned questions, I have used a special wartime source: a collection of Finnish soldiers' poetry. The Information Department of the Finnish Army High Command gathered the poems from 'ordinary soldiers' with the apparent aim to document an authentic, lyrical voice of the frontlines to be used for propaganda purposes. The unpublished, archived collection contains close to 850 poems.[19] It is somewhat unclear when exactly the gathering of poems started. In early 1943, the Information Department announced an official war poetry competition, but most of the archived poems seem to have been written during 1941–42. Probably they were subsequently submitted to the competition in 1943. In any case, they were written at the height of Greater Finland enthusiasm following the army's victorious advance to the east in 1941. But some soldiers also sent their earlier poems written during the Winter War in 1939–40, and new poems kept arriving until the spring of 1944, albeit in much smaller quantities. Many of the poems had been originally submitted for the divisional and regimental frontline papers, which were the army's semi-official publications printed for the soldiers of different front sectors.[20]

Later in June 1943, the Information Department decided to select a number of poems to be published. The anthology *Täältä jostakin: Suomen kenttäarmeijan runoja* ([From the Front: Finnish Field Army's Poems], 1943) included a total of 140 poems and was edited by the famous Finnish author Olavi Paavolainen, who was serving as a lieutenant at the Information Department. Interestingly, as the book was published in November 1943 – after Stalingrad and all the following German setbacks – its content is much more reserved than the overall collection would have allowed. By then Finnish officials had given instructions to avoid public rhetoric that would have unnecessarily antagonized the Allied Powers (Finland was not at war with the United States and wished to maintain this relation). Thus, for instance, the many enthusiastic poems on Greater Finland were never printed. This may also have to do with Paavolainen's own literary distaste with overly pathetic verses.[21]

As a historical source, the collection has its limitations: most importantly the fact that the poems were requested and gathered by army officials. The unpublished poems were not censored in any way; only the poems selected for the anthology had to be approved by wartime censors. But although the soldiers could send their texts under a pseudonym, this was clearly not the right place to be overly disillusioned or critical. Understandably, the poems are not representative of the overall mood among the troops, but rather of the most elevated, nationalistic perceptions of war. Yet as such they serve as an interesting contrast to the post-war reminiscences, which – written from the post-1945 perspective – have the tendency to downplay vigorous patriotism or anything resembling war zealotry.

Furthermore, borrowing anthropologist William M. Reddy's concepts, the poems can be read as emotives – as verbal expressions of feeling – with which the writers brought together their personal experiences at the frontlines and the socio-cultural norms of feeling in an 'emotional regime' of a nation at war.[22] Although I will not follow Reddy's theory systematically, I take two useful insights for understanding the poems: first, their character as in-between the personal and the cultural, and second, their role as acts or practices, which create emotions instead of just describing them. Seen this way, the poems offer a rare view into the reciprocal interaction between the national systems of meaning and the soldiers' personal feelings and attachments. Olavi Paavolainen wrote in his wartime diaries that the abundance of 'patriotic phraseology' in the poems showed how 'our official propaganda has been able to corrupt and stultify the fresh, original imagery of the common man'.[23] True as this may be, I think it is more fruitful to read the poems as an active response to the invitation to patriotic, martial masculinity,[24] demonstrating that the call had been understood.

Unfortunately the background information on the writers of the poems is very limited – usually only the name, military rank and the unit are given. Thus, not much can be said about the social distribution of the collection's authors. The number of junior officers, NCOs and lance corporals among the poets seems to be disproportionately high, which would make sense: the motivation shown by their above-average military rank reflected on their above-average dedication to the war effort and its national meanings. But the poems of ordinary privates are also very common.

Lyrical attachments I: addressing the nation

By its very nature, lyrical poetry provides a way to express sentiments which would seem too naïve, pompous and out-of-place in prose. Despite all its horrors, the battlefield's dramatic scenery, extreme conditions and existential challenges have often been glorified and aestheticized in poems.[25] In this regard, the Finnish soldiers had a rich genre of literature to draw from. Patriotic war poetry occupied a prominent place in the elementary school curriculum; most importantly pupils often learned by heart national poet J.L. Runeberg's (1804–1877) *Vänrikki Stoolin tarinat* ('The Tales of Ensign Stål'). This national-romantic collection of martial poetry – the canonic anthology for Finnish nationalism – depicted the sacrifice, bravery and stoicism of the Finnish soldiers in Sweden's lost war against Russia in 1808–09. Similar themes were repeated in a multitude of patriotic songs, poems and stories learned at school, in civic organizations and in the army. The traumatic memory of the Finnish Civil War in 1918 emphasized further the need to force a nationally cohesive curriculum upon the schoolchildren of the 1920s and 1930s.[26] It is also worth noting that those pupils especially who continued their education to secondary schools and gymnasiums, were often taught in the classical tradition, which cherished Latin and Greek literature and thus also the heroic virtues of the antiquity.

This cultural repertoire of patriotic verse echoes strongly in the collection of Finnish soldiers' wartime poems. The total of ca. 850 poems naturally includes diverse topics and styles; yet, more surprising is the collection's uniformity. Notwithstanding a few odd outliers, the collection is generically consistent. First, the poems can be tagged into two groups according to their type of address: 1) the poems addressing an abstract collective, usually the nation or an entity closely related to it; and 2) the poems addressing specific human individuals, the soldiers' close ones. In many poems, of course, both addressees are present, thus reflecting an intertwined attachment between one's nation and one's specific fellow citizens. The poems in these two groups can then be further tagged by their central themes, as will be detailed below.

Starting with the poems addressing the abstract collective, the first theme is narrative poems, or broadsheet chants, which tell the story of a given battalion or regiment in war, chronicling the main events, special incidents, remarkable personalities and famous commanders. The style of these poems is often rakish and humorous. They connect a unit's particular expeditions to world historical events, and especially in 1941 they depict the Finnish soldiers as taking part in making history. One's adventurous military unit and its personnel become subjects of attachment and affinity, expressing a joyful *esprit de corps*. A soldier's personal journey with his unit becomes aligned with the collective narrative of the nation, whereby the given regiment or battalion embodies both the individual soldiers as a group and the nation as a band of brothers, led by a charismatic commander. The military unit is an object of affection and pride, instilling its collective strength to individual soldiers.

In a similar fashion, albeit less folksy in style, many poems consist of heroic, march-type lyrics celebrating the victorious Finnish Army and its soldiers fighting and conquering to liberate the country and the 'Finnish tribe' from the threat of the East. These poems extol the 'dawning new day' and the 'bright future' of the Finnish nation, redeemed by the soldiers:

> We want to crush the Eastern hordes,
> our strong blows know no mercy.
> The spirits of our heroes
> from ages gone by
> join us in our struggle.
>
> Our girl remembers us with longing,
> for us her dear heart beating.

Do not worry,
soon we'll meet
when the heavy work is done.

We shall bolt and bar the border.
The Eastern filth to vanquish.
Therefore always forward side by side
the invincible regiment marches.[27]

As the poem shows, the collective theme (the regiment as the embodiment of the nation) and the quasi-personal addressee ('our girl') join seamlessly to create an image of male warriors crushing the nation's enemies under the longing gaze of young women. In this vein, many authors dedicate their writings to Greater Finland and to the liberation of Eastern Karelia. Although the ideology of Greater Finland has often been understood as the fanciful project of Finnish nationalist elites and therefore not influencing the common people, the theme of expanding Finland's territory inspired many in the rank-and-file, too.[28] The Greater Finland poems are one of the most common types in the collection, especially among the poems written in 1941–42:

To the bosom of mother Finland
return these dear brothers.
Borders on which it is easier to build,
with bolts against the Eastern threats.
It is our goal,
we will not leave undone,
we must make our Finland greater
twine together the roots of our kin.[29]

Here, references to the Finnic population of Soviet Karelia as 'our kin' and to the borders of Greater Finland expand the national attachment to new people and territory. Obviously, such an expansion has an aggressive edge as a revenge and final victory against the 'eternal enemy' in the East. Easily overlapping with the previous themes, poems of patriotic sacrifice, oaths and flag contrast the purity of the soldiers' mission to the dirtiness and destructiveness of 'Asian Bolshevism'.[30] These poems connect Finnish men on the frontlines with the ancient Finnish tradition of fighting against the East, with natural warrior skills and instincts, and with the demanding and timeless example set by the forefathers in sacrificing for the Finnish nation, now followed by their sons in arms:[31]

Look! past centuries watch you,
with brothers long since fallen,
and mothers, fatigued with woes...
See our orphans' ample tears.

Like a high priest you are destined
to sacrifice on your people's altar.
Swear in the name of freedom
that you will give it *all* you can.[32]

The ethos of these grandiloquent verses paints a dramatic picture of the front as a borderland of death, where men are ready to give their lives for the nation. The Christian motifs of sacrifice, martyrdom and redemption sound loudly through the whole collection, but the most explicitly religious poems often take the form of prayers or hymns, thus intertwining the transcendental qualities of religion and nationalism.[33] These poems ask for heavenly protection, usually for the soldier's fatherland and family rather than for himself. Christian themes easily integrate with national-patriotic passions. Especially later in the war some contain more desperate cries for God's help and guidance in an insecure future. Quite conventionally, the poems depict the soldierly sacrifice as a Christ-like offering:

The sacrifice of the warrior was great,
when he gave his blood.
So did the Saviour suffer,
carrying our sins to the cross.[34]

There is nothing disillusioned or ironic in these poems, not in the least. Instead, they substantiate a deeply felt attachment to the nation and its embodiments. They draw from a compound of 'traditional' religious and nationalistic cosmology.[35] Even though there is no similar collection of young men's poetry from the pre-war era at hand with which to compare the poems, it seems that the war experience had only intensified and concretized the nation as an object of affection. This reminds me of the debate concerning the consequences of the First World War to British culture. Although for the much-cited, highly educated poets such as Wilfred Owen and Siegfried Sassoon the shattering war experience led to a breakthrough of novel poetry, the Great War as a cradle of literary modernity seems too straightforward an explanation. In popular and 'less educated' war poetry, patently patriotic, romantic and religious motifs kept flourishing. Having witnessed devastating human losses, common people in 1914–18 and afterwards actually tended to return to traditional, classical verse to find consolation for their hardships.[36]

Similarly, the Finnish soldiers of the Second World War searched for assurance that their sacrifices had not been in vain and that they had a collective, lasting meaning. The heavier the losses, the more significant their purpose had to be. Taken together, the Winter War of 1939–40 and the offensive of 1941 had caused the loss of well over 50,000 Finnish lives (out of a population of ca 3.7 million). By addressing the nation and investing it with personal attachment, the soldiers bound themselves and their hardships to the fate of the collective. In the nationalist rhetoric and imagination, the young men at the front have been presented as in imminent contact with their parent community, as the 'chosen delegates' presenting the nation in its existential struggle. Their sacrifices have been placed at the centre of collective attention.[37] This first set of poems shows that Finnish soldiers understood this role and responded to it. One could claim – as author Olavi Paavolainen did – that the official war propaganda had turned the soldier-poets into simple automatons of nationalistic rhetoric. I would, instead, argue that as repetitive and unoriginal as these poems were, composing the verses, writing them down, and learning them by heart were acts of feeling the fatherland and giving this feeling an emotional expression. And in feeling the fatherland, the soldiers were also 'doing the nation' for themselves. In addition to Reddy's above-mentioned theory, I am drawing here from Monique Scheer's thinking on emotions as embodied practices.[38]

Lyrical attachments II: empowering and comforting

In contrast to the abstract, sublime poems of the first category, the second one subsumes more personal poems that tell of concrete events and impressions, and that are often dedicated to specific persons. Probably the most important addressees here are one's fellow soldiers and especially the fallen comrades. Such obituaries usually contain a mix of emotions: sorrow and bitterness come together with a defiant determination to uphold the memory and take revenge. Individual sentiments of loss often reach the collective level as the fallen comrades join the abstract army of the departed: the memory of the fallen in the Winter War challenges the still-living soldiers to continue the battle; the heroes under the grave mounds call the soldiers to follow their path. In this way the fallen are turned into an empowering resource, instead of causing depression or anxiety. Fighting and dying together as brothers-in-arms become a great leveller of earlier social and political boundaries:[39]

> The day has come, but the tired brothers
> still remain in the field
> In this night of battle they too have
> become equally big and rich!
> Together they have found the father's land.
> Forgotten their gaping wounds.
> It is enough – when they could die for their fatherland![40]

The poems for one's living comrades, on the other hand, embrace the warm and secure atmosphere in the dugouts. In contrast to the more pompous, patriotic poems of sacrifice and martial heroism, they depict the soldiers at the frontlines as the guardians of home, living and fighting side-by-side on the border of their national community. There is also a spatial dimension to the experiences of empowering solidarity at the front. For those soldiers situated on the River Svir front in Eastern Karelia, for instance, the great stream itself, separating the homeland and 'Finnish culture' from the unknown and 'cultureless' enemy territory, becomes a mighty, inspiring symbol for war's liminal experience.[41] As has been noted in cultural heritage and memory studies, the visitors of age-old battle sites often construct an affective, visceral relation to these places, which easily turn into sites of national sentiment and belonging.[42] It is no surprise, then, that the soldiers, who had seen several of their comrades die for an unmarked acre of forest or field, could create strong affective ties to such terrain. As the sites of battle, small rivers, tiny hills and unspectacular villages could grow into emotionally charged symbols of the whole nation. But for the soldiers risking their lives on these very sites, this affection was also a strongly embodied experience.[43]

Thus, the intimate vicinity to the violent, liminal battlefield was an identity marker for the brothers-in-arms. Another spatial dimension in the poems is constructed through geographical distance: even if the soldiers are taken away from their homes and sent to the far borders of the nation, this distance is overcome by the intensity of feeling. Just as prominent as the poems for one's comrades, are the verses dedicated to one's mother. The mothers seem to symbolize the essential idea of home and all its security and warmth. In these poems the mother is often praying, asking for protection for her sons. This emotional support worked both ways; many poems ask for endurance and consolation for the worried mothers. Even if the poems for mothers and homefolks often have a longing tone, they reassert, rather than question, the meaning of the war: ideally, the poems depict the sons at the front as protecting their praying mothers back home. It is interesting that poems written for wives are rare in the collection. This poetic silence traces back to the youth of the majority of the soldiers, but it may also illustrate the special symbolic and emotionally comforting role of mothers in the mindscape of war:[44]

> Mother, I recall your grey hair,
> recall your gentle care
> Here where the best of men now are
> I feel the beat of your heart.
>
> Mother, I ask you
> not to let sorrow break you
> Carry your burden like others do,
> I'll stand guard here for you.[45]

Besides their mothers, the soldier-poets write about other women, too, but more commonly than wives or even girlfriends the objects of these admiring, romantic 'serenades' are the *lottas* (members of the Lotta Svärd women's auxiliary corps), nurses and canteen keepers close to the frontlines; the soldiers' 'smiling flowers' and 'caring sisters'. Obviously, soldiers in the trenches actually talked about women in less sublime and less asexual ways,[46] but the poems tell, nevertheless, of the other aspect of feminine reinforcement for soldiers' masculine identities: women were offered the role of the admiring audience for manly heroism, reinforcing and encouraging the boys/men to fulfil their soldierly duties.[47] The idealized image of pure, innocent, gentle and beautiful maidens gives comfort to young soldiers:

> As the night grows dark above the hospital,
> the nurse is awake and tends to us all.
> Someone thanks her quietly, without words
> that friendly soul so busy.
>
> And as the night turns to dawn
> the sister goes, another takes her place
> And just like that nightly friend of ours,
> as gentle and sunny is she.[48]

Such an ethereal description of young women bears close resemblance to the Finnish Maid, a symbol of Finland at the turn of the twentieth century. This innocent maiden was the object of male fantasies and symbolically threatened by foreign aggression and rape by Russians (at that time Finland was a part of the Russian Empire). Furthermore, as Johanna Valenius has noted, we should not see the nation only as symbolized by a young woman, but also *as* a woman, a beloved virgin to be desired and protected by men.[49] This amalgamation of the national and the feminine is vividly present in the soldiers' poems, too.

Finally, we have impressionistic elegies, which ponder existential issues and often borrow their motifs from nature. Their direct addressee is more difficult to pinpoint than in the other poems: they seem to have been written for the author himself or for his anonymous peers. Although rarely directly pessimistic, they nevertheless create a more melancholic and reflective tone than do poems in the other sub-groups. The collection does not contain many of these poems, and they seem to be somewhat more common among the poems written later in war. This chronology hints at a change in the soldiers' way of seeing their service at the frontlines, although the poems from 1943–44 are too sporadic to allow for a more comprehensive comparison. The apparent change may also be due to the fact that the original collection of poems was supplemented later in 1943 by allowing soldiers to send their texts directly to officials at the Information Department and thus not through the hands of their own nearby officers, which seems to have been the earlier procedure.[50]

Summing up the poems' personal addressees, the gendered distribution of characters is quite revealing. Soldiers' fathers are mostly missing, or the fathers come to present some archaic 'forefatherhood' or the nation as the fatherland. Also the soldiers' biological siblings are rarely mentioned, but 'brothers' and 'brotherhood' are nonetheless key concepts referring to one's comrades-in-arms. As noted, both real and imagined young women are often attributed 'sisterly' qualities, and they overshadow the role of soldiers' wives. Together with their fellow soldiers, mothers are the single most important theme in poems referring to soldiers' concrete human relations.

It is worth noting in this regard that a great many of the frontline soldiers were too young to have had intimate relations with women, and that the most important person in their lives was still their own mother. In spite of all the boasting and tough guy talk in the trenches, women of the soldiers' own age were often distant and unobtainable figures, and the soldiers felt insecure of their manliness in relation to them.[51] It makes sense, then, that the Finnish wartime gender ideology was so focused on the role of soldiers' mothers. As historian Ilona Kemppainen (now Pajari) has shown, the idealized mother figure was central in the Finnish culture of conferring meaning to fallen soldiers. In public discourse the mothers' willing sacrifice of their sons to the fatherland overshadowed the more troublesome fate of war widows.[52] As the many affectionate references to mothers in soldiers' poems demonstrate, the image of a loving and caring mother, whom the young soldiers were expected to protect on the front, was an extremely important personal and cultural focus of emotions, even for older reservists. In order to make sense of all the filth and brutality of the frontlines, there had to be something good and pure to defend; motherly figures back home became both the concrete and symbolic repository of these essential, positive qualities.[53]

Personalizing the nation, nationalizing the personal

Taken together, what can be said about this plethora of overly patriotic, religious and passionate verses? It would be tempting to attribute the collection's elevated, almost naïve pathos to a marginal type of soldier, the outliers in their communities.[54] Yet this conclusion would not do justice to the poems. Most importantly, the poems are plentiful and still very uniform in their basic nature. This sameness reveals a strongly shared cultural and ideological ethos, not the idiosyncratic scribblings of a few odd poets. Even if the poems do not articulate an all-embracing sentiment common to all Finnish soldiers, taken in sum they do express the war effort as a personally and nationally meaningful endeavour; an experience at its strongest in 1941–42. We can justifiably interpret these poems as lyrical expressions of these high-flown sentiments, which were, in various degrees, familiar to a large body of soldiers.

If we agree that the poems can be used to analyse one aspect of soldiers' war experiences, what can we learn from them about the subject of this chapter, the attraction of nationalism to the common soldier? Quite clearly, the nation with its various symbols acts as an empowering collective force, which demanded sacrifices but also 'nourished' the soldiers:

> The Fatherland did not drink the blood
> of our fathers and brothers in vain.
> Your daughters fed us with that mighty blood
> and made us so much stronger.[55]

In the midst of violence, fear and personal insecurities such a national grounding anchored things in their right place and promised a reason for all the hardships. When the individual felt that he was at the mercy of forces beyond his control, the nation – often depicted as a mother figure – could be experienced as a protective cover which lifted the abstract moral and existential concerns from the soldiers' shoulders. It was enough to take care of one's immediate practical duties; the nation itself had given them larger meaning. Consequently, the nation as an imagined collective reflecting one's identity was an object of keen admiration and love; a kind of narcissistic object of attachment, as historian Tuomas Tepora has written. Invested with positive emotions, the nation helped individuals to define the nature of their belonging, to cherish this idealized self-image, and to draw a clear line to the destructive and negative emotions projected onto the enemy.[56]

A specific feature of the poems is how they nationalize individual relations as ties of family or friendship. A concrete mother–son relationship is raised to an abstract one between the soldier and 'Mother Finland'; a dead comrade comes to represent all the fallen 'brothers'; departed 'fathers' challenge their 'sons' to defend the nation. The soldiers themselves are not merely individual beings, but avatars of quintessential 'Finnish men' with their mythic qualities; they line up with the timeless national continuum of men from ancient times to the future. Thus, the poems tend to see concrete human relations as mirroring their nationally defined ideals – and vice versa.[57] If we apply Michael Billig's idea on how the everyday events, objects and experiences are discursively 'flagged' as national, thus constructing a national identity, then what happens here is a flagging of personal human relations and attachments as a matter of national belonging. As was noted earlier, such flagging must be rooted in the pre-war civic education and banal nationalism, so that the soldiers were already primed to nationalize the personal.[58] In the context of the front, this preparedness was then actualized with apparent ease.

The conjunction of the personal and the national illustrates the abovementioned aspect of experiencing the nation as an emotionally supportive entity, and it constructs a rhetorical device to describe the intensity of emotions – one feels for the nation as if it were one's mother. But it also tells of a need to imbue the actual war experience with lasting, transcendent meanings and to find comfort in them in the face of brutal personal losses. Through the concept of comradeship, for instance, the dead close friend at the front lives on as an abstract idea worth defending, and through the motherly attributes of the nation the bloody acts of soldiering become analogous to defending one's loved ones. By blurring the concrete and the abstract so effortlessly, the poems emphasize the extraordinary place of war and soldiers in the national cosmology: in having such collective meanings so readily at hand, the writers showed that they understood the mythic aspects of war and their own special role in the civic religion of nationalism.[59]

The high pathos and national-romantic voice of the poems invites contemporary readers to see them as an embellishment of war's brutal 'real' face.

To some extent this is true; there was, for example, no well-known Finnish literary tradition from which the soldiers could have drawn to depict the destructive experiences of violence and shock. The writers were inclined to use the same nineteenth-century Runebergian tone of patriotic, martial hero-ism they had learned about in classrooms and heard in public speeches. Yet the literary genre of war's romantic embellishment should not be understood only as something inauthentically superficial and learned by rote. The sol-diers used the public language most readily available to them for making their experiences meaningful. 'Embellishment' was also a coping strategy to counter the fundamental horrors of the front. Parallel with the experience of disillusionment ran the phenomenon of idealization; the violence and filthi-ness of the front required an embrace of a pure and beautiful *raison d'être* to make the horrible experiences meaningful.[60]

Rather than delusive imagination or manipulative retouch, the embellish-ment of war was actually a capacity to see an allegedly deeper, ideal content behind the concrete objects of war: the mutilated body of a comrade became an allegory for the body of Christ; the battered swathe of the frontline became an existential border between the warring nations; the spring flowers at the ruins in Eastern Karelia were a symbol of the dawning of Greater Finland. The poems throughout the collection are saturated with religious meanings and metaphors, either explicit or implicit. They position the soldiers within the violent, liminal outskirts of their society at the frontlines, but also within the historical continuum of the nation. The poems' connection to the army's ideological and religious education is evident.[61] Yet importantly, even if the poems echo and renew the nationalistic war discourse, no one had forced the soldiers to put pen to paper: this was a voluntary, deliberate act of imagining the nation.

Composing the poems, the soldiers were active participants in personalizing the nation and nationalizing the personal. Both by embedding their personal experiences within the collective imagery of the nation and in flagging their interpersonal relations as reflecting the national bonds of attachments, the soldiers created an empowering, comforting and binding nation for them-selves. As I have shown, this was a strongly emotional process.[62] Furthermore, following Monique Scheer, I see the acts of writing the poems as a practice which mobilizes the emotion. In so doing, they *are* the emotion – and it is thus rather irrelevant to ask whether or not the poems correlate with some 'genuine' feelings beyond the lyrical verses. Although the English translations cannot mediate the rhyme of the original versions, composing the stanzas and reading them was also a material exercise, which inscribed the poems' rhythm together with their national sentiments into the body and the mind.[63]

Concluding remarks: artisans of patriotism

In a nutshell, the stereotypical, idealized mindscape of war which the soldiers' poems depict can be quite easily described. The central ethos of the poems is to see the soldier and his group of comrades as manly guardians of the nation, most forcefully symbolized either as an omnipotent collective or as a motherly/fatherly figure. Thus the nation is, at the same time, a demanding and a protective entity. Especially in 1941–42, the poems have an aggressive edge in stressing the crusader spirit and the virility of the conquering soldiers, who come to represent the imagined ideal of ageless Finnish masculinity. Besides the caring mothers, the women in the poems act as objects and spectators reinforcing soldiers' martial masculinity. Through the concepts of frontline comradeship and patriotic sacrifice, the violence of the front turns from a destructive threat into a productive experience, fostering community under fire and strengthening the nation. Furthermore, the religious rhetoric of passion and martyrdom gives the soldier's death a spiritual aura and promises salvation. The Christian tradition is rich with the images of redeeming sacrifice, egalitarian brotherhood and martyrdom in ennobling suffering, and the poet-soldiers used this archaic cultural resource to make their hardships explainable and tolerable.

This is, in short, a Finnish example of canonic *pro patria mori* nationalism. The national cosmology, so vivid in the poems, is not without occasional gaps and ruptures. The poems include some moments of disillusionment, irony and doubt – and these moments do deserve an analysis of their own. But here, my key observation has been the poems' striking uniformity and cohesion, which tell of a shared cultural recognition of the national call to arms and of the strong emotional support provided by the nation amidst the soldiers' fears and insecurities. As foreign and unironically romantic the style and content of the verses may be for a modern reader, it is worth taking seriously the power of such nationalism to inspire, to give meaning, and to set the larger cultural framework for the soldiers' war experience. Indeed, I see the authors of the poems as the artisans of patriotism – not as passive receivers of nationalist manipulation from above, but as the active producers of the object of their own passions and attachment.

Notes

1 Acknowledgements: This chapter is based on my doctoral dissertation *Battled Nerves*. I am grateful to Hannu Tervaharju for the poems' English translation and to the Academy of Finland for financing my current research.
2 Anderson, *Imagined Communities*, esp. p. 7; Billig, *Banal Nationalism*, esp. pp. 1–2.
3 For a recent 'emotional history' of the Winter War, see Tepora, *Sodan henki*.
4 For concise English overviews on Finland in the Second World War, please see Vehviläinen, *Finland in the Second World War*; Kinnunen and Kivimäki, *Finland in World War II*.
5 Heikura, *Rintamajoukkojen mieliala*, pp. 88–97.
6 For the analysis of general emotional dynamics in the Finnish war experience of 1939–1945, please see Kivimäki and Tepora, 'War of hearts'; Kivimäki and Tepora, 'Meaningless death'.
7 On the immediate post-war 'emotional landscape' in Finland, Kivimäki, 'Hämärä horisontti'.

8 Kettunen, *Suojelu, suoritus, subjekti*, p. 371; Kivimäki, 'Militärpsykologi'; also Seeck, *Johtamisopit Suomessa*, p. 143.

9 Wessely, 'Twentieth-century theories', pp. 274–276. In 1947, Finnish sociologist Knut Pipping published his doctoral dissertation on the frontline soldiers' small-unit community, attitudes, and behaviour in 1941–44, based on his own observations as a wartime non-commissioned officer. This pioneering work was ahead of its time, and it posed very much the same questions and conclusions as the emerging American military sociology of the late 1940s.

10 Varpio, *Väinö Linnan elämä*, pp. 301–317.

11 See e.g. Kivimäki and Tepora, 'Meaningless death', pp. 254–264.

12 Kemppainen, *Isänmaan uhrit*, pp. 219–226.

13 Tuomaala, *Työtätekevistä käsistä*, p. 195 ff.; Nevala-Nurmi, *Perhe maanpuolusta-jana*, passim.

14 Ahlbäck, *Manhood*, pp. 107 ff., 199–200.

15 Kemppainen, *Isänmaan uhrit*, pp. 65–74; Kivimäki, 'Between Defeat and Victory', pp. 485–487.

16 E.g. Kärnä et al., *Arkielämän aseveljeyttä*; Kulha, *Aseveljien aika*; cf. Kühne, *Kameradschaft*; Mosse, *Fallen Soldiers*.

17 Cf. Tuomaala, *Työtätekevistä käsistä*, pp. 316–333; Ahlbäck, *Manhood*, pp. 207–220, 226–229.

18 Billig, *Banal Nationalism*, pp. 6–7.

19 National Archives of Finland (NAF), T 10602/16–17, Finnish Army High Command, Information Department (PM Ttus.os.), collection of soldiers' poems in 1942.

20 Pilke, *Korsu-uutisia*, pp. 226–234.

21 Paavolainen gives an account on his work with the anthology in his published wartime diaries *Synkkä yksinpuhelu*, pp. 590, 610, 634–637, 642–644, 655, 661–662, 669, 682, 684, 736.

22 Reddy, *Navigation of Feeling*, pp. 101–105, 124–129.

23 Paavolainen, *Synkkä yksinpuhelu*, p. 642.

24 For this invitation or 'call', see Ahlbäck, *Manhood*, pp. 141–144.

25 On poetry and the 'beauty of war', as well as on poems as means to contain and control the horrors, see Winn, *Poetry of War*, pp. 1–11.

26 Wrede, *Se kansa meidän kansa on*, p. 14; Jokinen, 'Myytti sodan palveluksessa', pp. 142–143; Tuomaala, *Työtätekevistä käsistä*, pp. 209–212; Viitasalo 2005.

27 NAF, T 10602/16, PM Ttus.os., Private M.N., untitled, dedicated to Infantry Regiment 6, 1942. All direct poem citations from Finnish have been translated by Hannu Tervaharju.

28 Kivimäki, 'Rintamamiesten Suur-Suomi', pp. 290–294. The pre-war Greater Finland activism was, indeed, mostly an academic phenomenon; Nygård, *Suur-Suomi*, pp. 234–238. But during the successful Finnish offensive in 1941 the expansion to the east was more widely accepted, even among some social democrats; Manninen, *Suur-Suomen ääriviivat*, pp. 222–227.

29 NAF, T 10602/17, PM Ttus.os., Lance Corporal E.K., 'March of Victory', 23.5.1942.

30 These enemy images come close to those represented in war propaganda of the Finnish conservative press at the same time; Luostarinen, *Perivihollinen*, passim.

31 On these same features in the Finnish war novels, see Jokinen, 'Myytti sodan palveluksessa', pp. 142–143, 147–150; on the similar ideological education in the pre-war Finnish conscript army, see Ahlbäck, *Manhood*, pp. 120–125.

32 NAF, T 10602/16, PM Ttus.os., Second Lieutenant H.O.L., 'To a rank-and-file soldier', 6 December 1942 (emphasis in original).

33 On the Finnish religious rhetoric of sacrifice in war, see Kemppainen, *Isänmaan uhrit*, pp. 223–225 and passim; Tilli, *Continuation War*, passim.

34　NAF, T 10602/17, PM Ttus.os., Lance Corporal Y.P., 'After the battle', undated.

35　The 'traditional' quality of this rather modern religious-nationalistic amalgamation must be observed with caution, of course; cf. Hobsbawm, 'Introduction'.

36　On this debate, cf. Hynes, *War Imagined*, esp. pp. 337 ff.; Fussell, *Great War*, pp. 86–90, 169 ff.; Eksteins, *Rites of Spring*; on the other hand, Winter, *Sites of Memory*, esp. pp. 2–5, 221–222; Bogacz, 'A tyranny of words'.

37　On the military community as delegates and border crossers, see Marvin and Ingle, *Blood Sacrifice*, pp. 98 ff.; Tepora, *Lippu, uhri, kansakunta*, p. 46; Siltala, 'Sodan psykohistoriaa', pp. 50–53.

38　Scheer, 'Are emotions a kind of practice'. On doing and feeling the nation, see also Heaney, 'Emotions and nationalism', esp. pp. 256–257.

39　Cf. Kivimäki and Tepora, 'Meaningless death', pp. 243–245, 252, 255–256.

40　NAF, T 10602/17, PM Ttus.os., Lance Corporal A.R., 'Night Miracle', 27.3.1943.

41　On war as a liminal experience, see Leed, *No Man's Land*, pp. 12–33.

42　See, e.g., Waterton and Watson, 'War long forgotten'; Raivo, '"This is where they fought"'. Cf. on war tourism and the feelings of empathy towards the 'enemy', McKay and Harman, '"It was like swimming through history"'.

43　In the Finnish case, for instance, the Winter War battle sites of Kollaa, Taipale, Summa and Raate became legendary already during the conflict and have remained so ever after. For the Finnish soldiers' emotional attachment to their site of battle, Jalonen, *Summan tarina*, pp. 159 ff. For recent initiatives on the spatial and material dimensions of national affections, see Merriman and Jones, 'Nations, materialities and affects'; Stephens, 'Affective atmospheres'.

44　Kemppainen, *Isänmaan uhrit*, pp. 233–243; Hagelstam, 'Families, separation', pp. 289–295.

45　NAF, T 10602/17, PM Ttus.os., Corporal O.R., 'Letter to mother', undated.

46　See e.g. Pipping, *Infantry Company*, pp. 183–187.

47　Goldstein, *War and Gender*, pp. 301–322; Braudy, *From Chivalry to Terrorism*, pp. 373–382; on the specific role of female nurses in this regard, see Hallett, *Containing Trauma*.

48　NAF, T 10602/16, PM Ttus.os., unknown author, 'In military hospital', undated.

49　Valenius, *Undressing the Maid*, p. 207.

50　Paavolainen, *Synkkä yksinpuhelu*, 634–635; openly critical or bitter poems are very rare, but not wholly non-existent.

51　Kivimäki, 'Ryvetetty enkeli', pp. 25–26.

52　Kemppainen, *Isänmaan uhrit*, pp. 233–245, 255.

53　For a similar analysis on British soldiers' maternal relation in the First World War, see Roper, *Secret Battle*, esp. pp. 1–4, 22–27, 250–254.

54　This is exactly what author Väinö Linna did in his *Tuntematon sotilas*: practically the only patently 'patriotic' soldier among his rank-and-file characters, Private Salo is described as a very naïve person, not taken seriously by his fellow soldiers.

55　NAF, T 10602/17, PM Ttus.os., Private T.M., 'To Fatherland', 1.1.1943.

56　Tepora, *Lippu, uhri, kansakunta*, passim; Kivimäki and Tepora, 'War of hearts', pp. 292–295, 299.

57　In the same vein, see Anderson, *Imagined Communities*, esp. pp. 142–144; Mosse, *Nationalism and Sexuality*, pp. 72–80.

58　Billig, *Banal Nationalism*, pp. 6–11, 93 ff.

59　On the cult and significance of soldiers and their sacrifices in nationalism, see e.g. Anderson, *Imagined Communities*; Koselleck and Jeismann, *Der politische Totenkult*; Mosse, *Fallen Soldiers*.

60　Cf. Winter, *Sites of Memory*, pp. 204 ff.

61　On the scope and content of the army's ideological and religious education, see e.g. Salminen, *Propaganda rintamajoukoissa*; Kemppainen, *Isänmaan uhrit*; Tilli, *Continuation War*.

62 See Cohen, 'Personal nationalism', esp. pp. 804–805, 808–812; for the role of emotions, Hearn, 'National identity', esp. pp. 666–667.
63 Cf. Scheer, 'Are emotions a kind of practice', esp. pp. 209–212, 218–220.

References

Ahlbäck, Anders, *Manhood and the making of the military: Conscription, military service and masculinity in Finland, 1917–39*, Surrey, Ashgate, 2014.

Anderson, Benedict, *Imagined communities: Reflections on the origin and spread of nationalism*, revised ed., original 1983, London, Verso, 2006.

Billig, Michael, *Banal nationalism*, London, Sage, 1995.

Bogacz, Ted, '"A tyranny of words": Language, poetry, and antimodernism in England in the First World War', in: *Journal of Modern History*, vol. 58, no. 3, 1986, pp. 643–668.

Braudy, Leo, *From chivalry to terrorism: War and the changing nature of masculinity*, New York, Alfred A. Knopf, 2003.

Cohen, Anthony P., 'Personal nationalism: A Scottish view of some rites, rights, and wrongs', in: *American Ethnologist*, vol. 23, no. 4, 1996, pp. 802–815.

Eksteins, Modris, *Rites of spring: The Great War and the birth of the modern age*, London, Houghton Mifflin, 1989.

Fussell, Paul, *The Great War and modern memory*, Oxford, Oxford University Press, 1975.

Goldstein, Joshua S., *War and gender: How gender shapes the war system and vice versa*, Cambridge, Cambridge University Press, 2001.

Hagelstam, Sonja, 'Families, separation and emotional coping in war: Bridging letters between home and front, 1941–44', in: Kinnunen, Tiina and Kivimäki, Ville (eds.), *Finland in World War II: History, memory, interpretations*, Leiden, Brill, 2012, pp. 277–312.

Hallett, Christine E., *Containing trauma: Nursing work in the First World War*, Manchester, Manchester University Press, 2009.

Heaney, Jonathan, 'Emotions and nationalism: A reappraisal', in: Demertzis, Nicolas (ed.), *Emotions in politics: The affect dimension in political tension*, Basingstoke, Palgrave Macmillan, 2013, pp. 243–263.

Hearn, Jonathan, 'National identity: Banal, personal and embedded', in: *Nations and Nationalism*, vol. 13, no. 4, 2007, pp. 657–674.

Heikura, Mikko, *Rintamajoukkojen mieliala: Tutkimus Suomen armeijan rintamajoukkojen mielialasta Suomen ja Neuvostoliiton välisen sodan aikana 1941–1944*, Research Report No. 85, Institute of Sociology, Helsinki, University of Helsinki, 1967.

Hobsbawm, Eric, 'Introduction: Inventing traditions', in: Hobsbawm, Eric and Ranger, Terence (eds.), *The invention of tradition*, Cambridge, Cambridge University Press, 1983, pp. 1–14.

Hynes, Samuel, *A war imagined: The First World War and English culture*, London, Bodley Head, 1990.

Jalonen, Jussi, *Summan tarina: Talvisodan ratkaisutaistelun ihmiset ja historia*, Helsinki, SKS, 2017.

Jokinen, Arto, 'Myytti sodan palveluksessa: Suomalainen mies, soturius ja talvisota', in: Kinnunen, Tiina and Kivimäki, Ville (eds.), *Ihminen sodassa: Suomalaisten kokemuksia talvi- ja jatkosodasta*, Helsinki, Minerva, 2006, pp. 141–157.

Kärnä, O.A. *et al.* (eds.), *Arkielämän aseveljeyttä: Kirja päivänkysymyksistä opettajille ja muille kansalaisille*, Porvoo, WSOY, 1944.

Kemppainen, Ilona, *Isänmaan uhrit: Sankarikuolema Suomessa toisen maailmansodan aikana*, Helsinki, SKS, 2006.

Kettunen, Pauli, *Suojelu, suoritus, subjekti: Työsuojelu teollistuvan Suomen yhteiskun-nallisissa ajattelu- ja toimintatavoissa*, Helsinki, SKS, 1994.

Kinnunen, Tiina and Kivimäki, Ville (eds.), *Finland in World War II: History, memory, interpretations*, Leiden, Brill, 2012.

Kivimäki, Ville, *Battled nerves: Finnish soldiers' war experience, trauma, and military psychiatry, 1941–44*, PhD thesis in Nordic history, Åbo Akademi University, 2013.

Kivimäki, Ville, 'Between defeat and victory: Finnish memory culture of the Second World War', in: *Scandinavian Journal of History*, vol. 37, no. 4, 2012, pp. 482–504.

Kivimäki, Ville, 'Hämärä horisontti, avautuvat tulevaisuudet: Suomalaissotilaat ja syksyn 1944 tunnemaisema', in: Kivimäki, Ville and Hytönen, Kirsi-Maria (eds.), *Rauhaton rauha: Suomalaiset ja sodan päättyminen 1944–1950*, Tampere, Vasta-paino, 2015, pp. 73–100.

Kivimäki, Ville, 'Militärpsykologi och föränderliga uppfattningar om män: Finländska soldater som föremål för psykologiska observationer 1944–1956', in: *Historisk tid-skrift för Finland*, vol. 97, no. 1, 2012, pp. 95–126.

Kivimäki, Ville, 'Rintamamiesten Suur-Suomi: Odotukset, kokemukset ja tunteet jat-kosodassa', in: Näre, Sari and Kirves, Jenni (eds.), *Luvattu maa: Suur-Suomen unelma ja unohdus*, Helsinki, Johnny Kniga, 2014, pp. 259–319.

Kivimäki, Ville, 'Ryvetetty enkeli: Suomalaissotilaiden neuvostoliittolaisiin naissotilaisiin kohdistama seksuaalinen väkivalta ja sodan sukupuolittunut mielenmaisema', in: *Naistutkimus – Kvinnoforskning*, vol. 20, no. 3, 2007, pp. 19–33.

Kivimäki, Ville and Tepora, Tuomas, 'Meaningless death or regenerating sacrifice? Violence and social cohesion in wartime Finland', in: Kinnunen, Tiina and Kivi-mäki, Ville (eds.), *Finland in World War II: History, memory, interpretations*, Leiden, Brill, 2012, pp. 233–275.

Kivimäki, Ville and Tepora, Tuomas, 'War of hearts: Love and collective attachment as integrating factors in Finland during World War II', in: *Journal of Social History*, vol. 43, no. 2, 2009, pp. 285–305.

Koselleck, Reinhart and Jeismann, Michael (eds.), *Der politische Totenkult: Krie-gerdenkmäler in der Moderne*, München, Wilhelm Fink, 1994.

Kühne, Thomas, *Kameradschaft: Die Soldaten des nationalsozialistischen Krieges und das 20. Jahrhundert*, Göttingen, Vandenhoeck & Ruprecht, 2006.

Kulha, Keijo K., *Aseveljien aika: Suomalaisen asevelihengen ja aseveliliikkeen historiaa 1940–1945*, Porvoo, WSOY, 1980.

Leed, Eric J., *No man's land: Combat and identity in World War I*, Cambridge, Cam-bridge University Press, 1979.

Luostarinen, Heikki, *Perivihollinen – Suomen oikeistolehdistön Neuvostoliittoa koskeva viholliskuva sodassa 1941–44: Tausta ja sisältö*, Tampere, Vastapaino, 1986.

Manninen, Ohto, *Suur-Suomen ääriviivat: Kysymys tulevaisuudesta ja turvallisuudesta Suomen Saksan-politiikassa 1941*, Helsinki, Kirjayhtymä, 1980.

Marvin, Carolyn and Ingle, David W., *Blood sacrifice and the nation: Totem rituals and the American flag*, Cambridge, Cambridge University Press, 1999.

McKay, Jim and Harman, Serhat, '"It was like swimming through history": Tourist moments at Gallipoli', in: West, Brad (ed.), *War memory and commemoration*, London, Routledge, 2017, pp. 17–36.

Merriman, Peter and Jones, Rhys, 'Nations, materialities and affects', in: *Progress in Human Geography*, vol. 41, no. 5, pp. 600–617.

Mosse, George L., *Fallen soldiers: Reshaping the memory of World Wars*, Oxford, Oxford University Press, 1990.

Mosse, George L., *Nationalism and sexuality: Respectability and abnormal sexuality in modern Europe*, New York, Howard Fertig, 1985.

Nevala-Nurmi, Seija-Leena, *Perhe maanpuolustajana: Sukupuoli ja sukupolvi Lotta Svärd- ja suojeluskuntajärjestöissä 1918–1944*, Tampere, Tampere University Press, 2012.

Nygård, Toivo, *Suur-Suomi vai lähiheimolaisten auttaminen: Aatteellinen heimotyö itsenäisessä Suomessa*, Helsinki, Otava, 1978.

Paavolainen, Olavi, *Synkkä yksinpuhelu: Päiväkirjan lehtiä vuosilta 1941–1944*, Porvoo, WSOY, 1946.

Paavolainen, Olavi (ed.), *Täältä jostakin: Suomen kenttäarmeijan runoja*, Porvoo, WSOY, 1943.

Pilke, Helena, *Korsu-uutisia! Rintamalehtien jatkosota*, Helsinki, SKS, 2012.

Pipping, Knut, *Infantry company as a society*, Swedish original 1947, transl. by Petri Kekäle, Helsinki, National Defence University, 2008.

Raivo, Petri J., '"This is where they fought": Finnish war landscapes as a national heritage', in: Ashplant, Timothy G., Dawson, Graham and Roper, Michael (eds.), *Commemorating war: The politics of memory*, New Brunswick NJ, Transaction, 2004, pp. 145–164.

Reddy, William M., *The navigation of feeling: A framework for the history of emotions*, Cambridge, Cambridge University Press, 2001.

Roper, Michael, *The secret battle: Emotional survival in the Great War*, Manchester, Manchester University Press, 2009.

Salminen, Esko, *Propaganda rintamajoukoissa 1941–1944: Suomen armeijan valistustoiminta ja mielialojen ohjaus jatkosodan aikana*, Helsinki, Otava, 1976.

Scheer, Monique, 'Are emotions a kind of practice (and is that what makes them have a history?): A Bourdieuian approach to understanding emotion', in: *History and Theory*, vol. 51, no. 2, 2012, pp. 193–220.

Seeck, Hannele, *Johtamisopit Suomessa: Taylorismista innovaatioteorioihin*, Helsinki, Gaudeamus, 2008.

Siltala, Juha, 'Sodan psykohistoriaa', in: Kinnunen, Tiina and Kivimäki, Ville (eds.), *Ihminen sodassa: Suomalaisten kokemuksia talvi- ja jatkosodasta*, Helsinki, Minerva, 2006, pp. 43–68.

Stephens, Angharad Closs, 'The affective atmosphere of nationalism', in: *Cultural Geographies*, vol. 23, no. 2, 2016, pp. 181–198.

Tepora, Tuomas, *Lippu, uhri, kansakunta: Ryhmäkokemukset ja -rajat Suomessa 1917–1945*, Helsinki, University of Helsinki, 2011.

Tepora, Tuomas, *Sodan henki: Kaunis ja ruma talvisota*, Helsinki, WSOY, 2015.

Tilli, Jouni, *The continuation war as a metanoic moment: A Burkean reading of Lutheran hierocratic rhetoric*, Jyväskylä, University of Jyväskylä, 2012.

Tuomaala, Saara, *Työtätekevistä käsistä puhtaiksi ja kirjoittaviksi: Suomalaisen oppivelvollisuuskoulun ja maalaislasten kohtaaminen 1921–1939*, Helsinki, SKS, 2004.

Valenius, Johanna, *Undressing the maid: Gender, sexuality and the body in the construction of the Finnish nation*, Helsinki, SKS, 2004.

Varpio, Yrjö, *Väinö Linnan elämä*, Helsinki, WSOY, 2006.

Vehviläinen, Olli, *Finland in the Second World War: Between Germany and Russia*, Basingstoke, Palgrave, 2002.

Viitasalo, Jenni, *'Laulaen Suomi sun särkyneen pesäsi korjaamme': 1920-luvun kansakoulun laulukirjat suomalaisen yhteiskunnan kuvastajina*, unpublished MA thesis in Finnish history, University of Tampere, 2005.

Waterton, Emma and Watson, Steve, 'A war long forgotten: Feeling the past in an English country village', in: *Angelaki*, vol. 20, no. 3, pp. 89–103.

Wessely, Simon, 'Twentieth-century theories on combat motivation and breakdown', in: *Journal of Contemporary History*, vol. 41, no. 2, 2006, pp. 269–286.

Winn, James Anderson, *The poetry of war*, Cambridge, Cambridge University Press, 2008.

Winter, Jay, *Sites of memory, sites of mourning: The Great War in European cultural history*, Cambridge, Cambridge University Press, 1995.

Wrede, Johan, *Se kansa meidän kansa on: Runeberg, vänrikki ja kansakunta*, Jyväskylä, Gummerus, 1988.

9 Emotional communities and the reconstruction of emotional bonds to alien territories

The nationalization of the Polish 'Recovered Territories' after 1945

José M. Faraldo

In a seminal review of historians working on emotions, Carolina Rodríguez-López addresses the opposition between the Berlin Max Planck Center of History of Emotions and the Madrid CSIC Center headed by Javier Moscoso to establish the two main directions of research. Rodríguez-López describes the former's approach as

> in favor of a bio-cultural model that suggests the confluence of innate and learned components [...] it is understood, therefore, that as historians, we will be more interested in the learned component or, in other words, in how emotions are framed, acquired, negotiated and experienced in a cultural context.[1]

The focus is on cultural structures and discourses.

Javier Moscoso's team, by contrast,

> brings a regional and disciplinary variation with respect to [...] the history of emotions [...] in France, Germany or the USA. Thus, [...] the Group of Emotional Studies of the CSIC has opted [...] to focus on the history of experience. This approach studies the cultural forms of subjectivity, including emotions but also sensations, passions and instincts, and is especially interested not in what the emotions initially mean but in the cultural forms that make them possible.[2]

This implies that studying experiences, and not only emotions, has a deeper medical and neuroscientific basis, a view that dovetails with the radical interpretation of emotions as biologically determined. Some researchers think that the main 'modes' of emotions were 'constructed' in prehistory and 'frozen' to the present day.[3] This idea is rooted in the work of two neuroscientists, Leda Cosmides and John Tooby, and is supported by the influential psychologist Keith Oatley. Oatley says that if we take the adage of Tooby and Cosmides – 'the past explains the present' – and run it backwards, we can look at what we recognize as modern emotions – happiness, love, sadness, anger, and so on – and project them back into the past.[4]

A third way between the two poles, which Jan Plamper in his important book defines as "constructivism" and "universalism", might be William Reddy's "navigation of feelings".[5] Reddy argues that "the Western concept of emotion represents a well-developed method for talking about the complex multipathway activations that are an omnipresent aspect of waking life. Such activations spread well beyond the capacity of attention".[6]

What should be asked is, if this kind of perspective might be useful to understand nationalism. We can legitimately ask if such a theory is but one of many 'turns' that will pass, as other now forgotten perspectives, trends and fashions. The answer is, however, evident: nationalism has a lot to do with emotions; nationalist emotions *drive* individual behaviour. Moreover, nationalism researchers have always worked on emotions, albeit often without theoretical cover. Ute Frevert begins her book on emotions by describing French president Nicolas Sarkozy's 'humiliation' and anger in Brussels when the European Commissioner for Justice and Fundamental Rights sharply reprimanded the French government for the campaigns against illegal Roma camps in September 2010. He was not able to 'hold back', because it felt that it was an 'attack' on 'his' country. Such expression of emotions linked to nations has been common for centuries.[7]

The other problem is how to find a way to explore the nexus between emotions and nation, beyond the empirical description of testimonies about emotions. As Reddy put it: "A coherent account of emotional change must find a dynamic, a vector of alteration, outside the discursive structures and normative practices that have monopolized ethnographic attention."[8]

In this chapter, I assume that national narratives, expressed as speech acts – real words, repeated through time in a given community or even beyond – are the key to connect the biologically grounded, culturally modulated phenomena we call 'emotions' and the political entity we understand by 'nation'. As a case study, I have explored this subject by way of the settlement of the Polish 'Recovered Regions' that I have been researching for almost two decades.[9]

The 'Recovered Territories'

In the chaos at the end of the Second World War, a large part of the former East German territories, around 103,000 km², a space three times the size of the Netherlands, fell under the authority of the re-born Polish state.[10] The area was completely devastated by war. Marauders and plunderers ran wild. According to the Potsdam Agreement (1945), all Germans remaining in Poland, Czechoslovakia and Hungary (around eight million persons) had to be transferred to occupied Germany.[11] Millions of Polish newcomers flooded into the territories, many of them transferred from the former Polish Eastern lands, now part of the Soviet Union. The cities and villages they found there were alien to them. They needed to find a way of coming to terms with the spaces they had to inhabit, and with the people who lived around them. It was a difficult task. They had to develop emotionally positive bonds with the place and forget the negative feelings associated with towns and villages that were still impregnated with German life. They found themselves in a complicated cultural and emotional situation. One of the questions explored in this chapter is, how the new research on emotions might help to understand how the new settlers invested an emotionally alien place with new feeling to make it 'theirs'.

The regions were first called 'Recovered Territories', a nationalist label drawing upon the supposed medieval belonging of the regions to a primitive Polish state. With time, they came to be named 'Western and Northern Regions'. These urbanized and industrialized areas had a distinct and plural cultural (German) character. The new inhabitants encountered a landscape that, although progressively losing its population at the time, to them had a strange, alien, structure associated with the 'Germans', the people who had occupied their country and provoked so much pain in their recent history. They needed to get used to a physically unfamiliar territory that was now said to be part of their nation. Constructing emotional links to these territories was a very difficult process, which the authorities wanted to achieve through nationalization.

Many of these people had an ambiguous identification with the new Polish state because they came from rural areas of the former Eastern Poland, ethnically a very mixed territory with hybrid languages and plural cultures. Their 'Polish nationality' was still under construction. Therefore, it was necessary for the state to develop common signs of identity while reconstructing the space. Integrating these diverse populations into a new society, and shaping emotional bonds with the territory, was a multi-faceted process that in some ways was made possible through the reconstruction of emotions.

A note on sources

In order to research such emotions, I have used around 400 diaries and memoirs – from a total of 800 – preserved at the 'Western Institute' (*Instytut Zachodni*) in Poznań, the capital city of the Wielkopolska region, in Poland. They are testimonies of the time or subsequent remembrances by people who settled, after the Second World War, in the 'Northern and Western Regions' or who were born there during or immediately after the war. The memoirs were collected through diverse competitions, which were announced in radio broadcasts, newspapers, posters and other means of advertising. These contests drew on a methodology initiated by Polish-American sociologist Florian Znaniecki[12] and developed by his Polish disciple Józef Chałasiński.[13] A common strategy of Polish sociology in the after-war years (which continues to the present), it resulted in an incredible accumulation of material in many archives and institutions in Poland. Changes in sociological methodology in Poland in the 1980s and the rejection of almost all research made under Socialism after 1989 implied a certain ostracizing – or at least oblivion – of the memoirs. However, with the increasing importance of biographic methods in the social sciences in the last few years, such materials have recently been receiving more attention – also from historians.[14]

The *Instytut Zachodni* was founded in 1945 by Zygmunt Wojciechowski, a pre-war nationalist and ideologue of the so-called 'Western Thought', a political movement which advocated the expansion of Poland to the West.[15] In his view the Institute had to be an instrument of defence of Polish historical, economic and geopolitical rights to the annexation of the former German regions.[16] As complementary tasks, the Institute should monitor Germany and its developments and also document the destructions of Hitler's occupation.

After a few months in Warsaw, the Institute was moved to Poznań, where before the war a dynamic 'Western Thought' movement had been active. Since its inception the institute had published a journal (*Przegląd Zachodni*, 'Western Affairs') and some important series of books. The beginning of Polish Stalinism, in 1948–49 caused the Western Institute some problems: the sociological department was dismantled and many of its employees had to work in other institutions, even as school teachers. As sociology was abandoned at Poznań University too, some scholars had to finish their PhDs in other departments (history for example).[17]

Shortly after the political changes of 1956, in which the worker's revolt in Poznań played an important role, the sociological department was reopened, and the Institute initiated a frenetic series of activity. Throughout the 1960s the Institute developed a very interesting and complex series of experiments and research projects, including three memoir competitions and several questionnaires and reports about the Polish–German border region.[18] This research should have been continued in the 1970s, but the political situation changed. New studies about the territories were subtlety forbidden – by such means as informal pressure and the freezing of funds.[19] The official explanation was that the Western Regions were fully integrated and there was no longer any reason to research them. The accords between Poland and the German Federal Republic of 1970 had ended the insecurity about the borders, allowing the Polish Government to conclude all scientific work of political legitimization. The negative result of these projects, from the official point of view, that is, must have also played a role. Indeed, the research presented a much more problematic view of the Western Regions than the Communist officials wanted to see.[20] Over time, however, this sociological and anthropological treasure trove has been opened to investigation. In this chapter I use a selection of accounts from the 1957 and 1966 competitions.[21]

Settlement and emotional communities

In his memoires, written around 1957, Jerzy K., a teacher in a little village near the Oder river, explained how the post-war resettlement had happened:

> The first inhabitants of Sławnikowice were people returning from Germany [where they had been requisitioned as forced workers, JMF], although they came originally from various parts of Poland. [...] Near the school on the hill, some large and nice buildings were taken by Sz., a man from the central Polish regions. On the left, a Pole from Germany settled in a quite destroyed farm; on the right, people I think from Podolia settled; there were many settlers from the Vilnius region, Belarusians as they were called. Ukrainians, as the people from Vilnius called people from Podolia and Wołyń, came with their whole family. Each of them brought their own dialect, flair, and culture. The connection of all these groups was the Roman Catholic religion, although there were practitioners of other faiths, mostly Orthodox. And despite the predominance of the Belarusian and Ukrainian languages, which the newcomers from the East commonly used (there were many who did not know Polish at all), they considered themselves Poles, and for this reason only the Orthodox thought themselves to be Belarussians. Catholicism was a feature of Polishness here.[22]

Indeed, at the beginning of the area's re-population the territories were a culturally mixed society, where people did not know each other, and suspicions always thrived. The adaptation to the territories was difficult. Some of the settlers came from backward rural areas and they were alien not only to German culture, but to modern technology as well:

> Sławnikowice had electricity, and therefore machines moved by its energy, cookers, electric ovens. Many of the new settlers saw such things for the first time. There were funny stories, like the old man blowing on a light bulb to extinguish it. Quickly, however, they became accustomed to the 'materiality' of civilization, rushing with its spirit.[23]

Both culture and science had to be learned, but in time a real community was built where "the majority of residents quickly found a common language, rising from a necessity of neighbourly help and advice. Often the common ground was the experience of war". The war and its traumas connected people: every one of them had suffered similar experiences of violence, flight, refuge, persecution, forced labour, displacement. With time, people in the region were able to form an emotional community as a way of overcoming the trauma of this shared past.

According to Barbara Rosenwein, who coined the concept of 'emotional communities', there is a biological and universal human aptitude for feeling and expressing what we now call 'emotions'. However, what those emotions are, what they are called, how they are evaluated and felt, and how they are expressed (or not) – all these are shaped by 'emotional communities'.[24]

Rosenwein's theory is grounded in the belief that emotions are culturally modulated and as such are not part of biology but of social sciences and historical research. She proposes a 'social constructivism' of emotions and is very much opposed to biological explanations of emotions in history.[25] She defines 'emotional communities' as "social groups that share the same ratings of emotions and perceptions that express them", or in a different context, "as groups of people held together by common or similar interests, values, emotion styles, and emotion ratings".[26]

This theoretical basis is clearly applicable to our case study. Resulting from an atomized and running accumulation of newcomers, the new inhabitants of the Western Regions developed different strategies to shape their society. I am totally convinced that one such strategy was to build an emotional community. This emotional community connected to the nation because only a national community of feelings could convince a hardly enthusiastic population to stay there, in those very unstable and dangerous *Recovered Territories*. They felt a need to be connected, not only to the fellow members of their community – for this purpose a religious or local community might have been satisfactory – but to a wider world beyond as well: the nation outside the limits of the territories was deemed the only power – and authority – strong enough to defend and protect the community from the unsettling dangers of these alien lands.

The first emotion: fear of instability

After the war, one of the most common shared emotions in Poland was 'fear'.[27] All over the country there were emotions of fear, provoked by hunger, banditry, disease, violence, homelessness, unemployment and, above all, uncertainty.[28] Fear of the country's Communist collectivization, of its violence and the ensuing loss of private property was felt. Fear of being robbed, killed, raped or abused was also common after the war, but in this chapter I limit myself to a specific kind of fear. For the Polish state after 1945, the integration of the population in the Western Regions – related to the political security of the Oder-Neisse frontier – could only be successful if the Polish settlers truly believed in the regions as an integral part of Poland. At first, however, everything was alien to the people who arrived in those territories after the war. The presence of an important German-speaking population that only gradually left or was forced to leave, as well as the Prussian-German appearance of the region, led many Poles to be dubious about the area's future attachment to Poland.

There was fear about the return of the expelled Germans. Many considered their own presence in the Regions as something provisional and the result of post-war political confusion, rather than a lasting change of borders. Unsurprisingly, although millions of people streamed into the area after the end of the war, the settlements were very unstable for a long time. Many came, in view of the economic hardships of the post-war period, to find a higher income in the supposedly richer regions or simply to survive. But, as conditions worsened at the end of 1945, they returned to Central Poland.

The Warsaw government viewed this exodus with concern because it could threaten the integration project and embolden claims that Poland could not carry out the repopulation and administration of the Western Regions, and therefore demands of border review. Polish state propaganda did everything possible to combat the 'psychosis of provisionality' among the population. The objective was to instil confidence in the durability of the new frontier and to create the basis for a feeling of familiarity with territories perceived as alien. This was motivated by the fear of border revision that could benefit the Germans. The alliance with the powerful Soviet Union, which was the guarantor of the border, was considered vital for the new Poland. This argument also had other implications, which had to do with the establishment of socialism in Poland and the overcoming of anti-communist, anti-Soviet and anti-Russian sentiments widely shared by the population.

As another newcomer described it:

> the first ones who arrived did not take any care of agriculture, they would search through the ruins of the houses, the warehouses and shops of Głogów and trade with what they would find ... In the next village, Krzepów, they settled Poles from the eastern area, which brought aversion, conflict and often enmity for years.[29]

The Government used such fear as a way of getting rid of the surviving Jews that were returning from the Soviet Union after the Holocaust. They were concentrated at the border, presumably with the explicit intent to increase their fear for survival in post-war Poland and to push them to migrate to Palestine. As Irena P.-S., a civil servant in the town of Szczecin, wrote:

> I was surprised at why [they] were allocated in separate districts, a kind of ghetto ... A few days after that, Szczecin was full of Jews. On the streets, bazaars, in a few shops, at tram stops, there were plenty of them everywhere. They talked loudly, loudly, mostly in Russian or jargon, with their characteristic gestures. At that time, there were less than 50,000 inhabitants in Szczecin; Over 30,000 Jews arrived within a few weeks. It was strange and incomprehensible for me that Jews were not allowed to return to their home places of residence. Instead they were pushed to the German border. I doubted whether they could feel safe and secure in the face of our not really stabilized position in these lands.[30]

A local teacher from Szczecin, Franciszek B., described how various rumours circulated around the city about the fate of Szczeczin, e.g. "that Russians had given the town away to Czechs, that all Poles were going to be expelled from Szczecin and other stuff like this". The area "was devastated by war, not yet connected in any way with the motherland".[31]

Fear divided but also united. The construction of the emotional community of the new settlers began with fear of Soviets and Germans. Janina J. tells a story of violence. Janina was born in 1924 in the Eastern Ukraine and had been in Germany as a forced labourer. When she and her fiancé tried to come back to Poland and reached the territories, they were constantly attacked by Soviet soldiers. One day a soviet soldier attempted to rape her. She only avoided the abuse because another older woman voluntarily went to bed with the soldier. Another day Janina did not go to the fields because she felt ill.

> It was all my happiness, because they would do with me like they did with the girls who went with the cows: a truck came up, threw them on the car, and there were pigs, so they took them on the pigs nobody knew exactly where. Nothing helped, asking nor pleading. They came back only on the third day, but they did not tell anyone, and nobody knew what had happened to them.[32]

Fear was an emotion able to divide the new community and the others. And although the fear was omnipresent, the dividing lines were predominately ethnic and national because the only shelter was in their own community. As Janina J. says, "But we were afraid all the time."

A case for emotional communities: landscape

A different part of the process of constructing an emotional community was the need to create emotional bonds to the territory, bonds that might be shared by most of the population. For this process the authorities were able to draw on a full treasure trove of images, stereotypes and discourses about the region from the old German culture. However, this could only be shared by the new inhabitants if they found something to embrace about their Polish national identity. A possibility was the use of the presence of some Polish-speaking minorities on the territories, the so-called 'autochthones'. This was proof of the 'eternal' belonging to the mother country. Poland was 'returning' to former 'Polish' territories.

Barbara R., a young girl from Warmia, in the north-eastern part of the Regions, wrote her reminiscences of childhood and early youth in 1966. She answered a call of the Western Institute in a competition addressed to "the young generation of Polish *autochthones* (natives) in the Polish Western Regions".[33] In a letter to the organizers, Barbara R. declared that she did not write her memoir specifically for the competition, but because "in life there are moments when people need to analyse the past, maybe aiming to fill at any price their dull void, to try to explain themselves why they wasted half their lives". She wrote in her memoir "about everyday life" and it seems that she understood very well what the mission of the competition could be, because

> maybe this everyday life is the best image of Polish Warmia's new natives. Banal everyday life, joy, sadness, work, love, common life, a life that is strongly linked to our homeland, a homeland that is being built here, on Warmian land.[34]

Barbara construed a wide range of emotions – nostalgia, homeland attachment, sadness – focused on the landscape, but with the objective to connect her to the 'homeland'. This was due to Barbara's specific situation.

Barbara had been born on September 27, 1939, at the very beginning of hostilities. In her small village of birth, German was the everyday language. Only later, she discovered that Polish remained spoken in church and that her grandmother wrote a "black book" (a diary?) in Polish.[35] Moreover, according to her, one of her grandparents probably came from Lithuania.

When the front reached the village, her mother fled with her to a little town in Masuria, the neighbouring region. Some Soviet soldiers helped them find a home and she lived there through her childhood. Times were hard, and when the war ended the first 'szabrownicy' (plunderers) came.

Her first playmates were casual acquaintances, always new because the natives "travelled beyond the Oder into the Reich and settlers often moved". In her little town, settlers took power: "Those who knew and wanted, could rule." There were permanent nationality issues: "People were not Masur or Warmiak, they were 'szbaw' [a pejorative word for 'German' J. M. F]. They were not Poles but 'warszawiak' [from Warsaw J. M. F.], from Kurp [another region, J. M.] or from Vilnius. Nobody concealed that they were there provisionally."[36]

Barbara started school because she wanted to learn Polish. She admits that she spoke only a mix of Polish, German and Russian 'dialects' from different regions.[37] This is a patent sign of the enormous plurality and *anomia* of the new local society, where there was no clear ethnic majority. However, integrative processes were already under way: in school she learnt, among other things, the famous verses "Who are you? A little Polish child", the Polish nationalist children's catechism since the late nineteenth century.[38] Moreover, she "learnt to speak in literary Polish very fast". Books from the library were her best aid.

In her memoir Barbara frequently addresses aspects of her national identity and her ties to the homeland. She did not find friends in school because of her 'nationality' ("I was abused with the word 'szwab'") and she tried to defend herself, invoking the Slavic name of her grandparents and great-grandparents. Her mother could not manage the situation and she never talked about the past. But she did not consider the possibility of migrating to Germany, because "her motherland was the land of her forefathers". As former German citizens, she and her mother could settle in Western Germany. This opportunity was, in the hard conditions of post-war Poland, a dream for many natives and a source of permanent conflict with the Polish settlers who did not have this prospect.

After some incidents at school, they only spoke Polish at home. In fact, "we did not speak [Polish] dialect". This created problems from both sides since Warmian and Masurian people hated them for wanting to be Poles and the settlers considered them Germans. "I felt myself more Polish than some of the settlers, always griping about the motherland, the government, the system."

The first source of Barbara's identity came to be the landscape – the town, the region. She constantly describes the sadness and the beauty of Warmia, using these geographic identifications to affirm her right to be Polish too. The historically stereotyped emotions the Warmian landscape elicited – 'sadness', 'melancholia' – were part of her repertoire of shared emotions. She developed an ideological construction of the new Polish nation, her own nation, through the connection between the literary and folkloric stereotypes of Warmia. Emotions about the landscape led to emotions about the nation.

After graduation Barbara decided to become a nurse ("only one year of studies, free dormitory, a uniform") and left for school. When she arrived there, her first journey into the unknown, she was so overcome with fear that she considered going back home. Again, the landscape helped her: She looked through the window and saw such a wonderful view ("a fairy tale landscape") that she decided to stay.

In classrooms and dormitories, there were "nationality issues", as she writes. Some Masurian girls isolated themselves from the rest by forming a German-speaking group, while some other 'natives' – such as Barbara herself – tried to find their place in the general society of the school. A Ukrainian girl was constantly abused and held responsible for "all crimes of the fascist band UPA [Ukrainian nationalists, JMF]". In one course they talked about war nurses' duties and Barbara writes: "I felt in [the other girls'] words not the fear of war, but the conviction that these lands are alien. It hurt me. I never limited Poland: there in Poland, here in Masuria." For Barbara, Masuria – as her Warmia – was an integral part of Poland, but other girls, coming from older Polish territories, felt alien there.

After finishing her studies, Barbara found a job in a neighbouring town. She lived in a hostel for single nurses. The bed she was given had belonged to a girl who had committed suicide only a few days before. The work disappointed her, mainly because of the difference between theory and practice. People around her did not tolerate that she was Lutheran: "a Good Pole is a practicing Catholic", they said. And she even heard once that "Luther was a devil with horns". Under this pressure, she gave up her practices. But the landscape was again an element of joy. Trying to lose a bothersome "admirer", she became used to walking and exploring the town, making the castle, the parks and the streets a part of her life.[39]

Her 'admirer' worked at the same hospital. He had been expelled from the former Polish Eastern Regions, now in possession of the USSR. He was always yearning for his native land. Barbara contradicted him when "he allowed himself to alter the Polish borders", making the suggestion to exchange the Western Regions with Russia for Vilnius. When she defended the then borders, he tried to soften his suggestion, saying that for her it would be better if the territories would go back to Germany. She cried. "I did not want any changes. The border problem was solved, in my opinion."

Later on, she met a young man at a ball and fell in love. One day, he came to the hospital to visit her.

> He began to talk freely only when I praised the beauty of the town. He vividly told me how much he was connected to it. He knew every stone, street, path. He grew up here. Not even once he said: 'in our Poland, Recovered Lands'. He, as I and thousands of boys and girls who grew up here say 'Our town, our lands'. Border problems don't concern us.

For Barbara, it was this attachment to his land that made the boy attractive to her. In an environment of frustrated settlers who considered her an alien, this young man did not give any importance to that aspect. And he loved the landscape, exactly as she did.[40]

For Barbara R., the shift from Warmian regional feelings to the new Polish nationalism, the necessity to re-define her identity as a primarily national one, went hand in hand with a very real destruction of her old community and the slow rising of a new one. She had to find her place in the new society, but she could not renounce her regional identity so easily. In a State-socialist country like the People's Republic of Poland, where all public (and even private) life was under strong centralization and homogenization pressures, Barbara tried to link her (old) *Land* to her (new) nation by turning her gaze to the landscape. Connecting the emotions she felt for her mother country to the bigger Polish nation reconciled her to the norms and values of the emotional community of the Polish newcomers. Belonging was a form of survival in a hostile environment.

National emotions through historical narration: pride

How do emotions become linked to a nationalist project? The question is embedded in a different one: how is an emotional community created? For Barbara Rosenwein, emotions have a social function and follow social rules. William Reddy writes about the performative function of 'emotives' (verbal expressions of feeling) beyond the pure descriptive role of many linguistic communications of emotions. For Reddy and Rosenwein, language is essential for understanding how socially shared emotions function. I am aware that emotions have a strong biological and neurological aspect, which means that physical sharing is part of the construction of emotional communities: a child sees, touches, smells, repeats, imitates and, in the end, learns a way of constructing its belonging to a given community. But beyond this, articulated discourses are the main instrument for transmitting values, thoughts, ideas and modes of behaviour. And this is absolutely central for nationalism.

An example of the use of language as a way to construct national emotional communities is the autobiographical writings of Zbigniew M., one of the contributors to the Instytut Zachodni's contest. As a youngster Zbigniew wrote some letters to a (West) German pen pal.[41] I am not sure if this friend was real or not, but this is unimportant in the given context. What counts is the rhetoric of the letters, which is in line with narratives and stereotypes of the time about Polish national identity. Such narratives were certainly promoted by the state and taken on board by the young writer, even if they were not necessarily assumed entirely.

Zbigniew was born four years after the end of the Second World War, in Świdnica, "in the so-called Polish Recovered Lands", as he wrote. His parents had moved there in 1946. The former German Regions were an object of permanent symbolical conflict for their inhabitants who were committed to preserving their and their homeland's identity. So, Zbigniew's narration begins with a perfect rhetorical figure:

> I didn't know, and that is a surprise to me, that your grandfather and your father were born in Świdnica. Your father's remains are old history and the name 'Schweidnitz' (so you write it) has disappeared from the map without possibility of return and that's why a solution to the question of 'the right to the homeland' is no longer necessary, as you expressed in your letter. But on the other hand, I understand your ignorance and your one-sided approach to the problem.[42]

Even though Zbigniew was hardly in a position to remember the first post-war years in Świdnica, he did his best to describe them. Settlers came to the former German lands "above all from the Republic's former eastern territories and from Central Poland" and they worked very hard to reconstruct the destroyed factories of the Old Town.[43] Heroic work to rebuild the country and the restoration of the Old Town are recurrent topics of the *Odbudowa* (Reconstruction) mythology of the post-war years. They are indicative of an effort to integrate Polish society more through the discourse of highly visible accomplishments than through promises of the socialist project. Such a discourse is present in a great number of the memoirs and diaries I have come across.

Another important subject of Zbigniew's writings is local history.[44] He described his hometown, its medieval church ("with the highest tower in Lower Silesia") and its wooden church ("the Church of the Peace"). He also wrote about medieval history, about the way his home region had become a foreign land: "That was the fault of the King of Poland who was absorbed with other conflicts and did not value Silesia that was at that time still a Polish and a Piast [the oldest Polish dynasty] territory."[45] Medieval history was proof that the town was Polish after all: "As you see, your father's 'fatherland' was not 'always German', it was only cut off from the Polish

Kingdom and it was slowly and gradually germanized."[46] As Zbigniew liked to read great men's biographies and books on history, he could not help adding: "*nota bene*, some of your compatriots claim that Copernicus was a German. Write, what do you think about this".[47]

But this was not at the centre of his attention: "I return now to the problem of 'the right to the homeland'. We, Poles, are living here, we are working, building new factories, schools, roads ... In a word: we feel at home, because we are at home." Still, there had been and there was always going to be a material presence of Germans: "You would certainly say, that you had been fashioning and administrating these lands. I would agree. But you destroyed them too. For example, Wrocław." He told the story of the destruction of 'Fortress Breslau' during the war,[48] claiming that the whole city had been razed.[49]

> We began from scratch. And now the *Festung Breslau* is a metropolis with nearly 500.000 inhabitants, with a developed industry and new residential areas. [...] We have the right to say that we fashioned these lands. If you add to this our historical rights to these lands, we can feel really at home here. And the people who live here have no doubts that these lands are genuinely Polish.[50]

But he did not want to dwell on politics: "This question is a little problematic, because I hadn't thought too much about it. [...] At this point, it is necessary to recall the saying that the future of the world rests only on peace, because this saying is true and accurate."[51]

Finally, Zbigniew wrote that he was sending reproductions of Jan Matejko's paintings. He emphasized that his friend had to have a careful look at Grunwald, a famous picture about the battle.[52] Matejko's historical paintings from the end of the nineteenth century exemplify popular Polish imagery of the past. Every Polish child knows these pictures, even today, because they continue to be reproduced in textbooks.

Zbigniew`s pride in his hometown reflected upon his greater fatherland. In a very clever way, the young man connected the linguistic discourses about the nation – the classic cultural construction of Polish nationalism – to the small, everyday performance of stories about his own place of living. Many of these stories came from a reservoir of discourses created by official/unofficial institutions of nation-building. However, as a source of pride, Zbigniew was creative enough to use them and eventually transform them. The emotional community needed the emotion of pride to include the territories in its mental map. And Zbigniew's letters tell us a lot about the way emotional communities are constructed: through sharing of narratives.

Reconstruction of emotions through narratives

Mar and Oatley argue that "imagined settings and characters evoked by fiction literature likely engage the same areas of the brain as those used during the performance of parallel actions and perceptions", a way to explain that there are no differences in the mind between 'real' or 'imagined' stories.[53] Narrative shapes the world. Concrete linguistic expressions, repeated by a given population (usually at the local level), that operate as a model for telling stories of relevance for the community, are very common.[54] In fact, we can find rich narratives on a subject, even long stories repeated within a community, sometimes using almost the same words. In general, these narratives tend to assemble a discourse of identity that is found at the local level. As Anthony Giddens writes: "A person's identity is not to be found in behaviour, nor – important though this is – in the reactions of others, but in the capacity *to keep a particular narrative going*."[55]

It seems that it is socially necessary to keep such particular narratives going too. In this way, discourse possibilities (that is, the verbal formulations – the *stories* – that the individual has at hand) shape possibilities to understand, and to construct, the social world. Stories, repeated time and again – and in this way, distorted too – are transmitted *independently* of their origin, and are used to forge the *Lebensraum*, the social space of the individual. Analysing these stories is a reasonable means to trace the shaping of national consciousness in a given human community.

Identity discourses are organized into narratives that are not necessarily closed and homogeneous. Contradiction and ambiguous interpretation are an integral part of such narratives. The way national narratives are made part of an individual's store of resources is through national images. They are suggestions or proposals of self-identification that can be accepted or not, but they are always present in a given nation(ality). Self-identification with a national image ensures the individual of a place in the world (national genealogy) and in society and tends to legitimize (and eventually to challenge) the social structure in a form that is very close to religion. A 'corpus' of general common (standard) national images envelopes the individual, and it is possible to suppose that a particular individual can share such a corpus.

What is the place of emotions in this? Suzanne Keen argues that

> the growth of therapeutic psychology during and after World War I – including but not limited to Freudian psychoanalysis – had established a relationship between the narrative expression of emotionally charged experience and restoration of health, resting on a theory of emotions as suppressed impulses that could burst forth in a return of the repressed.[56]

Emotions *are* expressed narratively, and narratives are constructed, attached and linked to the individual through emotions. However, Keen contends that narrative emotions differ from representations of emotional responses: she asserts that narrative emotions "are involved in readers' experience of both fiction and life writing".[57]

In our case study, it is possible to find different narratives, connected to emotions that are linked to the terrible circumstances of the memoir writers:

many of the individuals were teenagers living a difficult life in a settlers' society after a war. They used the opportunity given by the authorities to explain themselves through narratives, using plots derived from specific national narratives, readymade for them. As Keen put it:

> plots consist of related events and their beginnings allude to states of affairs that are undergoing change. Change and disruption are thus the natural states of narrative, which cannot exist for long in stasis. Something has to happen in order to stimulate the unspooling of related events that constitute plot, and those changes of state invite readers to experience versions of affect. Although a dictionary definition of affect (as a noun) makes it synonymous with feelings or emotions, its Latin root (and its meaning when it is a verb) emphasizes affect's role in influencing action. This is one reason why the core narrative affects, curiosity, surprise, and suspense, relate to narrativity.[58]

Constructing an emotional community means to develop socially relevant narratives able to shape and to form emotions, even as they are primarily of a biological nature, in order to adapt them to actual circumstances. An emotional community is both an answer to a historically given situation and a construction of bonds to a different, more abstract project, beyond the local and regional level. This is the way in which emotions connect to national ideologies: both share similar narratives.

Narratives and emotions

The focus on emotions and on their connection to the nation implies a different debate in nationalism research. It is the question of how nationalist meaning is produced, and how this meaning translates to the individual.

I believe that there is not a one on one transmission of state-run ideas, and that people are able to resist propaganda. However, I also argue that the state does have a role in the construction of individual identities, and in shaping the way people see themselves. People are creative. They transform everything they receive, but many *self-images* are believed and accepted even by ideological opponents because they fill a psychological need of *self-stereotyping* or because they are part of a long tradition.

Neuroscience suggests that learning processes are linked to emotions. Emotionally charged discourses have more chances of being accepted and assumed by the individual.[59]

A socialist state, as the Polish People's Republic, with its aspiration of controlling the whole life of its inhabitants, seemed to me the best case to investigate the relationship between nation, emotions, identity, state propaganda and the construction of social reality. The key in the relationship between all these factors is *narratives*, and the most successful political narrative of the nineteenth and twentieth centuries was, without doubt, nationalism or, rather 'the national'.

By 'the national' I do not simply mean narratives or images of the nation. There exists a large plurality of narratives and images of older ethno-symbolical or newer nationalist traditions. But from an observer's perspective not all narratives are equal: in order to be accepted, the narratives usually have to be part of a broader socially accepted cultural *corpus*. Only a discourse that is part of a given corpus can establish itself as a piece of *concrete* language, or a speech act.[60] Mechanisms of discrimination – for example social prestige – allow the individual to choose between different narratives. They can rely on it when shaping – and reshaping again and again – their responses to the outside world and their vision of it, or as scientists use to call it: their *identities*.

Thus, the process of adopting a certain identity and the process of changing it – if we speak about national identity – is not only an action of self-identification, but of acceptance, refusal or reworking of social narratives arising in the practice of public discussion. The nation is, per se, a public space, and a virtual one for that matter, because the nation – despite its economic, social and territorial basis – takes place only in the discussions of the public space – as, indeed, almost social communities do. Individuals talk about the nation, feel the nation, act in life while being guided by discourses of the nation. The displayed emotions and their structuration in shared narratives are the building blocks for emotional communities. The ensuing narratives and discourses mark the wide field of a social common discursive area where the debate between nation and emotion takes place.

Emotions might be mainly biological but for a historian this is irrelevant. Emotions are part of the historic dimension only because they are performative responses to situations. Such responses may get a correlate in social action: an example might be a criminal act, like a political murder, in an emotionally charged situation like a strike or revolt. This action might have an influence in the lineal development of the physically embodied social action. These consequences are part of the historical development and, in so far, of interest to the historian. However, usually, emotions are only relevant to the historian as narratives. If they are expressed, they exist.

National identities are built by state-run propaganda (sometimes openly implemented from above, sometimes as hidden rhetoric), discourses empowered by tradition (sometimes part of state purposes, sometimes positioned against it) and grassroots cultures (sometimes as a product of state politics, but often constructed upon other materials). The key to connect all of these different fields of meaning is emotions. Emotions are culturally modulated beyond their biological origin by narratives. A nationalist narrative on emotions is a national emotion itself. Emotional communities might be national if they find a link between the emotions related to the community and the national narratives that describe the community as a nation or part of it. As argued in this chapter, building a new society in the 'Western Regions' was only possible by constructing an emotional community based on narratives of emotions.

Notes

1 Rodríguez-López, 'Historia de las Emociones', p. 13.
2 Ibid.
3 Cosmides and Tooby, 'Evolutionary psychology'.
4 Oatley, *Emotions*, p. 28
5 Plamper, *The History of Emotions*.
6 Reddy, *The Navigation of Feeling*, p. 96.
7 Frevert, *Emotions in History*, p. 3.
8 Reddy, 'Against constructionism'.
9 Faraldo, 'Identidades conflictivas'; Idem, 'Autoimágenes e ideologías'; Idem, 'Die Nation als ein Traum'; Idem, 'Gloomy landscapes'; Idem, 'The teutonic knights'.
10 Thum and Faraldo, 'Las Regiones Occidentales Polacas'.
11 Curp, *A Clean Sweep?*
12 For the first time in the classical Thomas and Znaniecki, *The Polish Peasant*, but he developed this method in interwar Poland from his Chair at Poznań University.
13 Chałasiński, *Drogi awansu*, and above Idem, *Młode pokolenie chłopów*.
14 See Chamberlayne, Bornat and Wengraf, *The Turn to Biographical Methods*.
15 Krzoska, *Für ein Polen an Oder und Ostsee*.
16 Guth, *Geschichte als Politik*; Choniawko, *Instytut Zachodni w dokumentach*.
17 See Connelly, *Captive University*.
18 See: Dulczewski, *Tworzenie*; Idem, *Społeczeństwo ziem zachodnich*. Dulczewski, which was the promoter of this works, spoke with sadness about the impossibility of doing any further research after 1973 (author's interview, Poznań, 8.12.2000).
19 Interview with Dulczewski and various conversations with Zbigniew Mazur (Poznań, December 2000).
20 As in the last important research campaign of the Institute in 1973, the questionnaires on the Polish–German border region, whose results disappointed the communist officials.
21 See Faraldo, 'Materials of memory'.
22 Archiv Ziem Zachodnich i Północnych Instytutu Zachodniego im. Zygmunta Wojciechowskiego w Poznaniu (hereinafter 'AIZ'), Pamietnik 7 (hereinafter 'P'), p. 2.
23 AIZ, P 7, p. 2.
24 Rosenwein, *Generations of Feeling*.
25 Rosenwein, 'Problems and methods'.
26 Rosenwein, 'Problems and methods'.
27 Bourke, *Fear*.
28 Zaremba, *Wielka trwoga*.
29 Józef Galczyniak in *Mój dom nad Odra*, vol. 4, 1973, p. 38.
30 AIZ, P 210, pp. 22–27.
31 AIZ, P 165, p. 4/p.12.
32 AIZ, P 193, n.p.
33 See Dulczewski, 'The young generation'.
34 AIZ, P 246–17, *Letter to the Judges*, p. 1.
35 On languages in Warmia: Szyfer, *Warmiacy*.
36 AIZ, P 246–17, p. 5.
37 I have found this phenomenon in other memoirs, such as Anna L. See AIZ 271–42.
38 See Porter-Szűcs, *Faith and Fatherland*, p. 3.
39 AIZ, P 246–17, p. 28.
40 AIZ, P 246–17, p. 53.
41 AIZ P 344–116. Born and living in Świdnica Śląska in 1966, he was a 17-year-old high-school student at the time. He wrote that he wanted to be a 'humanist'. In a confession typical for this kind of memoir he declared that he had no friends and that

he had seen his German pen pal only once. There are three letters from Zbigniew in the archive.
42 AIZ P 344–116: 1a.
43 AIZ P 344–116: 1b.
44 About Swidnica's history see Jońca, 'Zarys Dziejów Ziemi Świdnickiej'.
45 AIZ, P 344–116: 2a.
46 AIZ, P 344–116: 2a.
47 AIZ, P 344–116: 3a. The debate about Copernicus' nationality was one of the main conflicts between Polish and German historians in the nineteenth century.
48 The Nazis ordered that Breslau should hold out up to the last man. They destroyed a good deal of the city to build defences and even an airport in the city itself. See Jońca, 'Destruction of "Breslau"'.
49 Indeed only certain suburban areas were totally ruined. The general estimation for the whole town is 68 per cent of destruction. See Thum, *Uprooted*.
50 AIZ, P 344–116: 3a.
51 AIZ P 344–116: 5b.
52 AIZ P 344–116: 6a.
53 Mar and Oatley, 'The function of fiction'.
54 See García García, 'El uso del espacio'.
55 Giddens, Anthony, *Modernity and Self-Identity. Self and Society in the Late Modern Age*, Cambridge, Polity Press, 1991, p. 54 (emphasis added).
56 Keen, 'Introduction'.
57 Keen, 'Life writing', p. 12.
58 Keen, *Narrative Form*, p. 153.
59 Deak, 'Brain and emotion'.
60 In this aspect, I owe a lot to Searle, *Speech Acts*; Idem, *The Construction of Social Reality*.

References

Literature

Bourke, Joanna, *Fear: A Cultural History*, London, Virago, 2006.
Chałasiński, Jósef, *Drogi awansu społecznego robotnika*, Poznań, Skład główny w księgarni św. Wojciecha, 1931.
Chałasiński, Jósef, *Młode pokolenie chłopów, procesy i zagadnienia kształtowania się warstwy chłopskiej w Polsce*, 4. vol., Warsaw, Spółdzielnia wydawnicza Pomoc Oświatowa, 1938.
Chamberlayne, Prue, Bornat, Joanna and Wengraf, Tom, *The turn to biographical methods in social science: Comparative issues and examples*, London, Routledge, 2000.
Choniawko, Andrzej (ed.), *Instytut Zachodni w dokumentach*, Poznań, Instytut Zachodni, 2006.
Connelly, John, *Captive university: The Sovietization of East German, Czech, and Polish higher education, 1945–1956*, Chapel Hill, University of North Carolina Press, 2000.
Cosmides, Leda and Tooby, John, 'Evolutionary psychology: A primer', 1997 (http://www.cep.ucsb.edu/primer.html, accessed 16 June 2019).
Curp, T. David, *A clean sweep? The politics of ethnic cleansing in Western Poland, 1945–1960*, Rochester NY, University of Rochester Press, 2006.
Deak, Anita, 'Brain and emotion: Cognitive neuroscience of emotions', in: *Review of Psychology*, vol. 18, no. 2, 2011, pp. 71–80.

Dulczewski, Zygmunt (ed.), *Społeczeństwo ziem zachodnich. Studium porównawcze wyników badań socjologicznych w województwie zielonogórskim*, Poznań, IZ, 1971.

Dulczewski, Zygmunt (ed.), *Tworzenie się nowego społeczeństwa na Ziemiach Zachodnich. Szkice i materiały z badań socjologicznych w województwie zielonogórskim*, Poznań, IZ, 1963.

Dulczewski, Zygmunt, 'The young generation of Polish autochthones in the Polish Western Territories', in: *Polish Western Affairs*, vol. 8, no. 2, 1967, pp. 430–444.

Faraldo, Jose M., 'Autoimágenes e ideologías en Polonia', in: Flores Juberías, Carlos (ed.), *De la Europa del Este al este de Europa*, Valencia, UV2007, pp. 615–631.

Faraldo, Jose M., 'Die Nation als ein Traum. Eine Erinnerung', in: Stokłosa, Katarzyna et al. (eds.), *Soziale und wirtschaftliche Konflikte und nationale Grenzen in Ostmitteleuropa. Festschrift für Helga Schultz zum 65. Geburtstag*, Berlin, Berliner Verlag, pp. 17–26.

Faraldo, Jose M., 'Gloomy landscapes. Everyday strategies of identity in 1960's Poland. A case study', in: *Berliner Osteuropa Info*, vol. 23, 2005, pp. 51–57.

Faraldo, Jose M., 'Identidades conflictivas. Discurso autobiográfico y nación en las Regiones Occidentales Polacas', in: Flores Juberías, Carlos (ed.), *España y la Europa oriental: tan lejos, tan cerca*, Valencia, UV, 2009, pp. 621–634.

Faraldo, José M., 'Materials of memory. Mass memoirs of the Polish Western Territories', in: Faraldo, José M., *Europe, Nationalism, Communism. Essays on Poland*, New York – Frankfurt, Peter Lang Verlag, 2008.

Faraldo, Jose M., 'The Teutonic Knights and the Polish identity. National narratives, self-image and socialist public sphere', in: Rittersporn, Gabor T., Behrends, Jan C. and Rolf, Malte (eds.), *Sphären von Öffentlichkeit in Gesellschaften sowjetischen Typs*, Frankfurt, Peter Lang, pp. 279–306.

Frevert, Ute, *Emotions in history – Lost and found*, Budapest, Central European University Press, 2011.

García García, José Luis, 'El uso del espacio: conductas y discursos', in: González Alcantud, José A. and González de Molina, Manuel, (eds.), *La tierra: mitos, ritos y realidades*, Barcelona, Editorial Anthropos, 1992, pp. 400–411.

Giddens, Anthony, *Modernity and self-identity. Self and society in the late modern age*, Cambridge, Polity Press, 1991.

Guth, Stefan, *Geschichte als Politik der Deutsch-Polnische Historikerdialog im 20. Jahrhundert*, Berlin – Boston, De Gruyter Oldenbourg, 2016.

Jońca, Karol, 'Destruction of "Breslau": The final struggle of Germans in Wroclaw in 1945', in: *Polish Western Affairs*, vol. 2, 1961, pp. 309–339.

Jońca, Karol, 'Zarys Dziejów Ziemi Świdnickiej', in: Jońca, Karol (ed.), *Wysiedlenia Niemców i osadnictwo ludności polskiej na obszarze Krzyżowa-Świdnica (Kreisau-Schweidnitz) w latach 1945–1948. Wybór dokumentów*, Wrocław, Leopoldinum, 1997, p. 13–35 (in Polish) and pp. 59–78 (in German).

Keen, Suzanne, 'Introduction: Narrative and the emotions', in: *Poetics Today*, vol. 32, 2011, pp. 1–53.

Keen, Suzanne, 'Life writing and the empathetic circle', in: *Concentric: Literary and Cultural Studies*, vol. 42, no. 2, 2016, pp. 9–26.

Keen, Suzanne, *Narrative form: Revised and expanded second edition*, Houndsmills, Palgrave Macmillan, 2015.

Krzoska, Markus, *Für ein Polen an Oder und Ostsee. Zygmunt Wojciechowski (1900–1955) als Historiker und Publizist*, Osnabrück, Fibre, 2003.

Mar, Raymond A. and Oatley, Keith, 'The function of fiction is the abstraction and simulation of social experience', in: *Perspectives on Psychological Science*, vol. 3, 2008, pp. 173–192.

Oatley, Keith, *Emotions: A brief history*, Oxford, Blackwell, 2004.

Plamper, Jan, *The history of emotions: An introduction*, Oxford, Oxford University Press, 2015.

Porter-Szűcs, Brian, *Faith and fatherland. Catholicism, modernity and Poland*, Oxford, Oxford University Press, 2011.

Reddy, William M., 'Against constructionism: The historical ethnography of emotions', in: *Current Anthropology*, vol. 38, no. 3, 1997, pp. 327–351.

Reddy, William M., *The navigation of feeling: A framework for the history of emotions*, Cambridge, Cambridge University Press, 2001.

Rodríguez-López, Carolina, 'Historia de las Emociones. Introducción', in: *Cuadernos de Historia Contemporánea*, 2014, vol. 36, pp. 11–16.

Rosenwein, Barbara H., 'Problems and methods in the history of emotions', in: *Passions in Context I: International Journal for the History and Theory of Emotions*, 2010, vol. 1, (http://www.passionsincontext.de/index.php/?id=557&L=1%2F%2Fa sse...images%2Fpit-id.txt, accessed 16 June 2019).

Rosenwein, Barbara H., *Generations of feeling: A history of emotions, 600–1700*, Cambridge, Cambridge University Press, 2015.

Searle, John R., *Speech acts. An essay in the philosophy of language*, Cambridge, Cambridge University Press, 1969.

Searle, John R., *The construction of social reality*, London, Penguin, 1995.

Szyfer, Anna, *Warmiacy. Studium tożsamośći*, Poznań, SAWW, pp. 157–159.

Thomas, William I. and Znaniecki, Florian, *The Polish peasant in Europe and in America*, vol. 1–2, Chicago, University of Chicago Press; vol. 3–5, Boston, Badger Press, 1918–1920.

Thum, Gregor and Faraldo, José M., 'Las Regiones Occidentales Polacas. Experimento social y arquitectura de las identidades', in: *Cuadernos de Historia Contemporánea*, vol. 22, 2000, pp. 325–346.

Thum, Gregor, *Uprooted: How Breslau became Wroclaw during the Century of Expulsions*, Princeton, Princeton University Press, 2011.

Zaremba, Marcin, *Wielka trwoga: Polska 1944–1947: ludowa reakcja na kryzys*, Krakow – Warsaw, Społeczny Instytut Wydawniczy 'Znak' – Instytut Studiów Politycznych Polskiej Akademii Nauk, 2012.

Conclusions

National(ized) emotions from below

Xosé M. Núñez Seixas, Maarten
Van Ginderachter and Andreas Stynen

This volume has tried to relate the history of emotions to the analysis of nationalism 'from below'. The different chapters offer a kaleidoscopic image of case studies and highlight how the boundaries between the emotional ascription to a nation and to other spheres of territorial, social and gender identity are often blurred. They also display the great variety, malleability and instability of sentiments of allegiance and the attendant ambiguities and contradictions. Despite the chronological evolution of nationalized emotions and their change over time, this volume makes clear that the transitions between the early modern and the modern 'emotional regimes' are not always clear-cut. The different contributions decisively contribute to illustrate the many ways in which, on the one hand, nationalism and national identity are translated into emotions, and, on the other hand, emotions can be used to reinforce national belonging. They have done so with different research strategies, methodologies and sources.

A first angle is that offered by the textual analysis of ego-documents, in order to study how national ascription is reflected in letters and diaries written by travellers, army officers and people belonging to the middle and upper echelons of society, but also by soldiers, sailors and ordinary people. This is illustrated by the complementary approach taken by Moreno Almendral's, Oddens', Niedhammer's and Kivimäki's chapters. As their contributions deal with different periods, they allow us to trace an evolution in the relevance of both emotions and national sentiments. Thus, the analysis by Oddens of the dozens of petitions written by poor people in the Netherlands around 1800 mostly expresses their rootedness in a pre-national environment, where sentiments of local, religious and monarchic allegiance tended to predominate. Some decades later, the diaries, memoirs and travel books written by British, French and Spanish individuals between 1780 and 1830, revealed, first, the growing importance of national identity, and, second, the increasing individualization of emotions and their free association with the nation. Thus, for many of these individuals becoming national, to quote Suny and Eley,[1] also meant becoming individual (within the new liberal order) and, to some extent, becoming masters of their own emotions, as well as masters of the way in which the public and the private sphere were connected by each member of the nation. This also included negative emotions ascribed to other national-ities, as a process of 'othering' which, to some extent, also implied different emotional frameworks.[2] Stereotypes, jokes and other narrative strategies, as well as 'emotives', those propaganda slogans that could be adopted and function as mechanisms of emotional identification in individual memoirs and ego-documents, served to enhance the process of emotional othering.

However, as the chapter by Niedhammer on the dozens of letters by admirers and fans to the Occitan poet Frédéric Mistral shows, 'othering' did not always mean a passionate, emotional exclusion. The process of defining borders became increasingly complex in multi-ethnic settings, as evident in the case of the French South and many other European regions at the end of the nineteenth century.[3] The letters of supporters of the Occitan movement suggest that the span of emotions varied from a high appreciation for the minority language they loved (and did not always speak themselves) to a loyal commitment to French national identity, though strongly rooted in local pride. A possible conclusion is that the borders between regional and national narratives are extremely blurred and malleable, and not always subject to a well-defined hierarchy of emotional prio-rities. At the time, the idea that many people were ready to die for their nation, but not for their region, was not self-evident, or rather these two ideas were intricately intertwined. For many people the nation was a local passion, and love for the terroir equalled patriotism.

By the interwar period of the twentieth century, in most of Europe the nation had apparently become a basic element of socialization and a framework for collective emotions. However, Kivimäki's chapter shows how national identity did not necessarily triumph in the context of war experience and in the war poems written by Finnish soldiers during the Second World War. If the patriotic feelings of conscripted soldiers had been reinforced during the pre-vious Winter War against the same enemy (the Soviet Union) and triggered through the wartime propaganda discourse of 'war nationalism', they did not find a direct translation into those literary pieces. This goes to show that ambiguity did not disappear in the twentieth century. Emotions were cer-tainly linked to the nation, on the one hand, and comradeship feelings often tended to see the trench community as the best expression of the national community in arms. But, on the other hand, soldiers were so subjected to brutalization, boredom and disillusionment, that they were well aware of the gap between bombastic nationalist slogans and images, and everyday senti-ments and physical perceptions. Thus, war experience does not always rein-force national(ist) emotions, but on the contrary the collective experience of extreme situations (danger, suffering, cold, etc.) may contribute to trigger contradictory feelings about 'us' and 'them'. As in the case of the French and Flemish trenches of the First World War, soldiers on both sides often felt positive emotions towards their enemies, as human beings subject to similar war machineries.[4]

A second approach of our authors is that of trying to go deeper into the relationship between the body and national emotions, by exploring how the body of the nation was also internalized and translated in individual terms. Hoegaerts' chapter, for instance, analyses the teaching strategies the primary schools of late nineteenth-century Antwerp used to turn love of the fatherland into an embodied practice for school children. Excursions, the act of singing, sports, walking, connected pupils with a given territory. These educational practices were not only associated with emotions, but they also linked physical, bodily experiences with particular places and moments, thus providing landmarks on their emotional map of remembrances and affections. Beyond the school period, Blanck and Cârstocea also demonstrate the importance of rituals, public performances and theatralizations for rooting national emotions into young people's minds. Undoubtedly, fascist ceremonies constitute a classic example of how rituals leave traces among the true followers, as the cases of Gabriele D'Annunzio's proto-fascist legionnaires in Fiume (1919–20) and the Romanian supporters of the Iron Guard in the 1930s convincingly demonstrate. Masculinity, a cult of heroism and sacrifice but also the promise of future redemption, was intimately linked to bodily practices, inner revigorization and triumph over death – an implicit conclusion from the morbid practices of Romanian fascists, who seemed to externalize their fear of death by associating their own lives with that of the nation.

A third approach, which is very present in Marzec's and Faraldo's chapters, is that of addressing the relationship between autobiographies, emotions, personal memory and national allegiance, an element which is also dealt with by Moreno Almendral and, to some extent, by Blanck. As they all demonstrate, personal memory came at odds with the 'margins' and borders of national identity. This became particularly evident in the case of Polish workers in late Russian Poland and Polish settlers in the 'Wild West' of post-war Poland. While the former had to justify preferring national allegiance over internationalist and 'socialist' emotions inherited from their parents, the latter tended to adopt much of the nationalizing state's rhetoric to give meaning to their personal experience. The settlers' personal biographies and lived experiences were profoundly marked by rootlessness – as they mostly came from the former Eastern Polish regions – and negative sentiments towards a territory and its pre-war inhabitants that were regarded as foreign and German. In this context, a new self-proclaimed image arose of pioneers of the Polish national spirit in strange, 'foreign' lands, which had been previously inhabited by Germans. This became a myth to live by, a collective enterprise that gave meaning to family stories broken by the impact of war and destruction. National emotions that were to some extent dictated by the national state and its officials, from schoolmasters to party bureaucrats, were thus interiorized by many individuals and presented as their own. These chapters present the subtle contrast between contemporary ego-documents and later autobiographical writings as a very promising research avenue to deal with the ambiguities of emotions, as well as with the temporal mechanisms that give meaning to emotions in a particular chronological setting. This also opens up the question of how national emotions change and are redefined in tandem with other factors, such as life cycle, ageing process and social mobility. National nostalgia and melancholy deserve to be further explored, as they are particularly relevant for brokering national identification among migrants, soldiers and displaced persons.

All contributions in this volume use sources of a different nature and scope to investigate how emotions were expressed and represented. Some grasp the immediate traces left by emotional reactions, others reflect on the expression or remembrance of national emotions from the distance, at a later stage of the life cycle. German war historians have established a classic division between *Kriegserlebnis*, the immediate impact of events on individual reactions; *Sinnstiftung*, the attribution of meaning to those events, which also depends on comparison with others' perceptions and the values and cultural codes of each individual; and *Kriegserfahrung*, based on individual reflection and interpretation of active and passive reactions to events.[5] To some extent, a similar scheme can also be applied to the individual perception and reproduction of emotions linked to national belonging. While the instant expression of sentiments linked to the national community is all the more difficult for historians to investigate, due to the scarcity of appropriate sources, emotional experiences can be recorded and reflected on in diaries and letters, once the lived events and reactions have been compared with others', as well as with the collective background of national feelings. *Erfahrung* involves a thoughtful and performative reflection on the recent past, which is then incorporated in personal timelines and becomes naturalized. It is the outcome of a whole sequence of events, and the emotions shaped by that process are a selection of perceptions and reactions. Put differently, the constructed character of national emotions does not only confirm that nations are crafted by intellectuals, institutions and confrontations, but that their emotional appeal and its deep penetration is not determined by isolated events, but by sequences of shared experiences and collective expressions of fear, joy, expectations and frustrations, as well as by embodied practices.

***

The chapters in this collection clearly demonstrate the constructed character of emotions, and relate this to the imagined nature of national sentiments. They highlight the concrete ways through which emotions were nationalized. Feelings of national and territorial attachment may have seemed organic and natural to the people experiencing them. Instead, they were invested with embodied practices, and were nurtured by institutions, social movements, local environments, schools and the education system, and reproduced by ceremonies and performances.

This volume hints at a number of open questions for future research, one of which could be the object of a typical chicken–egg dilemma: to what extent are emotions nationalized, or are nations emotionalized? Do the emergence and consolidation of nationalism and national identities contribute to decisively change the 'emotional system' of the long nineteenth and the first half of the twentieth century? Or did already existent ways of expressing and embodying emotions simply transfer their frame of reference, as well as their object, to the nation? The answer is ambivalent. On the one hand, national identities give a stronger emphasis and new meanings to the attachment to the places of everyday interaction, to the local homeland, the family and the natural environment. Schooling, institutional performances and wars also contribute to definitively enlarge those spatial frames of reference and emotional attachment. In so doing, they also change the nature of those feelings. On the other hand, nationalism has a powerful ability to recycle and re-semanticize previous sentiments of belonging, either to the family or to the territory, absorbing their ways of expression. Both phenomena occurred at the same time, and operated in both directions, in an entangled way. This volume represents a step forward in understanding the ambiguities and modalities of that interaction, thanks to a wide variety of case studies that span the European continent and cover a wide chronological period, from the early eighteenth century to the mid-twentieth century.

Antwerp, Leuven and Santiago de Compostela, September 2019

Notes

1 Eley and Suny, *Becoming National.*
2 Berger and Lorenz, *The Contested Nation.*
3 See Núñez Seixas and Storm, *Regionalism and Modern Europe.*
4 See Leed, *No Man's Land*, pp. 115–162; Ziemann, *Gewalt.*
5 See Latzel, 'Vom Kriegserlebnis zur Kriegserfahrung'.

References

Berger, Stefan and Lorenz, Chris (eds.), *The contested nation: Ethnicity, class, religion and gender in national histories*, London, Palgrave, 2008.

Eley, Geoff and Suny, Ronald Grigor (eds.), *Becoming national. A Reader*, Oxford, Oxford University Press, 1996.

Latzel, Klaus, 'Vom Kriegserlebnis zur Kriegserfahrung. Theoretische und methodische Überlegungen zur erfahrungsgeschichtlichen Untersuchung von Feldpostbriefen', in: *Militärgeschichtliche Mitteilungen*, vol. 56, no. 1, 1997, pp. 1–30.

Leed, Eric J., *No man's land. Combat and identity in World War I*, Cambridge, Cambridge University Press, 1979.

Núñez Seixas, Xosé M. and Storm, Eric (eds.), *Regionalism and modern Europe. Identity construction and movements from 1890 to the present day*, London, Bloomsbury, 2019.

Ziemann, Benjamin, *Gewalt im Ersten Weltkrieg: Töten-Überleben-Verweigern*, Essen, Klartext, 2014.

Index